MW00748741

JOURNEY INTO TIME

By
Dwight Johnson

Dwight Johnson

TEACH Services, Inc.
Brushton, New York

2007   08   09   10   11   12   ·   5   4   3   2   1

Copyright © 2007 Dwight Johnson and TEACH Services, Inc.
ISBN-13: 978-1-57258-452-5
ISBN-10: 1-57258-452-1
Library of Congress Control Number: 2006933540

Published by

TEACH Services, Inc.
www.TEACHServices.com

To Jonna and Stephen

CONTENTS

INTRODUCTION

Over the past eight years, my wife and I have made numerous trips from British Columbia to Ohio, Texas and California, visiting friends and family. Before we leave home, we go over the map and set out the route that we plan to follow, and as always we decide where we will stay each night barring any unforeseen circumstances, and make note of the highway numbers we will have to switch to as we travel along. The various States have made our trip more enjoyable by adding mileage signs as well as direction signs to guide us and help us arrive at our destination safely. For instance, as we drove through Montana a sign read, "Bozeman 64 miles", further down the road there was another sign, which read "Bozeman 32 miles". Every few miles there was another sign letting us know how close we are getting to our destination. As we pass each sign our anticipation grows, knowing that soon we will reach our goal for that days drive. Every day we set another goal to reach until all of a sudden, we see the sign that reads "Dayton 10 Miles", then comes a street name, and finally a house number, and we have arrived safely at our destination.

On one trip to Texas, we got away on time as planned and everything went well the first day. That night we were told that there had been a train wreck and some chemicals had spilled, causing a potential hazard along the road that we would be taking the next day. Authorities decided that the road should be closed until the spill was cleaned up, an alternate route was provided via a fifty or sixty mile detour. The following day we came to the detour sign and along with other traffic, had to drive the extra miles around the danger zone. Soon we were back on I–90 and continuing our journey.

Everyone in the world is on a journey, unfortunately, many do not know it, and some do not care while others have no idea where they are going. There are those who realize that they are on a trip of some sort, and have an idea where they want to go, but have no idea how to get there. So it is with some Christians today, they have not taken the time to study the road map to have a safe arrival at their destination. God wants each one of us to have a safe trip as we go through life on our journey to heaven. In His great love for mankind, He decided to give each of us a road map so plain that there is no chance of us making a wrong turn, and winding up at the wrong destination. This road map is the Bible. As with most maps, there is the flip side, which gives us finer details of the cities that we will pass through, along with exit numbers, street names, along with points of interest. Revelation, the last book in the Bible is like the backside of a map, it gives the finer details of our trip as we near the end of our journey. It is this portion of the map that we will be concentrating on.

This road map, including Revelation is like a puzzle, there are many different pieces to it. The key to understanding it, and having a safe journey, all depends on whether we can fit the pieces together in such a way as to make a complete, and perfect picture, with every piece of the puzzle in the right place. On this trip through the Revelation, there will be times when we will take a detour, and maybe even have to back track some. Eventually we will be back on course and on schedule as we continue to study the road map, preparing for the ultimate journey

God saw the events that would take place in this world before Christ could come to claim His bride. He knew that His people would also have to wait, and go through a time of soul searching and trouble before He could come for them. To prepare them for this apparent delay, He gave a message to John for those who were looking for his soon return. This message is the map that will guide, support and strengthen us as we travel through the trying days that are just ahead of us. If we fail to plot our course, study the signposts and mile markers that He has given us in Revelation, there is the chance that we will be deceived. We will miss out on the most glorious event ever to take place in this earth's history.. So with this thought in mind, and using the Bible only, we will open our road map and begin plotting our course to our Heavenly home.

It is my desire that each one will take their Bible, and read it along with this book, to help keep things in perspective. You may use whichever translation you prefer. I have used the King James version, so some of the wording may be a bit different than in your Bible. Happy travels.

Chapter 1

THE MYSTERIOUS VISITOR

Let us open our Bibles to the first chapter of Revelation to begin our travel plan. Here in verse 1 we read, "The Revelation of Jesus Christ, which God gave to him, to shew unto his servants things which must shortly come to pass; and he sent and signified by his angel unto his servant John". Many Bible scholars read the first part and stop there, "The Revelation of Jesus Christ", and then they prepare Bible studies and sermons around the thought that the book of Revelation was given to John to reveal the character of Christ. In so doing the real purpose of the book is covered over or blemished so badly that Gods people could be deceived or detoured to a route that will lead them to destruction. So let us take a closer look at what verse one is really talking about.

The word Revelation comes from the word "reveal", and whatever Jesus had to reveal was given to him by God, who intended him to pass it on to his servants. If we look at the last part of the verse we find that Jesus passed it on to an angel, who in turn passed it on to John, who was to pass it on to us. What was the 'things' that John was to reveal to us? Let us read the middle part of the verse "to shew unto his servants things which must shortly come to pass", so the subject is "things which must shortly come to pass", not the revealing of Jesus. Jesus and his character were revealed throughout Old Testament times in all his dealings with the Children of Israel, and in a more direct way when God sent him to live among men for thirty–three years. God did not need another book written to reveal His Sons or His character. His main concern in this book was to let us know what would be facing us in the closing days of this earths history, so that we would not become discouraged with the apparent delay in His Second Coming.

In verse 2, John was told to "bare record" of everything that he saw or was going to be shown. Then going on to the 3rd verse we find a direct message to us. This message is of the most importance to us today and the reason for the writing of this book. It has always been God's desire to give us good things, He wants us to have the very best of everything. The thing that He wants to give us the very most, is Eternal life, and the next thing he wants to give us are his blessings. In His great love for us, He will not force them on anyone who does not want them. So, in verse 3, we find blessings for those who want them, 1. blessed is he who reads, 2. blessed is he who hears and 3. blessed is he who keeps those things which are written therein. There is something we must do to receive these blessings and in this way we show God that we want them. What we must do is the reading (studying), hearing (learning), and keeping (memorizing) the things that are "written therein" and then John concludes with "for the time is at hand."

Now John turns his attention to the seven churches and he indicates that he has a special message for them in verse 4. It was a message of grace and peace from "him which is, and which was, and which is to come", (God the Father), the seven Spirits from before the throne and from Jesus, the faithful witness. Then in verse 5 and 6 John continues on by praising Jesus for cleansing our sins with his blood and then he climaxes these few short verses with verse 7, "Behold he cometh with clouds; and every eye shall see him, and they also which pierced him: and all kindreds of the earth shall wail because of him". Let's consider one item of interest in this verse before we move on. In this description of Christ's second coming, it states that every eye will see him come, that is, everyone that is alive when he comes, will see him appear. The interesting part is the next statement, where it says that "and they also which pierced him." These six words tell us some sinners now dead will come alive for the second coming. That would indicate that there will be a special resurrection for those people that were involved in his death on Calvary. This will most likely include the members of the Sanhedrin, as well as the mob that cried, "crucify him". It may even include Pilot and

Herod, as well as the soldiers who guarded the tomb. Perhaps this could also include other individuals who have violently opposed Christ and persecuted his followers. These people will have the distinct privilege of being resurrected twice and dying three times. After they have seen the one they crucified return in the clouds of heaven, they will die again, along with rest of the wicked, at the voice of Jesus. As he ends verse 7 with "Even so, Amen," he makes the declaration, "Even so I believe." In verses 5 to 7 we are shown a brief but yet complete rundown of the plan of redemption. In verse 5, John takes us quickly from the cross and the shedding of Christ's blood for our sins, making each one of us Princes and Princesses of the King of the Universe, right down through the ages to the glorious climax of His second coming. He had complete confidence in what God had revealed to him. Now God makes a declaration in verse eight, "I am Alpha and Omega, the beginning and the ending, which is, and which was, and which is to come, the Almighty," confirming the message that was started in verse 4.

Things now start to pick up momentum and get more interesting in verse 9. John is addressing the seven churches saying "I am your brother and companion in tribulation and in the kingdom and patience of Jesus. He wanted them to know that he was familiar with the trials and heartaches that they were experiencing or going to experience because of their love for God and the testimony of Jesus. He had been banished to the Island of Patmos for this very reason, in the hope that his influence with the fledgling church would die out. So it was here in exile that one Sabbath he was given a vision.

In verse 10, he continues "I heard behind me a great voice, as of a trumpet." As we travel on through the book of Revelation, John refers back to the voice that he heard in the beginning, a number of times.[1] The voice that John heard while in vision was that of Jesus, the "I Am", the Alpha and the Omega, the beginning and the end. Alpha is the first letter in the Greek alphabet, while Omega is the last one. Jesus wanted John to know that he was the beginning and

---

[1] Revelation 4:1; 10:8

he will be, forever. He instructed John to write down in a book or a letter, what he was about to see, and send it to the seven churches that had been started in Asia, by the Apostles while on their missionary journeys through this region of the world.

As the voice is speaking, John turns around to see from where the voice is coming. As he does so, he sees Jesus standing in the middle of seven golden candlesticks. In his right hand, he held seven stars. It is interesting to note that as we travel through the book, we will find that God communicates with John in various and different settings. Here in this vision, John remains on this earth as God delivers the message that he wants John to write down and distribute to the churches. This is evident in the fact that Christ is seen as standing among the golden candle sticks. Further on, we will see John taken up into heaven in vision and will record for us, what he saw, while there.

We will come back to this scene and continue with our study of this chapter in a short while, but first we need to set out some guidelines to follow so we do not wander around and become lost in our travels

Two patterns have started here that will run through the book of Revelation, first is the number "seven." We will be seeing this number quite often as we travel on our journey through this great manuscript. The other pattern is that of the use symbols, to help us have a better or fuller understanding of the message that John was asked to convey to those living in the closing scenes of this earths history.

We will not only be dealing with the seven candlesticks and the seven stars, but will also be looking at the seven churches, seven seals, seven angels, seven trumpets, seven last plagues, and seven vials of the wrath of God. So you see we have a lot of signposts to study and memorize if we are to have a safe journey to the Promised Land.

God has communicated with the human race in various ways since He created them. Before Adam and Eve sinned, God talked face to face with them, but as time went on, he used prophets to convey his messages to mankind. He also spoke audibly at times, and at least on one occasion, he spoke through an animal.[2] Some of these messages were in the form of dreams, sent to the prophets. At other times the prophet was taken off in vision, where they were shown events or happenings, that were going to take place at some time in the near or distant future. In dreams or visions, the use of symbols were often employed to help us understand more fully, the message that God was trying to get across to us.

In dealing with prophecy and the use of symbols, we need to have these guidelines to follow. Many speakers and theologians have fallen into the habit of trying to symbolize everything from our rising up from sleep in the morning to driving past McDonalds on our way to work. Often they take the same liberty when presenting the Word of God from the pulpit or in Bible studies. It is very important to study the Bible and find out how it deals with the use of symbols.

Throughout the Bible when the use of symbols were employed, God not only incorporated the symbol into the message, but in his great love for us, he also interpreted those symbols. If we accept his explanation of the symbols we will not be misled in our search for the true meaning of the message that he is trying to get across to us.

There are two words and their root words that are used in the process of translating visions and dreams or prophecies. These two words are positives, they are "are" and "is" and the Bible is very plain in the use of them. We will look at a number of examples of these in a few moments, but first I want to mention a couple of other words that are often used erroneously when explaining prophecies while giving sermons and Bible studies. These words are "as" and "like", these are both comparative words and we will explore the use of them along with the words "are" and "is".

In Genesis 40 we find the story of Joseph interpreting the dreams of the butler and the baker. In verse 12, Joseph tells the butler "the three branches are three days". Notice how positive that word "are" makes the statement. From this we can see that the branches were symbols, representing the three days, they told a story, conveyed a message that was imprinted

---

[2] Numbers 22:28

on the mind of the butler. Throughout the Bible, these words have been used to help us understand Gods message.

Now let's take a quick look at the other two words, "like" and "as". In Psalms 90:5,6, it says, speaking of man, that "in the morning they are like grass which groweth up, in the morning it flourishes...in the evening it is cut down". Many times these verses are used to promote the idea that grass is a symbol for man. However, the word "like" is used , it is only comparing the man to the grass of the field. We grow up, get old and die just like the grass does. The same goes for the word "as", and you can check that one out in Psalms 128:3.

Many times a prophecy will have its own set of symbols that are relevant only to itself. We have to look at each section, story or prophecy to make sure that these really are symbols, and that they are in context with the subject that we are reading or studying about. A good example of this would be the story where Jesus says to his disciples "I am the vine and you are the branches".[3] Now if we applied the "branches (days)" of the butlers dream above to these branches that Jesus mentioned, we would really be confused as to what he was talking about.

In Daniel chapter 2 is the story of King Nebuchadnezzars' dream of a great image made of gold, silver, brass, iron and clay.[4] When we read a little further on we find that these metals and the clay represented, or were symbolic of kings or kingdoms.[5] Daniel told the king "thou art this head of gold". Not all prophecies are as clear-cut as this when it comes to figuring out what they mean, but when we ask the Holy Spirit to stand by our side and to guide our mind and our thoughts, he will lead us into all truth.

Now lets pick up the story of Revelation where we left off above and continue on our journey.

John had walked with Jesus for three and a half years, listening to the lessons that he taught, seeing the miracles that he did, and his crucifixion. John, the beloved had taken Jesus' mother and looked after her through the latter years

---

[3] John 15:5

[4] Dan.2;32,33

[5] Dan. 2;38-41

of her life as Jesus had asked. From his close connection with Christ on this earth, it is no wonder that now as John sees him walking among the candlesticks that he recognizes the Son of man.

The description of Christ that John records in verses 13 to 16 is simply breathtaking. One can hardly envision the glory of his being and we will not fully understand what John saw until we behold Jesus with our own eyes, when he returns to claim us as his own. No wonder that John fell as a dead man at Jesus feet when he saw the Master in this vision. Jesus reaches down with his right hand, touching John as He speaks to him saying, "don't be afraid", its me, the first and the last, the one who was alive, who died and now I am alive again and will be forever. How that must have thrilled John while he was in vision and on through the rest of his life as he looked back on the event.

Jesus continues to speak to John in verses 19 and 20, asking John to write down the things which he had seen, and the things that were happening at that time, and also the things that were about to happen in the future. He did not want his followers to be left in suspense, wondering when he was going to come for them. He wanted them to know what was going to take place before they were to see him coming in the clouds of heaven, as King of kings and Lord of lords. In Matthew 24 he had told the disciples about the troublous times ahead, and what would be the signs of his soon coming, however he had not gone into the fine details of the event with the them. Now he knows that the time has come to prepare his children for the final conflict with evil.

Jesus knows that John doesn't understand exactly what he was seeing, so spells it out in very plain language. Jesus wanted John and everyone else on down through the ages who read this account, to know without a doubt, what the seven candlesticks were and also the seven stars. The seven stars are the angels of the seven churches Jesus told him about, and the seven candlesticks are the seven churches.

These candlesticks are similar or the same as the lamp stands, that are mentioned elsewhere in the Bible. The translators used the term "candlesticks" in the King James Version of the Bible, while most other translations use "lamp stands." As oil lamps were the norm in Bible times, it was probably these that John saw in his vision. He had grown up with them from a child and he knew, wherever there was a candle, the darkness was dispelled. He saw how the world was sinking deeper into spiritual darkness. He was the last of the twelve apostles still living, and had been exiled on the island of Patmos, cut off from the rest of the world, he didn't know how things were with churches. Christ used a lamp stand as an object lesson, or as we know it, a symbol of a church. John now knew that the church was a light shining in a dark place, a lamp stand radiating the love of God to the world. Better still, there were seven of them out there somewhere, and he was to write to all of them.

The seven stars were the seven angels of the seven churches. The word "angel," comes from a Greek word, which means "messenger," either heavenly or earthly. In the context of this last verse in chapter 1, it would mean a human messenger, probably the local elder or deacon of the church to which the letter was sent. Now John had the complete picture in his mind of what he was to do, he just needed the messages to write and that was about to be given to him.

Chapter 2

SIN IN THE CHURCH

When John was in vision, he was told to write letters to each of the seven churches, and he was told what he should say to each of them. It appears that John was instructed to write a cover letter, and send a copy to each church; this cover letter included the entire vision of what he was shown, and the things he heard in Chapter 1, verse 4, and continuing on to verse 20. He makes mention in his opening statement to each church, of a different feature in the vision he had seen. In each of the letters to the seven churches, Christ first commends them for their faithfulness to the cause of the church, and in a number of the letters, he also has words of censure for their weaknesses.

Now John takes up his pen and begins to write a letter to the leader of the church in Ephesus. These churches were not buildings, as we think of churches today, but were the congregation.

John immediately identifies who the message is coming from in his opening statement. "To the church in Ephesus, from him that holds the seven stars in his hand and walks in the midst of the candlesticks". The elder or deacon, whoever received the letter, recognized the origin of it. He had already read the covering letter, and noticed the similarity of the opening remarks to that of the seven stars and the seven golden candlesticks in John's vision.

This group of believers had worked very hard for the cause of God, they had been patient with new members in their congregation, but at the same time, they were not afraid to call sin, "sin". There were a group of people in the church who claimed to be apostles, however their lifestyles were such as to bring disrepute on the young church. These members, in Ephesus, appear to have had reason to doubt the sincerity of this group. They found out either by a church hearing, or by the deeds that these so called apostles had done, that they were a bunch of hypocrites and liars and as such could not stand having them around. Through all this, the church showed the love of God, in the way they had dealt patiently with these self acclaimed leaders.

Sadly enough, the church had slipped back into a lethargic condition, had lost the zeal for the Lord they had once had, and this brought a reprimand upon them. They were told to think back to the time they had first heard about him and how they had loved the message. They had been on fire for him, witnessing to all they came in contact with, of the love of God for mankind. Now in verse 5 they are told to repent, and practice those things that they had done before they became legalistic. If they refused to get back on track, Christ told them that he would remove the candlestick out of their midst. They would no longer be a light, shining in a dark place for the Lord.

Christ now broadens the scope of this message, to include all mankind, right down to the end of time with the use of the word "he" in verse 7. This word implies that any or all who has an ear, are to listen to what was said to the churches. This message was good for all time as Christ saw that these same problems would keep raising their ugly heads, right down to the time of the end. He ends the letter to the Ephesians with a promise to them and all others that should follow after. To each one that overcomes sin, I will give them the privilege of eating from the Tree of Life which is in Heaven where I live. O, what a promise for you and I, a promise far surpassing any of what the world has to offer us today.

Christ now instructs John to write to the leader of the church in Smyrna, saying, "These things saith the first and the last, which was dead, and is alive". Notice that here again, the attention of the church is turned back to the vision where John was instructed to write them, and these words corresponded with those in chapter 1, verses 17 and 18. They recognize that this message is coming from Christ, the head of the church.

The people here in Smyrna were encountering tough times. From all appearances, it looked like God had withdrawn his spirit from them. Christ told them that he knew their works, they were witnessing to those around them but they were not having much success, in fact, they were going through some very hard times, both spiritually and financially. They had been subjected to persecution for their faith and this probably was the cause for their poverty. Usually when things go bad for someone, there are those who are ready to point their fingers and ask, "What did you do that caused God to remove his protecting hand from you"? Today we would call them "down and outers", they were doing their best to be good witnesses, they were being persecuted, and they had no money. Christ knew all this and he didn't waste any time letting them know how he felt towards them. "You are rich", he told them, implying that money wasn't the thing that was of most importance, it was their relation with him that really counted.

As the message to the church continued, they were told that Christ was aware of the blasphemy of those who claimed to be Jews, but were of the synagogue of Satan. It was probably these people who were causing the hardship on the church.

Things did not look good for the church members from a standard point of view, even though they were on the Lord's side. He told them not to be afraid of the things that would cause them suffering, the devil will cast you into prison, that you may be tried. This was a purifying time for the church, a time of Jacob's trouble, a time for self-evaluation. As the members wondered how long they could hang on under the circumstances, they were told that they would have persecution for ten days. Using the "day for a year" concept[1], they were looking at ten years of trouble and trials. However if they were faithful and willing to give up their lives for God, they were given the promise that they would receive a crown of life. They understood this to mean life eternal with Jesus their Savior and Creator, in heaven and the earth made new.

Again, the message goes out, not only to the church, but to all mankind, "he that hath an ear, let him hear". Everyone who overcomes the tempter in the name of Jesus Christ will

---

[1] Ezekiel 4:5,6..Numbers 14:34

not have to worry about dying the second time, when Satan and all the evil hosts along with those who refused the free gift of salvation from Christ are burned when the earth is cleaned up with fire.

The church in Smyrna is the only one that did not receive a reprimand. They had accepted the gospel, lived it to the best of their ability and came through conquerors in Christ. O, that all the churches had lived such lives, how different our world would be today.

The members of the church in Pergamos received their message also. These folks had also received the cover letter from John, so they knew from who the message was coming. In the introduction to the letter, it was spelled out that this message was from him who had a sharp sword with two edges. This sword comes from the mouth of Christ.[2]

They were told their works or deeds, were known by God, also where they were living. Apparently, Pergamos was a hot bed of Satan worship, as such, it was very difficult to live Christian lives, and witness to those around them. Even in the face of ridicule towards them, and the martyrdom of one, Antipas, the believers held fast to the name of Christ and would not deny their faith in him. Christ commended them for all that they had done in upholding the faith, even in the face of such opposition as they had.

All was not well though, with the church. They had allowed some members to join up with them, who brought into the church, false doctrines. These people were followers of the doctrine of Balaam, and they taught that it was all right to eat food that had been offered to idols, and also to commit fornication. When the members discovered that these things were being taught, they should have taken action and rid the church of these false teachers. Because they had failed to do this, Christ had to bring it to their attention and reprimand them for their lack of action.

There was another group of people there in the church, who followed another doctrine, that of the Nicolaitanes. These folks were also a thorn in the flesh of the church and the message from Christ made it very clear that he hated

---

[2] Revelation 1:16

these doctrines also. The church in Ephesus was also plagued with the same problem, but they at least hated the deeds of these offshoots, whereas the members here in Pergamos, allowed them to believe these false teachings and still remain in the church. Christ's message to them was, "repent", and straighten up, get rid of these false teachers or I will have to come into your midst and deal firmly with them.

Again a message goes out to everyone, whoever hears or reads this letter to the churches please pay attention, there is a promise coming up for you. If you overcome, I will give you spiritual food to eat, you may have to search for it because it is hidden but, it will stay with you longer, you will not hunger so much. This food is comparable to the water that Christ offered the woman at the well in Samaria.[3]

Not only will the overcomers receive the hidden manna, they will also receive a new name as well. This name appears to be the same one that is promised to the members in the church at Philadelphia.[4]

John is then instructed to write to the church in Thyatira saying, "these things saith the Son of God, who hath his eyes like unto a flame of fire, and his feet are like fine brass".[5] Here again, attention was drawn to the one who is sending this message to them.

These members were a zealous group of workers who lived up to the name "Christian". Everything that they did, showed their love to God and their desire to follow him. Their works stood out in the community and the people around them felt the love of God radiate from each member of the church. They loved each other and those around them. The evidence of this could be seen in the service they rendered to everyone they came in contact with. They witnessed to others, of their faith in Jesus, and along with this they showed a great deal of patience towards others. It was this patience, that brought a lot of heartache into the church.

Christ now lets these church members know there are a few things that he is not completely happy with. Because of

---

[3] John 4:10–14
[4] Revelation 3:12
[5] Revelation 2:18

their attitude of love and not wishing to hurt anyone's feelings, they had allowed some new members to join them, who had some false doctrines. These people immediately set to work tearing down the church by introducing a false religion, one that included the eating of food that had been offered to idols. Christ referred to these people as "that woman Jezebel". They claimed to have a prophet or the spirit of prophecy and because of this, they had deceived the church there, in Thyatira. By accepting the doctrines of this false group of so called Christians, the members were committing spiritual adultery or fornication with this false church. God had given these false shepherds warnings and time to turn from their evil ways, but they had refused to repent. He then promised that he would allow the false church and everyone who followed her, to go through a time of great tribulation, and any of her children, those groups or churches that might spring up from the mother church, he would kill or destroy. All the other churches would know, that He is the one who knows what is in the their hearts. He will give a reward to everyone according to their lifestyle and deeds.

Christ then addresses these dear folks in Thyatira who had remained true to him, and had not followed the strange doctrines. He told them that he would not put any other burdens on them, but that they should hold fast to the faith until he would come back for them.

Christ's Church all down through the ages has been faced with the same or similar problems, which faced the early Christian Church. Even today Gods people have to be on guard for false prophets and doctrines of devils. Little things creep into the church almost unawares, and once it gets a toehold, it grows until all of a sudden it is no longer a little thing but has grown into a monster that is hard to deal with. The admonition to "hear what the Spirit saith unto the churches," is of just as great importance if not more so today than it was two thousand years ago. As we get closer to the end of this world's history, Satan will renew his efforts to sow seeds of discontent and conflict among God's people. We should be spending more time reading and studying these messages, so that we will know how to deal with problems that will arise in the near future.

Chapter 3

WHEN GOD GAGGED

In chapter 3 we have the messages to the last three churches. It would be nice if we could say that they were all perfect but that is not the case. Wherever God's work is going forward Satan is there to try to hinder it and stop it if at all possible.

The church in Sardis was in trouble, they had been a strong group of believers and it looked like everything was going smooth for them. They were like some churches of today, they had a group of people who attended regularly but were only bench warmers, they had died spiritually. O, they had good doctrines but some of these beliefs were possibly in question, that is why in verse 2 they were admonished to be watchful and strengthen what they still had or it would die or disappear also, because what they were doing was not what God wanted them to do.

Christ then asks them to think back to when they had first heard about him and accepted his free gift of salvation. They had been on fire for him but the fire was dying down, so he asks them to hold on to what they have left, and turn away from the course they were following. The main thrust of his message to them was to watch and be ready or they would not be ready when he comes.

A few of the folks there in Sardis had been faithful to his cause and had not followed after the strange teachings nor become complacent. They were still on fire for his cause, and were trying to live up to the things that they had learned. Christ told them that they would have white robes and walk with him because they were worthy, and that he would not blot their names out of the Book of Life. He also promised that he would stand between them and his Father as their Intercessor.

The sixth message was given to the leader of the church in Philadelphia, oh that we would receive a message like this one today. In verse 8 they are told, "I know thy works: behold, I have set before thee an open door". This door, because it is open is an invitation for the people to pass through and carry on, in the way they are going. No one could shut it on them as long as they continued in their love for God. In the last part of the verse he tells them that they have kept his word, done the things that they learned and were good representatives of his character and love for mankind.

In many of the early churches and even today there are people who call themselves "Christian", but do not live up to the name. The name implies that the bearer has the character of Christ in his or her life, showing to the world and those around them what God is really like. These church members in Philadelphia had personal relationship with him and shared their knowledge of him with those they came in contact with.

Wherever God's children are, there are those who claim to be followers of him, but their lifestyle and actions, show that their real leader is Satan. In the area around Philadelphia, as in a number of the other churches, lived people who claimed to be Christians, but because of their actions, life style or business dealings, they were not living up to what they claimed to believe. Christ, in his message to the believers referred to these people as members of Satan's church. In some way he was going to make these backsliders acknowledge that he was the leader of these people, that they loved him and above all, that he loved them and was their God.

Christ knew that his people were going to have difficult times ahead of them, that they would face temptations. Because they had been so faithful to him, he gave them the promise that he would keep them from the trials that were to come upon the inhabitants of the earth. These troublous times were to be a test to all who were living on the earth.

The promises that were given to the people in verses 11 and 12 are also for us living in the closing scenes of this earth's history. Each and every one who is true and faithful to the end will be accounted worthy to receive the rewards that are spoken of in these verses.

Now we come to the last church, Laodicea. It must have broken God's heart to look at these church members and know the condition of their hearts. The Creator of this world was about to speak to his people. The message that he was about to give, was not a pleasant one.

Here was a group of people that were claiming to be followers of him, and yet there was a great difference between what they preached and what they actually did. They claimed to love him, attended church on a regular basis, gave their tithes and offerings and from all outward appearances were true and faithful, but inwardly they had a problem. They were not on fire for the Lord, today we would call them "bench warmers", so the message to them was very severe. "I know the condition of your hearts, your works, your thoughts, and what I see makes me sick to my stomach". You are not for me and you are not against me, you are like lukewarm water. Now water is good for the body but very few people enjoy a drink of lukewarm water I will have a hot drink on a cool day once in a while, but for the most part I want cold water. A glass of lukewarm water makes me gag. Christ felt the same towards these lukewarm people, so he told them that because they were neither warm nor cold he would spue them out of his mouth. The word "spue" in the King James Version is a very mild word for how he felt towards them. If Christ were to use the language of today, he would put it somewhat like this. "Because of the way you are, very easy going, wishy-washy never standing up for principle, you make me sick to my stomach and I will vomit you out. You gag me."

If this sounds revolting to you then I have gotten my message across. The people in this church were in a bad way and they didn't even know it. In verse 17, the problem is spelled out very plainly to them and is a warning for us today. You may say, "well I don't have very much money and I do need a lot of things that I haven't acquired yet, so this doesn't apply to me." Think again.

Lets take a look at us as Christians today. We have freedom of worship, we have the Bible, we follow the ten commandments, we have great schools of learning, we have magnificent churches to worship in, we have publishing houses, and fantastic missionary programs. Is it possible that we might become so wrapped up in the things we have as a church, that we lose sight of our goal? Is it possible that we could become satisfied to attend church and sit in a nice comfortable pew to listen to a polished preacher, give an eloquent sermon, and still be lost?

The members in the church at Loadicea were content with their spiritual condition and their relation with the Creator. They did not recognize how far they had slipped away from the Divine plan for them. Christ told them that they were wretched, and miserable, and poor, and blind, and naked. What a contrast with the church of Philadelphia

Admonition was then given to them to open their eyes and take a look at the condition that they had fallen into. Christ advised them to "buy of me gold tried in the fire, that you may be rich, and white raiment, that you may be covered so you will not be ashamed of your nakedness". The gold that he was referring to here was not the kind of gold that most men seek after. In fact as we look at the next few texts we will find that very few people want that kind of gold of which Christ spoke.

Peter, writing to the members in Asia, Cappadocia, Galatia, and Bythnia, told them that the trials that were testing their faith are of more value than gold, though it had been purified in the fire.[1] Here faith is being compared to gold. Both of these have to go through a time of purification before they reach their ultimate value. God says, "...I will bring the third part through the fire, and will refine them as silver is refined, and will try them as gold is tried: they shall call on my name, and I will hear them: I will say, It is my people: and they shall say, The Lord is my God".[2] This is what Christ was referring to when he said, "buy of me, gold tried in the fire".

The Christians were then counseled to also buy white raiment, that they might be clothed. We find the term "white

---

[1] 1 Peter 1:7
[2] Zechariah 13:9

robe" used in several passages of scripture and we will look at several of these. In chapter 4:4 we see 24 elders sitting, clothed in white raiment in the throne room in heaven. The martyrs cry out with a loud voice, "How long, O, Lord, holy and true, dost thou not judge and avenge our blood on them that dwell on the earth? And white robes were given unto every one of them; and it was said unto them, that they should rest yet a little season, until their fellow servants also and their brethren, that should be killed as they were, should be fulfilled".[3] Here again we see that Gods people had to go through a time of trouble before they could receive the "white garment".

The white raiment, robe or garment mentioned in these passages is, none other than the righteousness of Christ.[4] This is what he wants us to buy and the purchase price of his righteousness is faith in, and acceptance of his perfect life and death on the cross for our sins, so we now have a twofold purchase plan for eternal life with our Creator. He bought us with his blood shed on Calvary and we buy his righteousness with our faith in that shed blood. Many who read this will immediately say, "but salvation is free and can't be bought". It's true that you can't buy salvation with money or good works, the only currency that heaven accepts is "faith." That's why Christ advises us to buy from him, gold tried in the fire, buy from him, white raiment, He is the only one who can offer it for sale.

Let us finish verse 18 and combine it with verse 19. Here we are asked to anoint our eyes with eye salve, so that our eyes are opened up to see clearly that, as many as he loves, he rebukes and chastens or corrects. This takes in everyone who has ever been born. Not all however will accept his invitation or his unlimited love for mankind. We need to spend more time studying these principles and getting them cemented in our minds so no one can take them away from us.

In the closing message to the church, Christ says, " Behold I stand at the door and knock". Here is shown one of the greatest attributes of his love, he doesn't gain entry into

---

[3] Revelation 6:10,11
[4] Revelation 7:14

our lives by force. When one goes to visit at a friends house you don't go up to the house and walk in without announcing your arrival. Upon knocking, you wait for someone to come and invite you in, and only then do you enter in and visit with your host. Here in verse 20 we see that Christ honors our personal wishes. We can refuse him entry into our lives or we can open the door to our hearts and let him come in so that he can communicate with us and we with him. In his great love for mankind, he allows each one of us to have the freedom to accept him or reject him. What a great God he is.

There are many great promises scattered throughout the Bible for each and every one of us, but probably the one that means the most to us, is here in the 21st verse. "To him that overcometh will I grant to sit with me in my throne, even as I also overcame, and am set down with my Father in his throne." Oh what a promise that is to his children, the hope it holds for each of us, is almost incomprehensible.

The final message that was given to each of the churches is again repeated to the Laodiceans, He that hath an ear, let him hear what the Spirit saith unto the churches. All of these councils were given to people of all ages, from Johns time right down until the coming of Christ in the clouds of heaven to receive his own people who have washed their robes white in the blood of the Lamb.

John has finished writing the cover letters to the seven churches. Some theologians have suggested that each one received a copy of the complete book, thus making sure that at least one copy, was preserved to be past down to us in the end times. This train of thought comes from the statements found in chapter 1, verse 19, "and the things which shall be hereafter", and also Revelation 22:16.

Thus ends the messages to the seven churches throughout Asia and to all churches down through the ages since that time. It is up to each one of us individually as to what we do with them, in applying them to our own lives as we prepare for his appearing.

Chapter 4

THE UNSOLVED MYSTERY

John draws our attention to the fact that the vision in the previous chapters is over, by using the words, "After this I looked". Today we would say, " later on", indicating that the first vision is over and a new one is about to begin. He now sees a door opened into heaven, and he hears the same voice that he had heard in chapter 1. This voice spoke to him, inviting him to come up to heaven, promising to show him the things that were about to happen in the future.

It is interesting to note the difference between this vision and the first one John had. In his first one, he was already in vision when he heard the voice behind him. Here in chapter 4, he sees heaven opened, hears the voice of Jesus, and then is taken up in vision into heaven to see what is taking place there.

As soon as John was taken into heaven via this vision, he sees a throne set there with some one sitting on it. He does not seem to recognize the person sitting there, if he does, he never mentions the name directly in this chapter. However, he gives a very beautiful description of the being that is seated there. John does not describe the being as tall, dark, and handsome, using physical features to tell us what the person looked like. He instead uses comparisons to precious stones and gems, to draw our attention to the beauty of the one on the throne. I like the way the Phillips translation puts it, "blazed like diamond and topaz".[1] I like to believe that, not only was this description one of appearance but also one of the beautifulness of the character of Him who sat on the throne. When we get into chapter 5, we will find that the one on the throne is God the Father.

John continues to describe the scene in heaven. Around about the throne was a rainbow, which also appeared like a gemstone. When we hear the word, "rainbow", immediately

---

[1] Revelation 4:3, Phillips trans.

we think of the rainbow of promise that was given to Noah. One that consists of a half circle, starting at ground level on one side, and circling over top to the other side. This rainbow was not over the throne, but "around about", indicating that it was like a halo, a complete circle over top of the throne, and maybe even over the twenty–four seats that John saw, surrounding the throne. It is interesting to note that the same terminology is used to describe the rainbow and the twenty–four seats, they are both "around about" the throne, and both appear to be on a horizontal plain. However it may be a vertical rainbow encircling the entire throne room scenario. John did not elaborate on it.

We need to take a few moments to talk about this throne room, and to find out what it really is. After the Children of Israel had crossed the Red Sea and were travelling through the desert, Moses was called, to come up on Mt. Sinai, to meet with God.[2] There he was shown the Sanctuary where God dwelt in Heaven. He was instructed to make a copy of it down on the earth, as a dwelling place for God, so that God could dwell among them while on their travels to the Promised Land.

Moses was instructed to build the Sanctuary with two compartments, the first compartment was known as the Holy Place, in which the Priests ministered, on a daily basis, transferring the sins of the people to here. The second compartment was known as the Most Holy or Holy of holies, where the mercy seat was. This was the visible dwelling place of the Most High God. Once a year, the High Priest would transfer all the sins from the Holy Place into the Most Holy Place, where they would be presented to God and then placed on the scapegoat. The scapegoat was then sent out into the wilderness to die. This was known as the taking away of sins or cleansing the sanctuary.

From this record in Exodus, dealing with the Sanctuary, we know that wherever God the Father is or dwells, is the Most Holy Place, the Heavenly Sanctuary. This throne room that John sees in the vision is none other than the Most Holy place, the same Sanctuary that Moses was shown hundreds

---

[2] Exodus 24:18, 25:8,9, 40.

of years before. Earthshaking events were about to take place here shortly.

Back in the throne room, we are listening to John as he describes some more of the things he saw while there. As mentioned earlier, there were twenty–four seats around about the throne. Twenty–four elders, dressed in white garments were sitting on these chairs, each one wearing a crown of gold. There are two interesting items of apparel, that are brought to our attention here that we need to look at. First, we will look at the white garments these elders are wearing.

Isaiah talks about being clothed with a robe of righteousness, which God gives him.[3] In Philippians we read, "And be found in him, not having mine own righteousness, which is the law, but that which is through the faith of Christ, the righteousness which is of God by faith".[4] Job also talks about righteousness that is given to man, by God.[5] From these texts we see that those who love God and have faith in his promises, will receive a robe or garment of Christ's righteousness. There are many more texts that refer to the righteousness of God or Christ, being imputed or given to mankind, who seek him with all their heart. These twenty–four elders around the throne are seen as wearing white robes of righteousness, a symbol of Christ's purity.

In considering the "crowns of gold", there appears to be several different kinds or types of crowns that will be given to Gods people. Just to name a few, there is the Crown of Righteousness[6], Crown of Life[7], and the Crown of Glory.[8] The crowns that these saints are wearing could be any one of the above, or they may all be one and the same. I am sure if a person were to dig deeper into the subject, they would find many more references to crowns with other names attached to them. We do know that this group of people, were a very special group, and they had a special job to do. Who were

---

[3] Isaiah 61:10

[4] Philippians 3:9

[5] Job 33:26

[6] 2 Timothy 4:8

[7] James 1:12, Revelation 2:10

[8] 1 Peter 5:4

these elders and what were they doing, seated around the throne of God in the Sanctuary of heaven?

The Bible does not give us a cut and dried answer, as to who these elders are, nor does it say what they are doing there in the throne room. To get an idea as to the possible identity of these beings, we need to look at a number of texts in the Bible, then we will have to draw our own conclusions and leave it at that.

In chapter 5, verses 8 and 9, we read that the twenty- four elders fall down before the Lamb and worship Him. Then they sing a "new" song. The last part of that song says, "and hast redeemed us to God by thy blood, out of every kindred and tongue and people and nation". Now we know that these beings were humans from this sinful world, but, had been redeemed by the blood of Christ. We know this by the fact that these elders are wearing white garments, which we learned earlier, was the righteousness of Christ. The next question is, how did they get to heaven before John was taken there in vision?

We are going to look at several different stories to see the possibilities, of identifying who these elders are. In the Bible, are recorded instances, in which various people were taken to heaven with out seeing death, in other words, they did not die, God just took them to heaven under special circumstances. They were not raptured secretly, otherwise we would not know that they were up in heaven at this time. You see, other people either saw them go to heaven, or were shown that they were in heaven. The first one mentioned in the Bible to be taken to heaven from this earth was Enoch.[9] In reading the accounts of all the patriarchs in the book of Genesis, you will note that each one is mentioned by name and it also tells how long each one lived. When it finishes talking about that particular individual, it simply says, "and he died", but when it comes to Enoch, it says, "and Enoch walked with God, and he was not, for God took him." You will note that the word "was" is italicized, indicating that it is a supplied word by the translators. It would have been more correct if they, the translators had used the word "died" in place of "was". Read

---

[9] Genesis 5:21-24.

the text again and replace the word "was' with "died", and you will get a clearer picture of what Moses was saying when he wrote this book. So we know that Enoch is in heaven, and there is nothing secret about him.

Next we have the story of Elijah,[10]a prophet of God who was taken up to heaven in full view of Elisha. It is interesting to note that in this story, not only Elijah and Elisha knew what was about to happen, but also, all the students from the school there in Jericho, knew as well. This knowledge of Elijahs' soon departure from the earth seemed to be well known amongst the people of the area. Nothing secret about his trip to Glory either.

Then we have the story of Moses, and how he died, just short of crossing over into the Promised Land.[11] He had just finished blessing the Children of Israel, the Bible record indicates he left the plain of Moab, where the Israelites were camped, and went up on Mt. Nebo, to a knoll called Pisgah. God came down and communed with him, and showed him the land that had been promised to Abraham, Isaac, and Jacob generations before. God gave Moses the opportunity to look at that land, but told him that he could not go over to it. After all that he had gone through, leading this rebellious people for forty years, and now all he could do was look at it.

God buried Moses there in a valley, in the land of Moab. In his wisdom, he didn't allow anyone to know where the grave site was. Moses had lived for a hundred and twenty years and had not lost his eyesight or his vitality. God had preserved him through all the wanderings and hardships as he led the people through the desert. God had a greater plan for Moses than Moses ever expected. Jude, verse 9 gives us a glimpse into the surprise that awaited Moses as he slept there beneath the sod in that foreign valley. In this verse, we find Michael the archangel having an argument with Satan as to who owned the body of Moses. Satan claimed his body, as he didn't want the body removed from the grave, however Michael had other orders. He was to raise up Moses and take him to a better Promised Land than the earthly one, and Sa-

---

[10] 2Kings 2:1-13
[11] Deuteronomy 34:5,6

tan was not at all happy about this turn of events. Moses had a work to do that was very important to you and me.

One day Jesus took Peter, James, and John up to a high mountain by themselves as he needed to be alone with them for a little while.[12] While on the mountain Jesus was changed, or transformed, for a short while. His face shone and his clothing became dazzling white. The three disciples had never seen anything like this before. Suddenly, two other people appeared on the mountaintop with them, Moses and Elijah, and they talked with Jesus, and he with them. These two men had come down from heaven as God's representatives to encourage Christ in his mission to save mankind from their sins. It is believed that Moses represented those who die before being taken to heaven and Elijah represented those who would be translated without seeing death. There is no Bible verse to verify that thought, but it has been the accepted understanding for as long as I can remember. Christ saw in these two men, how high the stakes were in the great controversy between him and Satan, and this encouraged him to go through with his plan to redeem the millions upon millions that believed in him.

So now we have three people that we know of, that are in heaven, who could be sitting in some of the twenty–four seats around the throne, but that still leaves twenty–one seats empty. We have to do some more searching to see if anyone else might have been taken to heaven, who could fill these seats.

In the book of Matthew, we find the account of the death of Christ.[13] At the moment that he died several things took place, but the one we want to look at is the earthquake. In the last part of verse 51 and the first part of 52, we find that the earthquake broke apart the rocks and the graves were opened. Remember that in Bible times people buried their dead in tombs carved out of rock or else they used existing caves. This is why the account says the rocks were torn open or rent. You can just imagine how the soldiers and their captain as well as all those around there, felt when they saw this happen. It must have really shook them up to see the graves

---

[12] Matthew 17:1-3
[13] Matthew 27:50-53

opened and all those bones laying around and those skulls with their haunting empty eye sockets staring at them. I can just see these "brave" soldiers huddled close to their fires as they guarded the tomb of Jesus over the weekend.

Early in the morning on the first day of the week, another earthquake hit the region, and I imagine that the soldiers who were guarding the tomb, expected some more eerie eye sockets to be staring at them. However something even more fearful appeared. An angel had been sent from heaven to re-move the stone from the tomb, Christ had arose.

Lets go back now and look at the last part of verse 52 and also verse 53. Here we read that "many" bodies of the saints, which slept, or were dead arose or were resurrected, and came out of their graves "after" Jesus arose, and they went into Jerusalem, where many people saw them. Though the Bible does not say so in as many words, many theological scholars believe that when Christ went back to heaven, he took these resurrected saints with him as first fruits, to pres-ent to the Father. The word "many" in the verse that we read does not mean a few, or some, but would indicate a great many or lots of saints. In the book of Ephesians, Paul writing to the church refers to the fact that Christ took those who were captives in the grave as his captives to take to heaven.[14] We can now see who might be sitting in those other seats around the throne and comprise the twenty-four elders.

Let's get back to the book of Revelation now, and con-tinue on our journey. In verse 5 of chapter 4, the throne is brought to our attention again. Lightning and thunder and voices are heard coming from it, and in front of it there are seven lamps of fire that are burning or lit. We do not have to wonder what these lamps are or represent because the next sentence tells us what they are. These seven lamps are, notice the word "are" the seven Spirits of God. We know that the number seven is a complete or perfect number in the Bi-ble. God does everything in sevens, thus in this verse, we see the perfect Spirit of God or the Holy Spirit. Now we know that the Holy Spirit is in the throne room, along with the twenty–four elders.

---

[14] Ephesians 4:8

John now draws our attention to some strange looking creatures that are around about the throne. These are in addition to the twenty–four elders that we read about earlier in the chapter. In the King James translation, they are called "beasts", while other translations call them "living creatures", and John tries to describe as best he can in human language, what they looked like.

It was when I arrived at this point in my study of the map leading to the kingdom, that I ran into a problem. Who were these beast like beings? How did they get there? And where did they come from? John never gave us any answers, and in fact I could not find any concrete answer anywhere I looked in the Bible. Then I came up with what I thought was a very ingenious plan to get it straightened in my mind before carrying on any further.

My wife and I were working at a church camp for the summer. I figured that if I asked a number of pastors, what these creatures were, that I would get a pretty good idea as to their identity, and where they came from. I cornered my first victim one afternoon and asked him who these creatures were, I received a very courteous, vague definition, but it didn't really answer the questions in my mind. I asked four more pastors the same question, now I had five different answers to choose from. These ranged from, "the four spirits of God" all the way to "the all seeing eyes of God". Now I was confused and I didn't know if I was on the right road or not. Had I taken a wrong turn and gotten hopelessly lost? I decided I would ask one more pastor and see if I could get back on the right road again, so I could continue on my journey.

I was walking along the road at the campground one afternoon a few days later, when I saw Pastor X driving towards me. Ha! Now was my chance, so I waved him down and told him of my dilemma. I then asked him the same questions I had asked the other five pastors. His answer absolutely shocked me, "I doubt there is one pastor in this conference that fully understands the book of Revelation, and I haven't had time to study it either". He then went on to tell me, that he felt the key to understanding Revelation, was hidden somewhere in the 12th chapter of the book of Daniel. He then gave me some of the best advice I have ever received, "continue to study and pray and the Holy Spirit will guide you in your search for the answers to your questions".

I will be honest with you, dear reader. I have not found a concrete, absolute answer to the identity of these four living creatures or beasts. I have found in the book of Ezekiel[15], a description of similar looking creatures, however it appears to be describing Christ. Also here in Ezekiel, each of the creatures have four heads and four wings, whereas in Revelation 4, each creature has only one head and six wings. One thing we must be cautious about is, not to symbolize every passage in the book of Revelation. For an example, these beasts do not represent kings or kingdoms as they did in the book of Daniel, or even further on in the book of Revelation. What John was viewing was an actual event taking place in the heavenly courts, and not a prophetic historical vision dealing with earth's political history. However, looking at it from John's perspective, the events which were being depicted as the seals are being opened before him, are, or could be termed prophetic, in nature.

Another interesting aspect of these creatures is that they worship the Lord God Almighty, as we read in verse 8. Seeing as these creatures give worship to God, we know that they are not God. If they were, then God would be worshiping himself, and that would be going against his heavenly principals. Another piece of the puzzle can be found in chapter 5, and verses 8 and 9. Here we find that both the four beasts and the twenty–four elders fall down before the Lamb and worship Him. In this worship song that they all sing, they make the declaration, "...Thou wast slain, and hast redeemed us to God by thy blood, out of every kindred, and tongue, and people, and nation". Because these four beasts or creatures sing this song they recognize or state that they were sinful beings at one time, but Christ died for them and paid the price on the cross of Calvary, to redeem them to himself. These two verses are the only clue we have as to who or where these creatures came from, that are around the throne.

---

[15] Ezekiel 1:4–28

Chapter 5

THE SECRET BOOK

Chapter 5, is a continuation of chapter 4, as the subject matter is still dealing with the throne room, and the events that led up to this point. Now we need to fasten our seat belts as the next part of the journey may get a little rough, and we may be shaken up a bit by some of the detours and reconstruction of the highway to heaven.

Verse 1, of this chapter, is just loaded with information, and this information raises just as many or more questions than there is information in it. So, lets take one thing at a time and hope that we don't have any breakdowns as we travel through this chapter. First of all lets read the verse so we know what we are going to be looking for, and talking about. "And I saw in the right hand of him that sat on the throne a book written within and on the backside, sealed with seven seals."

There are three main items of interest in this verse, that we are going to look at, the first one is the term "the right hand". It is interesting to note that the "right hand" was of great importance both in the Old Testament and in the New Testament times. Even today, in many cultures of the east, the right hand is held, in esteem over the left one.

King David talked often of the saving attributes of the right hand of God, as well as Paul, and John.[1] As we study the symbols of righteousness, and I use that term loosely, it is interesting to note the many aspects of it. In chapter 4 we talked about the "robe of His righteousness" and are given a "crown of righteousness". Now, Isaiah talks about being upheld by the "right hand of Gods righteousness".[2] Now here we have the one on the throne with a book in his right hand. So the right hand is significant in some way with salvation.

---

[1] Psalms 20:6 , 138:7; Hebrews 10:12; Revelation 1:17
[2] Isaiah 41:10

When I started studying this chapter and I read this verse, it struck me like a bolt of lightening, "the right hand". I've heard that term before, and then the picture came to me, clear as a bell. Jesus was talking to his disciples and telling them about his second coming. In the course of the sermonette, he told them about the gathering of all the people of the world[3], and how he was going to separate them. He knew the disciples were familiar with the ways of the shepherds of the area, how in the evening the shepherd would separate the sheep from the goats. He, being the Good Shepherd was going to separate his sheep from the goats, the sheep he would put on his right hand but the goats would be put on the left. The sheep follow the shepherd whereas goats tend to do their own thing. Then he proceeded to share with his followers just who were the sheep, and who were the goats. We will expand on this, a little further on in the chapter.

Now lets take a look at the next part of the verse, namely the "book". It is interesting to note that this is not just an ordinary book. There are two characteristics that make it stand out from other books that John is used to seeing in his day. The first thing we notice is that it has writing on both sides, the front and the back. If this were a common thing in Johns day, he would not have made a special mention of it here. Remember that in his day, the use of scrolls was very common. These scrolls were their books. The writer would unroll the scroll a little way and proceed to write on it much the same way as we do today on a piece of paper. When he got to the bottom of the scroll he would roll that page onto the handle on one side while unrolling a blank section from the opposing side. He would then write on that section until it was finished, and so, would repeat the whole process over again.

The scrolls were made out of either animal skins or papyrus paper, or other such material. Due to the fact that it was rolled on the handles so long, it would conform to a rolled up shape, similar to a roll of chicken wire or stucco wire. If these scrolls were then turned over, and rolled in an opposite direction, and written on, the fibers would be bent backwards. This wouldn't be so bad if it was only written on

---

[3] Matthew 25:32,33, 41.

and read once, but with repeated reading over many years, these scrolls would wear out just as wire does after being bent back and forth. Many Bible scholars feel that the scrolls were written on both sides to save waste of writing material. However, from my studies of scripture, and experience of rolling paper back and forth, I am inclined to believe that the books or scrolls were written on one side only.

We are going to look at a couple of other interesting parallels in the Bible where it is mentioned that there was writing on both sides of the writing material. There may be more than two other places, but these are all I have found so far.

In Exodus 32:15,16 is recorded the event of God giving Moses the Ten Commandments on Mt. Sinai, at the end of their communion together for forty days and nights.[4] These were written on two tables of stone, and were written on both front and back of the tablets, by the finger of God.[5] He had previously spoken these commandments audibly to them back in Exodus twenty, but he wanted them to have something that they could look upon and reread as needed, a written "standard of conduct". You can read the story for yourself [6], how Moses broke the two tables of stone and how God asked him to make a couple more like the first ones and bring them back up on the mountain. He did as God asked and spent another forty days and nights in Gods presence. At the end of their time together, God again wrote out the commandments on the two tablets with his finger.

The other instance in the Bible of writing on two sides is recorded in Ezekiel.[7] This scroll or roll, or book if you please, was not a literal, tangible book that Ezekiel could physically touch. It was one that he saw, while in vision, and was symbolic of a message that God wanted him to give to the nation of Israel for that time. This roll was also written on both sides, and it caught the attention of Ezekiel, to the extent that he made special mention of it also. It is interesting to note that in all three instances, it was God that did the writing and not mankind.

[4] Exodus 24:18
[5] Exodus 31:18
[6] Exodus 32
[7] Ezekiel 2:10

The third and last item of interest here in verse 1 is that this book is sealed with seven seals. If anyone wanted to open it and read it, all seven seals must be broken so that the contents could be revealed. John saw and heard a strong angel ask if anyone could open the book, but no man in heaven or on earth was able to break open the seals and read what was inside the book. This caused John a lot of unrest, being as he was a normal inquisitive human being. He wanted to know what was so important that it had to have seven seals on it. You remember what it was like when you were a child at Christmas time and all those presents were sealed up under the Christmas tree. How you tried to find out what was inside each box with your name on it by shaking, listening, and turning it over and over. John was in a worse state of mind, he wept because no one could open the book and read it nor even look inside it. If we didn't know better, we would class John as a spoiled brat, throwing a temper tantrum.

One of the elders now speaks to John, and tells him not to weep. There is someone who can break the seals and open the book, it is Jesus, the Lion of the tribe of Judah, a fitting symbol of the King of kings. Today we know the lion to be the king of the animal kingdom, fearless, strong, and in control of its domain, man is its only enemy. Christ is king of the universe and he is in control of his entire creation, however in his love he doesn't force mankind to obey him, and thus man has become his enemy also.

After the elder had spoken to him, John looked and all of a sudden he saw a Lamb in the center of the four beasts and twenty–four elders, near the throne. This Lamb looked like it had been killed, yet it was alive. John made note of that, and recorded it for us so that we would know without a doubt, that this being who had just entered the Most Holy place, was none other than Jesus, the Lamb that taketh away the sins of the world.

This Lamb had seven horns and seven eyes. These horns and eyes are symbols for the Holy Spirit. You will notice in the last part of verse 6, it says "which are the seven spirits of God". These are the same spirits that we read about in chapter 4, verse 5, that were around the throne. It then goes on to say that these seven spirits are sent throughout the earth. These are the same spirit, the Comforter, that Jesus promised to send to his disciples in John 15, verse 26. It is also the Holy Ghost that is mentioned in Acts 1:8, as he was about to be taken up into heaven from them.

Now Jesus "the Lamb that taketh away the sins of the world"[8], steps forward to the throne and reaches out, taking the book from the Father. He has at last entered the Most Holy place to begin the final phase in the redemption of you and me, and all those that who have looked for his appearing. His ministration now takes on a new angle and job. Not only is he our intercessor as a High Priest, but now he is to become our judge as well.

The twenty–four elders and the four beasts know that something significant is about to take place and with bated breath they watch as Christ takes the "book". Immediately, they all bow down before the Lamb. As they do, John sees that each one has a harp and a vial or bowl full of odours or incense. The odours that are in these vials are the prayers of the saints, which have ascended, up to heaven, and are presented, to God.

As the beasts and the elders are bowed before the thrones, they sing a new song that before now, no one could sing. This song was a song of redemption, you can read it in verse 9. The key points of the song are "you are worthy to take the book" and "worthy to open the seals on the book". This was due to the fact, that he had died to redeem mankind, or buy us back, if you please, and the purchase price was His blood on Calvary. His death paid the debt of every man, woman, and child that ever lived, in any country or nation, who spoke any language on this old planet earth.

It is in verse 9 that we find the first mention of the name of God, in this vision. Now we know without a doubt that we are in the Holy of holies, and that all three entities of the God head are present in the same room at the same time. Prior to this only the Father and the Holy Spirit were here, along with the beasts and the elders, as Jesus was ministering in the Holy place on behalf of man.

---

[8] John 1:29

The "book" has been mentioned eight times in the first 9 verses of chapter 5, only verse 6 makes no mention of it, as this verse is concerned with the arrival of the Lamb in the throne room. In all the other verses, the "book" is the key topic and subject, and it holds the attention of John, the twenty–four elders and four beasts, as well as all the angels in heaven.[9] John hears this great multitude saying, "worthy is the Lamb". He continues on in verse 13, that he even heard all the creatures that God had created, blessing and giving honour and glory to the one sitting on the throne. What is so special about this "book", that holds the attention of the entire realm of created creatures on this earth and in heaven?

Remember I mentioned earlier about the council one pastor gave me, who felt the key to understanding Revelation, was in the 12th chapter of Daniel. When I started studying the book of Revelation, I did not want to mix Daniel in with it, as I felt it was dealing mostly with history, and the rise and fall of ancient world governments or nations. If this were really the case, then it had no relevance in the study of Revelation and end time events. Many evangelists and Bible scholars, both in the pulpit and on TV kept referring to the "sealed book of Daniel", and this kept coming back to my mind, along with the council from my pastor friend. I decided that I had no choice but to turn to the book of Daniel, and study it over again and see if I could find the connection between it and Revelation. And so we must take a detour on our trip through the Revelation. Again, I must warn you, that all detours, are not necessarily smooth. Sometimes we may even be shaken up a bit.

As I studied Daniel over again, I found many of the old prophecies to be the same as I had heard them over the years, but none of them really had much to do with connecting it to the Revelation until I came to the 9th and 10th verse of chapter 7. Here Daniel was in vision, and he had just seen the four great world powers, represented by the four beasts, pass before him. The next scene that Daniel was shown was the thrones of these earthly kingdoms being cast down or destroyed and the Ancient of Days or God setting up his eternal kingdom. In

---

[9] Revelation 5:11

verse 10, Daniel saw an unnumbered amount of heavenly beings, and we assume that they are angels, ministering to God.
This "ministering to", was not necessarily supplying the needs
of God, but was the act of carrying out his work, both in heav-
en, and between heaven and earth. Then Daniel saw a courtroom scene, where a judgement was taking place and some
books were opened. Could this be the connecting link to the
Revelation? I decided I would continue on to the end of Daniel
and see if there were any more references to this event.

One of the most famous verses and probably the most
widely used by all students of prophetic writings, is found in
chapter 12, verse 4. "But thou, O, Daniel, shut up the words
and seal the book, even to the time of the end"…this is where
I ran into trouble. The general consensus of the majority of
Bible scholars, and this includes Evangelists, Professors, and
Pastors, both in the pulpit, the classroom, and on TV understand this to mean that Daniel was to seal up his book that
he was writing. This book would remain sealed until the time
of the end.

At some time in the future someone would figure out
what it meant and we would all be much wiser. As I attended
Evangelistic crusades year after year, I kept hearing that this
sealed book was the "little book" that John saw in the Mighty
angels hand, in Revelation chapter 10:2. A voice from heaven
commanded John to take the book and eat it. I can remember
thinking, "no wonder John had indigestion" after eating it, so
for the next thirty–five years I suffered along with John every
time I read these passages or heard them preached. Some
of the pieces of the puzzle were just not fitting into place, so
here I was, back in Daniel, studying to see if there might be a
clue to understanding what he was told to seal up.

As I went from prophecy to prophecy, I discovered that at
the end, or near the end of each vision, an angel or messenger
would come to Daniel and explain it to him. There were some
times when he had to wait awhile for it to be revealed to him
but, most of what he was shown was straight forward.

There were people who were not Jews who understood
the time prophecies of Daniel.[10] These men understood when

---

[10] see Additional reading # 1

the Messiah would be born, and so had to know the starting date of the 2,300 prophetic days of Daniel 8:14, to know how to figure in the 70 prophetic weeks of chapter 9:24, thus revealing the time of Christ's birth. It was very evident that this part was not sealed, so I had to go back to chapter 12:1–4 and start over again.

I read and reread chapters 7–12 every night for several weeks. Some nights I would go over the material two and three times, and still I was not able to tie the verses together. By the time the third week rolled around I was starting to wonder if I would ever find what I was looking for. I wasn't even sure, what I was trying to find.

As Daniel was told to "seal the book", I decided the book must have been open at some time. I started looking for other references to the "book" in the chapters I mentioned earlier. Of course there was the one in chapter 7, verse 10, where the judgement was set and the books were opened. Then I noticed the mention of "the book" in chapter 12, verse 1 that I had missed or overlooked in all the previous readings of this scenario. Now I had three texts which referred to "the book", but there was no indication that they were talking about the same book, that I could see.

I had spent a great deal of time in prayer, asking the Holy Spirit to open my eyes, so I could have peace of mind, and get back to the study of Revelation. Towards the end of the third week of wrestling with these verses, I was starting to have serious doubts as to whether or not I was going to find that "thing" that was bothering me about the sealed book. I believe it was a Thursday night. I had read over verses 1 to 4, of chapter 12, eight or nine times, still nothing came to mind that tied these together. In desperation, I fell on my knees and pleaded with God that he would send the Holy Spirit to open my eyes, so I could see the message that he had there in these verses for us. As I got up and took up my Bible again, I reread these texts and suddenly, like a flash of light, it hit me.

In chapter 7, verse 10, Daniel, in vision, saw God sit down with all the heavenly hosts at the end of this earth's history, to go over "the books", and judge the world. The information that was contained within "the books", was of a highly confidential matter. God had been keeping a record all down through the ages of the deeds of mankind, so he could prove to Satan, and the other universes that there were people on planet Earth who loved Him and kept his Commandments. Even Moses knew that God kept this record as far back as the exodus from Egypt. He asked God to blot his name out of "the book" instead of destroying the Children of Israel for their sin, when they had danced around the Golden calf.[11] What Daniel saw in this vision was the "Cleansing of the Sanctuary" also known as the "Investigative Judgement".

In Daniel 12:1 the vision is coming to a close, Daniel had been shown many of the events of this earth's history, how Gods people would be treated and persecuted, some even dying for their belief in Him. Now it is all over, everyone has made their final choice, and God has gone over the deeds of the last name in "the book". The judgement has ended, the decree has gone out, "He that is unjust, let him be unjust still, and he that is filthy, let him be filthy still, and he that is righteous, let him be righteous still, and he that is holy, let him be holy still".[12] So Daniel saw Jesus stand up when his work as intercessor was over. He saw a time of trouble such as never was since there was a nation, however he doesn't give us any details of that "trouble". He does say that it is at this time, God's people will be delivered, everyone who is found written in "the book".

What does this have to do with verse 4? How does it tie the whole scenario together? If we look at verse 2, we see that many of the saints will have been sleeping in their graves and will awake to everlasting life, while others will wake to shame and everlasting contempt, this is a result of the judgement that has just taken place. Daniel saw the judgement set and "the books" opened, he saw that everyone whose name was written in "the book" would be delivered, then in verse 4 he is told to shut up the words and seal "the book" until the time of the end. The book that he was told to seal up was the same one that he saw opened in chapter 7, the same one that contained the names and the deeds of all mankind in. As he

---

[11] Exodus 32:32
[12] Revelation 22:11

looked on this scene of judgement in heaven, he may have seen the name of Dwight Johnson, come up on a couple of pages. God in His mercy asked him to seal it, so no one could look in it until Jesus had blotted out all my sins. What a loving Father we have.

Someone is sure to ask, What are the "books", and what is the "book", that Daniel saw while in vision? Are they one and the same, or, are they two separate books? There are a number of books mentioned throughout the Bible that indicate that God is keeping an account of the lives of every individual that ever lived. This bookkeeping covers from the time of Adam, right down to our day and beyond until He comes to redeem us and take us home to heaven.[13]

The "books" that Daniel was shown in chapter 7 verse 10, were the book of deeds or remembrance, and the Book of Life. The "book" mentioned in chapter 12, verse 1 is the Book of Life, as noted by the preceding statement, referring to "thy people shall be delivered, every one that shall be found written in the book".

What was really sealed in the book of Daniel? The answer to that is beyond the scope of this book, but I will say that God did the sealing of that portion of the book, not Daniel.[14]

Now lets get back to John's vision and see if we can pull this all together. Daniel saw the judgement set and the "books" were opened. John sees the Lamb come into the Most Holy place and take the "book" written on both sides, from the Father. Notice that one book is mentioned in the plural, while the other is singular. However the single book is written on both sides. This would indicate that it is really two books in one, thus verifying that this scene in Revelation is the same event that Daniel viewed in his vision.

Daniel was not shown much detail about the judgement, while a great deal of the judgement was shown to John. He was living closer to the end time, and this message was for those living in the closing scenes of earth's history. Daniel was told to shut up the words and seal the book, and John saw the Lamb take the sealed book from the Father. All he

---

[13] Revelation 20:12
[14] Daniel 12:5-9

had to do now was break the seals and open the book, and the final judgement could begin.

Chapter 6

MYSTERY OF THE SIX SEALS

The summer that I turned five, we moved to a small farming and logging community that had a population of several hundred people, in southern British Columbia. It consisted of a train depot, a post office in the general store which also had gas pumps outside. There was a community hall, church, and school. The first winter that we were there, my parents heard that an evangelist was coming to hold some meetings in the community hall. We were church going people, so planned on attending the meetings each evening. My father would milk the cows early and supper would be over so that we could arrive at the meeting place on time.

As I was used to being around cows, and seeing the different breeds, I was familiar with seeing different colored ones. We had brown Jerseys and Guernseys which were heavy cream producers, while some of the farmers had black and white Holsteins for milk production. Being very young and not being able to read at that age, I had to have someone read the poster that was tacked to the bulletin board at the store, that announced the meetings. Of course as on any poster, the name of the speaker was in plain view. Elder Holstein, was going to present a series of studies on the book of Daniel and the Revelation. Why would anyone want a cow's name? Was he black and white? It is funny what goes through the mind of a child especially in the early 1950's before there was television in the area. Well the first night of the meetings rolled around and I was relieved to find that Elder Holstein looked just like everyone else. I never did find out how he got his name.

As the meeting got under way, the speaker unrolled a number of large charts with all kinds of funny looking animals on them. I recognized some of the parts of the various animals from my picture books but these animals seemed to be all cross-breeds. I had never seen a picture of a lion with wings before, nor a bear with ribs sticking out both sides of its mouth. Then there was a terrible looking creature that had a bunch of horns that seemed to have had some trouble and lost a few. I was one mixed up, frightened kid when that meeting was over and I can assure you, I had nightmares for weeks after.

One part of his sermon wasn't too bad, he talked about some different colored horses, and that, I could relate to. I had some trouble with the different riders on the horses, they seemed to carry funny instruments with them. By the time Elder Holstein had finished his meeting that night, he had scared all sin out of me and I vowed I would be good the rest of my life. Such was my introduction to the books of prophecy in the Bible. Since then I have come to love them and to spend much time in studying them.

As we open our Bibles to chapter 6, we will begin another segment of our trip through time to our heavenly home. We must ever keep in mind that a judgement is taking place, that we are in a court room in Heaven, along with John, viewing what is taking place there.

Let's do a quick review of the events so far; John is taken in vision to heaven, he sees a throne with someone sitting on it, there are twenty–four seats around it, with an elder sitting in each one, there are four Beasts there, and the one sitting on the throne has a sealed book in his hand. John wants to know what is in the book, but no one can break open the seals. Suddenly the Lamb, Jesus Christ, is seen in the room, and he takes the sealed book from the Father. All the elders and the Beasts fall down and worship Him, and now he proceeds to open the book.

At this point in our trip we need to pause a moment for a brief look at the pattern that has been set for us in the first few chapters of Revelation. Remember the seven churches, how they were representative of the seven eras of the Christian Church, from Christ's day, down to the end of time. We will be looking at the seven seals in much the same way. Each seal represents a period in history, in which people lived, and the judgement will begin with the dead and eventually pass on to the living.[1] God has set a day in which he will judge the world.[2]

This does leave some question as to, when did or does Christ judge those people who lived prior to the Christian era? One possible answer to this problem is that all the people who lived from the beginning of time, up until the Christian era, having gone through much the same trials and struggles in their lives, will be divided up into these first five seals.

As each successive seal is opened, we notice that they contain more information, and become more detailed. The first and second one are about the same length, then the third and fourth ones have a little more detail in them. Then when the fifth one comes along, it is longer. The sixth one continues from chapter 6 verse 12, to chapter 7 verse 17, while the seventh seal includes chapter 8 verse 1, to the end of chapter 16. This may all seem foreign to you at the moment, but as our study progresses you will see that the road map is complete and accurate in every detail, and every piece of the puzzle fits into its place, making a perfect picture.

There is no "cut and dried" explanation in the Bible, stating that the word "horse or horses" are people, in prophecy. However in the book of Zechariah, there is a lot of talk about "horse and horses" that seems to indicate or suggest that people are being referred to, when the term is used. The fact that there is a rider on each of the horses indicates that whatever the horse is, it is being guided or under the control of the one on its back.

The color of the horses seems to depict the condition of the times in which the people were living, that were being judged. We will see that plainly once we get into the study of them. Here in Revelation there is a white, red, black, and pale horse. In Zechariah the horses in chapter 1 are red, speckled, and white, while in chapter 6 of the same book the horses are red, black, white, and grizzled and bay. Here in Zechariah's vision, he is told what the horses represent, they "are the four spirits of the heavens", however we cannot use

---

[1] Revelation 20:12,   Acts 10:42
[2] Acts 17:31

this vision to interpret John's vision in the Revelation, as they are two separate and different visions.

As the Lamb opens the first seal, John heard one of the Beasts speak, and its voice echoed and re-echoed like thunder, as it rolled throughout heaven. It said, " Come and see". John looks, and he sees a white horse with a rider on its back. As this vision was not explained to John, nor was he told what the symbols represented, we must conclude that he understood what was going on in the courtroom. White is a symbol of purity, so the people, whose names are being gone over in this time frame were living in a time when the gospel was pure and undiluted. The rider on this horse had a bow in his hand, and a crown was given to him. He was going out to do battle with the enemy, and he was victorious over the enemy, giving him the right to wear the crown of victory, making him king. This rider was none other than Jesus Christ, the King of kings.

In verse 4, we have a much different scenario taking place, here the horse is red in color, and the rider has a much different character than the first rider. Here we see that some things were beginning to change within the church. The gospel, which had been pure and undiluted up to this time, was now beginning to be tainted. The fact that this horse was red, may symbolize the red blood that flowed freely during these troublous times in earth's history. Notice the word "may" in the preceding sentence, I must remind you dear reader, that we must be very careful when dealing with prophecy and symbols. There is no Biblical proof that the color red is symbolic of blood.

The rider on this horse was given a sword, and he was allowed to take peace from the earth. This was a time when everyone lived for himself. Life was very uncertain, wars and strife were rampant as the world came into the Dark Ages. Notice the term, "power was given him", he was allowed to take peace from the earth. This rider who was in control of the events taking place was certainly not Christ, so it had to be Satan who was in control at this time.

It is interesting to note, that each time Christ breaks open a seal, one of the four Beasts, or living Creatures, tells John to come and see what is happening. Now in verse 5, the third Beast gives him the same invitation, to come and see. John now sees a black horse with a rider on it. There is one thing different about this one. This rider was not given anything, instead we see that as he comes upon the scene, he has a set of balances in his hand, a totally different picture is presented here.

Let us take a quick look at the horse. This one is black in color, depicting the darkness that this world had slipped into, as it drifted away from God. People's minds were depraved, and many of them lived only a little ways above the animal kingdom. All we have to do is look back into some of the history books to find the stories of the atrocities and depraved lives of the early civilizations, if you can call them that.

The rider has a set of balances or scales in his hand. A balance has a specific job that it is used for. Yes it is for weighing things on, but more importantly, a balance is a judge. Let me explain. With a balance, there are the two trays, one on either side of the pivot point. Both of these trays are of exactly the same weight. When they are both empty, they hang at exactly the same level. When a person wants to weigh something on it, you must put a standard of weight on the one tray. This standard is a piece of metallic substance, or any other substance for that matter, that one places on one of the trays. Then by adding whatever it is, that you want to weigh to the other side of the balance, you are able to obtain the exact amount in weight, as the standard on the other side of the balance. This scale has now been used to judge, whether or not the substance purchased meets the weight of the standard.

In verse 6, John hears a voice from among the four Beasts talking about a measure of wheat and three measures of barley. The rider is going to weigh these measures on his balances to make sure that they are the right amount. Each of these amounts of grain were worth a penny, a day's wages back in Bible times. The rider is making sure that everyone is getting a fair amount of grain for their money. This scenario has a further application to it. As this was shown John, in the vision of the judgement, we get the picture that the one on the horse is wanting to let us know that the Judgment is going to be done fairly. Each one will get what he deserves. Each one of us, will be judged by God's great standard, the Ten Commandments.

Our words, our deeds, our thoughts, and in fact every facet of our lives will be placed on the balance to see if we measure up to God's great law of love. We want to be so in tune with God that it cannot be said of us, as it was to King Nebuchadnezzar, "thou art weighed in the balances and found wanting".[3]

It is quite evident, that the one riding this black horse is Jesus, and that he is the one, guiding the events in the world, during this period of earth's history.

Now the judgement enters another era of time, as another seal is broken open. The fourth Beast calls John's attention, to the last horse. This one is pale in color, which is probably the result of it's rider, who is Death. As we study this seal, we will see the pallor of death hanging over this period of earth's history.

This rider was not alone. He had another fellow riding with him. This second rider on the pale horses name was "Hell or Hades". It is interesting to note that these riders were also given power over the earth, the same as the one at the opening of the second seal. This indicates that they had not had power to do as they wanted, previous to this time. It is interesting to note that the riders on the first and third horses, "had" a bow and a pair of balances in their hands, while the riders on the second and fourth horses were "given" power. They did not have this power until it was granted to them. The riders, Death was Satan.

The power that he received at this time was to extend over a quarter of the earth. This "power", was the "right to do as he wished". He was given the freedom to cause people to be destroyed, by the sword, and by starvation, and by feeding them to wild beasts. This was a very dark time in the history of this world. People were being persecuted for their faith, and belief in Christ. As we look at this, we can see a very marked similarity to the Dark Ages, and the events that

---

[3] Daniel 5:27

took place between 538 AD and 1798 AD, when true Christians were persecuted and martyred for their faith.

In this scene that John is looking upon, he sees that the Judge is going over the names of all those who lived during this time, in earth's history.

It is interesting to note that when Christ opens the first four seals, a Beast speaks, and tells John to "look and see". Also, there are four horses with riders on their backs, while in the next three seals, things take on a totally different view. As we get further on into our study, we will find other instances where the number seven is divided into four and three.

The next three verses, 9 to 11, are really loaded with important information. Many times, we have skimmed over these without studying them in depth or detail. Some theologians tend to pass over them as if they were of no importance. However upon careful examination we will find at least one very important item of interest. The study of this seal will make our trip more interesting, and is a signpost along the way to the heavenly Kingdom, letting us know just how close we are to home.

Johns starts out with the opening of this seal, in the same fashion as the four previous seals, "And when he had opened the fifth seal", but there the similarity ends. No beast speaks up this time, telling him to come and see. No horse and no rider this time, he gets right to the point and says, "I saw under the alter, the souls of them that were slain for the word of God, and the testimony which he held". It is of utmost importance that we look at these seals, and in fact, most of the Book of Revelation, as taking place in a systematic sequence. For instance, the first seal must be followed by the second seal, if it were followed by the fifth seal, then the fifth seal would naturally have to become the second seal. That would foul everything up and we would become lost on our journey to heaven.

Let me tell you about a little side trip that we took one time, back in the early 60's. We were driving out to the Maritimes, on the East coast of Canada, to spend Christmas with my oldest brother and his family. We had dropped down into Washington, to get on No. 2 highway through Idaho, and across the plains. On our way East, I had noticed an Indian Museum at Browning, Montana. Being an avid student of native culture as a teenager, I wanted to stop and go through the museum, however my father had other plans. He wanted to cover a certain amount of miles before nightfall so didn't want to take the time to stop.

I logged the information in the back of my mind, hoping that on the homeward journey, we would be able to take a break from driving and go through the museum. As we neared Browning from the east I dropped a few hints that we weren't to far from the place I wanted to stop at. Dad didn't think that we were that close to the entrance to it, and he wasn't too thrilled with the idea of taking the time to stop. With all the talking going on back and forth as to where we should turn into it, we went past it. I said "we should have turned back there". Everyone was looking back and in that short time we went through a junction without noticing that we should have turned south-west. We drove for some time before I spoke up, and said "I think we are on the wrong road". Mom and Dad didn't think so and my older brother wasn't sure. The scenery didn't seem right to me, so after driving for another fifteen or twenty minutes or so, we stopped and got out the map to see just where we were. Sure enough, we had driven thirty miles out of our way, so we had to turn around and go back to the junction, which was right by the entrance to the museum. By this time I knew enough, not to even suggest going into it.

The point I want to make is this, we can get so wrapped up in our discussions that it is easy to take the wrong road. It is very important to keep our attention focused on the road map, and not be distracted by traditions that are taught as doctrines. We need to stick with a "thus saith the Lord".

Lets get back to verse 9. The souls (bodies , people) that John sees under the alter when this seal was opened, were there as a result of the events that had taken place in the previous seal. It is important to note, that they had been killed because of their love for the word of God. You see the continuity of these scriptures, the one event follows the previous event.

Verse 10 is one of those verses that is bound to bring up questions. For instance, how can dead people cry with a loud voice? This is just a figure of speech. Remember when Cain had killed his brother Abel, and God asked him where Abel was. Cain asked God, "Am I my brothers keeper"? Then God said to Cain that Abel's blood cried out to him from the ground.[4] Abel's blood didn't actually cry out, it was just a way of saying that he knew what Cain had done.

The question that is asked God in this verse has a lot more to it than first meets the eye. "How long" indicates that a long time had already passed by, since they had been martyred. It was time for God to judge and avenge their blood, to bring "every work into judgement".[5] The bottom line was, when are you going to even the score for us? The question goes on to make a statement. Notice carefully, the last part of their plea for justice. How long...dost thou not judge and avenge our blood on them that dwell on the earth? This is the first indication that we get, that suggests that the judgement has passed from the dead to the living. The word "dwell" is the same as "live". From this verse onwards John sees living people as each of the last three seals are opened. There is no reason to doubt that judgement passed from the dead to the living at the opening of the fifth seal, or very shortly thereafter.

Verse 11 continues talking about these martyred saints, as it says that "white robes were given to everyone of them". You will remember that back in chapter 4, the twenty-four elders around the throne were wearing white robes. These robes are given to those that have overcome temptation and sin and have accepted Christ's righteousness. At this point these people in verse 11 are told that they will have to rest, or sleep a little longer, until their fellow servants and their brothers should be killed as they were, should be fulfilled. The term "fellow servants" indicates that these are or were, co-workers or living at the time of the martyrs death, and would be judged under the fifth seal. Of course, these fellow workers have long since passed away and so have many others, but we are not finished with this verse yet.

[4] Genesis 4:9,10
[5] Ecclesiastes 12:14

This verse also includes the "brothers that should be killed as they were, should be fulfilled". If these brothers "should be killed", then it is reasonable to assume that they are still alive. It is also safe to say that these saints, that are still alive, are living with a death sentence hanging over their heads. This last half of verse 11 is a prophecy predicting that another time of persecution will come upon the world, just as the one in the Dark Ages did. The persecution that is to come on God's children in the last great conflict will be of a much greater magnitude than that which the early church went through. Much of the world had not been discovered at that time. The Gospel had not reached much of the New World, Australia, or the Far East, and had not gone into the islands of the seas. Therefore, the inhabitants of those regions were not even aware that there was persecution. The persecution that is mentioned in these verses will be of a universal nature. People will feel the results of it wherever the gospel is preached, around the entire world, and Jesus told his disciples that the gospel would be preached in all the world, and then the end would come.[6] This will be Satan's last ditch effort to squash God's plans to redeem mankind. That is why it is so important that we spend time in God's word , and develop a relationship with him. Only our faith in him will see us through the trying times ahead.

There are two more seals that have to be opened, that affects those of us that will be alive during the last days of earth's history.

We need to take our Bibles now and read all the verses from verse 12 through to verse 17, before we continue any further. Then we will look at it a verse at a time, this way we will not become confused as to what John is seeing, at this point in the vision.

The scenery along the route of our trip to the Promised Land is beginning to become more detailed and exciting as we get nearer the end of our journey. We need to spend more time studying the road map, looking at every little detail, locking them in the recesses of our minds. Then when our

---

[6] Matthew 24:14

road map is taken away from us, we will still be able to make our way safely to the Kingdom.

Let's just take a quick look at what Jesus told his disciples after they had asked him about the signs of his second coming. He said that immediately after the tribulation of those days, the sun would be darkened, and the moon would not give her light, and the stars would fall from heaven, and the powers of the heavens would be shaken.[7] The tribulation that Jesus is talking about here, is the time of trouble and persecution in which some of his children will be martyred, just prior to his coming. It is after this tribulation that the sixth seal is opened

As John sees the sixth seal opened, there was a great earthquake, the sun stopped shining and the moon was a blood red color. For years this earthquake was believe to be the great Lisbon earthquake of 1755, in which 50,000 people perished. We run into a problem at this point because of two discrepancies in our theory. First of all, the Lisbon earthquake took place in the time of the fourth seal, between 538 AD and 1798 AD (see page 57), so it does not fit in here, in the sixth seal, as all of these seals were being opened after 1844. The other problem we have with it is that there have been bigger earthquakes, in the same era that did greater damage and killed thousands more people than in Lisbon. Due to the lack of communications in those early days, many of these large earthquakes went unnoticed and undetected until recent times, but we still tend to cling to the traditions that were established over 150 years ago.

The earthquake that John saw will be of much greater magnitude than any that this world has ever seen up until the time it takes place. It will probably be a universal earthquake. If not, at least its effects will be universal. Let me explain a little further. The Bible was written for all mankind, in all countries of the world. The judgement includes all mankind, in all countries of the world. There is no Biblical proof that the earthquake is, or is not universal, but it is not unreasonable to believe that it could be. Due to the fact that everyone on this old planet is going through this judg-

---

[7] Matthew 24:29

ing period, everyone is being judged by the same standard, and people all around the world are studying the same Bible. As they read the same chapter as we are, they are looking for the same events to take place in their area of the world. Another point to ponder is the fact that this earthquake is going to take place during a time just before the judgement is over and probation for mankind closes. Also it takes place while people are living at the end time, as we shall see in a few moments.

Along with the great earthquake, John is also shown that the sun will cease to shine and the moon will appear to look like blood, and the stars of heaven fell like figs falling from a tree. This is exactly what Jesus had described to his disciples, while he was still with them. All of these events took place back in the late 1700's and early 1800's, but were localized in the eastern United States. The people in England never saw this phenomenon and there is no record of it being seen in South America, as far as I can find. These events that took place in North America were forerunners, warning the world of far greater events to take place just before the end of this earth's history.

John hasn't finished with his vision yet. He sees the heaven parted as a scroll when it is rolled together, and the islands in the oceans disappear. This is a universal cataclysmic event. The earthquake is what causes the islands to vanish.

I used to wonder how this verse could ever happen, until some years ago, when my family and I spent several years in the Marshall Islands as missionaries. On occasion we would ride the copra boats from our island of Namu Namu, up to Kwajalien, to get supplies. Several times we stopped on the island of Lib, which is the tip of an extinct volcano. This island was less than a mile across. When the copra boat would arrive there, a rope would be taken to shore and attached to a large rock in an effort to anchor the ship, as the ocean floor lay 7,000 feet below. This little island was just a pinnacle a mile and a half high, in the middle of the Pacific Ocean. As I would walk around on it, I often thought of what would happen if a severe earthquake should hit the region, and what would become of this tiny speck of land. Would it break off at the base and topple over on its side, disappearing forever under the waves of the ocean? I always felt great relief when I was back on the boat and heading for a larger piece of terra firma.

Before we go on further, we need to look at the first part of verse 14 for a moment. Here John saw the heavens unroll like a scroll when it is rolled together. Remember that he is trying to put something he has seen onto paper for us to read. He wants us to visualize what he saw taking place in his vision. In writing these events down, he uses various objects to compare them to, so that we can get a clearer picture of what he saw, if that makes any sense. In this scenario, he used a scroll, rolling and unrolling to describe what was taking place in the heavens. As we look at this whole scene, it is one of turmoil and destruction. Possibly what he saw was massive hurricanes or typhoons with the clouds rolling back and forth, torrential rain, and high winds buffeting the earth. Whatever it was he saw, was literal events taking place, with literal results.

This whole scene passes before John and as it does, he sees men of all walks of life, kings, rich men, great men, men of valor, free men, slaves, poor men, all terrified by the events that are surrounding them. They run to the mountains to hide, they hide in the storm shelters, the fallout shelters, or what ever place they think is a safe place to be. These people that John sees in the vision, know about God and the judgement to some extent because of their cry from the rocks, the mountains, the buildings, and air raid shelters that they are hiding in, to fall on them, so they don't have to face the one sitting on the throne.

All mankind have a built-in alarm system called conscience, and when something goes wrong, people immediately, whether they believe in God or not, tend to blame him for their troubles. The people living under this sixth seal recognize the power of God in the upheavals of nature that they have just witnessed, and as usual, they want to blame God for their troubles. They want to hide from him and from the wrath of the Lamb. All one has to do is read the headlines on the tabloids at the local check-out counter of any grocery store, and you will read of pending gloom and doom. People seem to know that a time of trouble is coming in the near future. So it was with the people that John saw in his vision. They were going through a frightening experience, but they seemed to know that there was something more fearful yet to come, which they called the "day of his wrath". They end their statement with a very thought provoking question, "who can live through the terrible days ahead, who can survive the upheavals of nature, the unrest of nations, who can live up to the standards that God has set in place?"

It has been thought and preached that the opening of the sixth seal heralded in, or was a description of Christ's Second Coming. There is a problem with this in that, if Christ came here, and at his coming, the wicked are destroyed, there would not be anyone left to ask the question, "who shall be able to stand the great and dreadful day of the Lord?" Also Jesus has to open the seventh seal on the book, before judgement is pronounced, "Over".

We will find the answers to these perplexing questions in the next few chapters as we continue our travels on this intriguing journey through time.

At this time it would be well for us to take a quick recap of the events that have taken place thus far in this chapter:

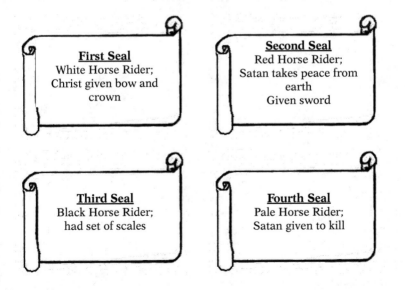

First Seal
White Horse Rider;
Christ given bow and
crown

Second Seal
Red Horse Rider;
Satan takes peace from
earth
Given sword

Third Seal
Black Horse Rider;
had set of scales

Fourth Seal
Pale Horse Rider;
Satan given to kill

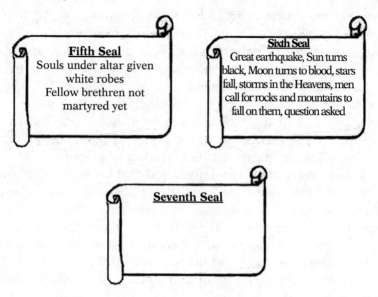

Christ still has one more seal to open, but before he can open it, the question that is asked in the sixth seal has to be answered. That answer will be found in the next chapter.

Chapter 7

THE GREAT CONUNDRUM

In our journey through this chapter, not only will we find some amazing events taking place, but some very special promises are made to those who have come through the trials and persecution of the preceding days. Many of God's children will have been martyred during the latter part of the fifth seal period as prophesied in chapter 6:11, but now John sees something of great importance taking place in the heavens.

In the last chapter, John had seen some awesome events take place. As he continues on in this chapter, he ties it in with the events of the last chapter with the opening words, "And after these things I saw". Here he was referring to the dark day, the great earthquake, moon turning to blood, and the fear of mankind. So what was it that he saw?

As he is looking on the scene in vision, he sees four angels standing at the four corners of the earth, holding back the four winds of the earth so that the wind would not blow on the earth, nor on the sea, nor on any tree. What were these winds that the angels were holding back? Were they real winds, or were they symbolic, and if so, what did they symbolize?

Wind can have a devastating effect on the earth when it becomes too strong. At one time or another, each of us have encountered, or heard of typhoons, hurricanes, or tornadoes. These storms wreak havoc with homes, farm crops, and lives. On several occasions while living in Micronesia, we have experienced firsthand, the effects of typhoons. We have seen homes destroyed, fruit crops destroyed, and trees blown down. It caused a lot of hardship and stress on the people who lived there. I am sure that each one of you have viewed many such scenes on the nightly news channels on our television stations over the past few years. There were the tornadoes along tornado alley, which swept through northern Texas and Arkansas up into the Ohio Valley. Then we all remember Hurricane "Mitch", that caused so much havoc across the Gulf of Mexico and Central America a few years ago. Are these the kind of winds that John was writing about in verse 1?

Many theologians translate the word "wind" or "winds" to mean strife, in fact many times it is referred to as the "winds of strife". I must be honest with you, dear reader, there is no text in the Bible that says, "winds of strife", nor is there a verse that says that the term, "wind" or "winds", are symbolic for strife, such as political strife, or strife of nations.

For interest sake, I looked up the word "wind" in a Concordance[1] and I discovered that it was used one hundred twenty-three times. The usage of it breaks down as follows. Twenty-nine times it was used to describe general wind, as the wind in the trees. It mentions an east wind, nineteen times, a north wind once, a west wind twice, and a south wind, five times. It referred to it as God's or the Lord's wind, ten times. It was used as a figure of speech, such as "on the wings of the wind" twenty-three times, twenty-two times, it was the cause of a great storm, such as the one on the Sea of Galilee[2], and the one that straightened Jonah up.[3] The term "wind", was used ten times as a comparative term, "life is as wind", "words as wind", etc. No place could I find, "the winds of strife" that I had heard so much about as a teenager and young adult attending evangelistic meetings.

I decided that it might be listed under the word "strife" so again I checked the Concordance, and again I was disappointed. I did discover however that strife is generally referred to as a struggle or disagreement between two or more people. There are thirty-nine verses throughout the Bible using the word "strife". No where was it tied to the word "wind".

So let's get back to verse 1 for a few moments and see if we can find anything else that might help us understand better what John was seeing. The four angels that he saw were

---

[1] Stongs Exhuastive Concordance pg.1220
[2] Mark 4:37
[3] Jonah 1:4

holding the winds so that they wouldn't blow on the earth, sea, or trees. The fact that they were holding them indicates that there were plans to let them go in the near future. In the event that these are literal winds there was going to be some great storms, causing disaster and destruction on land and sea. Let's carry on to verse 2.

John has seen the four angels holding the winds, now he sees another one coming from the east carrying or having something with him. That something is of very great importance to you and me. In fact it is of great importance to the whole world even though the majority of the world's population knows nothing about it at the moment. That something is the seal of the Living God. A little further on in this chapter, we are going to be looking at that seal in greater detail.

The fifth angel that John sees in this seal, cries out to the four angels that are holding the wind back. He tells them not to hurt the earth or the sea until we have sealed the servants of our God, in their foreheads.[4] It is interesting to note that this one angel having the seal with him, uses the language of pluralism. Notice that he said "we have sealed" and "servants of our God". Does this mean then that more than one heavenly messenger was helping to do the sealing? Or was this just a figure of speech? It is quite possible that many messengers go out from God to stand beside His faithful children during these trying times, to give encouragement. What was this seal and why were they going to be sealed in their foreheads? Was it a visible mark on their forehead that everyone could see, or was it an invisible one, that only they knew about? As we travel a little further on our journey through this chapter, we will discover what the seal is, and why the servants of God were sealed, and why they were chosen to receive the seal of God.

In the book of Matthew[5], Christ was talking to his disciples about his second coming. He told them that all the nations, referring to everyone on earth would be gathered before him. Some of the people would be following Him and

---

[4] verse 3
[5] Matthew 25:31-33

some would not. He would have to separate those that loved him and those that did not.

As the disciples were familiar with sheep and shepherds, Christ used these as an object lesson, to get across the message that there would be two groups of people when he comes back the second time. It was customary for the shepherds, in the evening when they brought the goats and the sheep in from the pastures, that they would separate them for the night. Whether this was for convenience of milking the goats, or to protect the sheep from the goats bunting them around, I do not know. I do know that the disciples knew about the practice, and that is why Christ was using the example for their benefit. He told them that he was going to separate all the nations or people at his coming just like the shepherds did, the sheep on his right hand and the goats on his left. It was these "sheep", the chosen ones of God that were going to be sealed.

As we travel on our heavenward journey through Revelation, we will notice that the gap between those following God and those that don't, becomes wider apart. Each group of people develop opposite characteristics to the other group. It is only reasonable to assume that if one group is distinguished by a seal, that the other group would also have a mark of some sort with which to identify it. A few chapters further on we will find and discuss the identifying feature called the "mark of the Beast"[6]. So now we know what the two identifying marks are, the seal of God and the mark of the Beast.

Our journey has brought us to some more rough road and we are going to have to take another detour for a little while before we get back on the main road again. I hope you will stick with us as I am sure you will enjoy the scenery along the way.

As a youngster growing up in a community of Christians and attending parochial school, I had always taken Bible studies both in school and in church. Being raised in the Seventh-day Adventist faith, I had always attended church with my family on Saturdays, which we called the Sabbath. Many

---

[6] Revelation 13:17

of our Christian friends attended church on Sunday, but this didn't bother us as we were taught that everyone was free to worship as they chose. As I got older I started to study the Bible more, trying to find answers to some of the question that I had in the back of my mind. Sometimes I found what I was looking for and sometimes I didn't.

Of course as in most churches we were expected and encouraged to memorize portions of the Bible, one of them being the Ten Commandments.[7] Most of the commandments started out with the words "thou shalt not". It was like being told, "you can't do this or you can't do that". It had a negative tone to it and of course with human nature involved, if you are told that you can't do something, it makes you want to do it all the more. There was one commandment that was different from the rest, the fourth one didn't start out with a "you shall not" it started out with "Remember", remember what? If you think back to the days when you were in school, and the teacher said to the class, "remember what we studied about division in math class last Monday"? Immediately your minds all went backwards to the day when you had learned to do long division. You remembered something that you had learned or known previously, and the teacher wanted you to think back to that time and pull that information out of the dark recesses of your mind. That is exactly what God was doing to the Children of Israel. They had some four hundred years earlier been worshiping him on the Sabbath. Due to the long period of slavery in Egypt, they had forgotten to worship him on the day that he had set aside at creation for them, to come apart from their usual affairs and spend time with him.

So it was that He said, "Remember the Sabbath day, to keep it Holy. Six days shalt thou labour, and do all thy work: but the seventh day is the Sabbath of the Lord thy God, in it thou shalt not do any work, thou, not thy son, nor thy daughter, nor thy manservant, nor thy maid servant, nor thy cattle, nor thy stranger that is within thy gates: for in six days the Lord made heaven and earth, the sea, and all that in them is,

---

[7] Exodus 20:3–17

and rested the seventh day: wherefore the Lord blessed the Sabbath day and hallowed it. (Exod. 20:8-11)

In this passage of the Bible, God was asking his followers to remember, think back to what they had learned from their forefathers about the creation of the world. Back to the time when he had made man and put him and his wife in the beautiful garden of Eden. Back to a time when there were no Israelites or Jews. Back to a time when everything was perfect and beautiful, Adam and Eve had just come from the hand of the Creator, and now he gave them a special gift. Genesis 2:2 says, "And on the seventh day God ended his work which he had made, and he rested on the seventh day from all the work which he had made". Verse 3 continues, "and God blessed the seventh day and sanctified it, because that in it he had rested from all his work which God created and made."

God spent the very first Sabbath this world had seen with Adam and Eve in the garden. It was his plan that for ever and ever through out eternity, it would be kept as a Holy day, as a weekly anniversary, if you please, to remind mankind not only of creation but that He, their creator, loved them so much that he wanted them to come apart on that special day to spend it with him. It was this special day that God asked his followers, upon the exodus from Egypt, to remember.

As I spent more time studying about this "special day", I discovered that as the Children of Israel traveled from Egypt through the Sinai desert on their way to the Promised land, that food was very scarce, and Moses wondered what he was going to feed the large group of people that he was leading. The people accused Moses of leading them into the wilderness to starve them to death. God had a talk with Moses and told him that He would send a special bread down from heaven every day. He instructed Moses to tell the people to go out every day of the week and gather, just what they could eat for that day, no more, no less. On the sixth day they were to gather twice as much, as God would not send any for them on the seventh day, the Sabbath. Most of the people did what they were told, but there were some who didn't trust Moses or God, so they gathered more than they needed. The next morning the extra manna, as it was called, had become wormy and stank. Some of the folks decided that if it came for six days, surely the Lord would send more on the seventh day. What a surprise they got on the Sabbath morning when they woke up and had to go hungry because they had failed to trust God, and obey his law. For forty years God supplied their food for them. For forty years they gathered it, six days a week. For forty years, no manna was sent on the Sabbath day. For four hundred and eighty Sabbaths, God impressed upon their minds, which day was the day that they were to meet with him in special communion. His plan worked, never again did the Children of Israel forget what day the Sabbath was. Today we still have, and use a seven day week. It includes the first day of the week, Sunday, the second day of the week, Monday, the third day of the week, Tuesday, the fourth day of the week, Wednesday, the fifth day of the week, Thursday, the sixth day of the week Friday, or the preparation day, and the seventh day of the week, Sabbath, known as Saturday. You can read the story in the book of Exodus, chapter 16.

As I studied this chapter, and saw how the people disobeyed God deliberately after he had just released them from four hundred years of slavery, I wondered, are we in the same spiritual condition today in the world. Are we determined that we are going to do it our way? Something that struck me as ironic in this story, was the fact that these people had just come out of Egypt and God asked them, "how long are you going to refuse to keep my commandments and my laws"?[8] He had not given them the Ten Commandments as yet, but he still expected the people to keep them. Did they already know them before they left Egypt? Were they in effect before He gave them to Moses on Mt. Sinai?[9]

As I went back further in the Bible to the book of Genesis, back in history before there were any Jews or Israelites, I discovered that it was wrong to kill.[10] It was also wrong

---

[8] Exodus 16:28
[9] Exodus31:18
[10] Genesis 4:8-15

to bear false witness[11], wrong to commit adultery[12], wrong to steal[13], wrong to have other gods.[14] In fact, I found that all the commandments and laws that God wrote on the two tables of stone, and gave to Moses on the Mount, were in effect from the very beginning of time, which began in the Garden of Eden.

No wonder God said "remember the Sabbath day". It had been in effect since creation, and would continue in effect until the end of time. In Exodus 31:17, referring to the Sabbath, God said "it is a sign between me and the Children of Israel forever". God reinforced this statement by repeating it a thousand years later through Ezekiel the prophet.[15]

Now back on the main road of our journey again. The Hebrew word for sign was "owth" which meant "a flag, a monument, a mark", thus " I have given you my Sabbath as a sign, a mark, a monument forever". This sign, or mark, or monument, was a contract, a legal document between God and his children.

Now we will attempt to find out what the seal of God is and then we will tackle the issue of the forehead. What denotes a "seal"? There are several kinds of seals, the one that first come to mind are the furry little fellows that live in the ocean. They don't quite fit the picture here in Revelation so we will have to look at a different kind of seal. If this seal belongs to someone, it must be something like a legal seal that we would find on a legal document. One dictionary describes it as "an emblem or figure of authority", to decide irrevocably, a private mark. The word "seal" comes from the Greek word "sphragis", which means, "mark of privacy" or "genuineness".

Thus it was, that I arrived at the conclusion that the "seal of God" was the keeping and the observance of the seventh day Sabbath. It was to be kept for several reasons, one was to commemorate the completion of creation, and another was because God had rested on it and blessed and sanctified it.

[11] Genesis 12:12,13
[12] Genesis16:1,2
[13] Genesis 27
[14] Genesis35:2,4
[15] Ezekiel 20:12

This was good enough for me, I believed that the seal that the angel had in verse two was none other than the "Sabbath day observance". Little did I realize the surprise that God, had in store for me, nor the method in which he would reveal how his people would be sealed in the end time. It happened this way.

It was the winter of 1994, our son and daughter were going to school at Southwestern Adventist College, in Keene, Texas. Just before Christmas our son got married and his bride and he, left on their honeymoon for several weeks. This left us to spend Christmas with our daughter. As she had several weeks of vacation to relax from her studies, she wanted to do something other that sit around Keene. My cousins son and family lived out in Knoxville, Tennessee, and my cousin and her husband were out there for Christmas. After Christmas was over we decided to run over to Tennessee and spend a few days with them, so we loaded up our little car and away we went.

It was great to be with our relatives that we hadn't seen for some time. As usual when John and I get together it isn't very long before the Bibles are out and we are in a good old fashioned Bible study. So it was that the second evening, after the table was cleared off and the dishes were done, that John, and I got into a discussion. I don't know how we got on the subject of the sealing of God's children in the end time, but we did. John was quite excited about some verses that he had found in the Bible, which he thought pertained to the sealing. He had taken a class in Inductive Bible study, so he had an edge on me, and being as he was older than I was, I felt that he was more studied in the Word.

As we got into the study, it became apparent that he was taking a different view on the sealing than I was accustomed to. He pointed out to me that the seal of God which was mentioned in verse 2 and placed in our foreheads, verse 3, was the name of God. He had a Bible text to prove it, Revelation 14:1, last part. It read, "having his Fathers' name written in their foreheads". This was talking about the 144,000, the same group that the angel was going to seal back in the first part of the chapter. Could I have been wrong all these years about the seal being the seventh day Sabbath?

John then took me on a study through the Bible dealing with the word "name". First we got out Strong's Concordance and looked up the term "name" in it. We found that in the Greek it meant "authority or character", while in the Hebrew it meant basically the same but added that it also meant that one's name stood for a mark or memorial of individuality. We then looked at several names in the Bible, like Eve, meaning "mother of all living"[16], Jacob, "heel-catcher".[17] He pointed out, that a name, reveals one's character. He then went on to show what God's character was like. We turned in the Bible to 1 John 4:16, where we read, "And we have known and believed the love that God hath to us. God is love; and he that dwelleth in love dwelleth in God, and God in him." This says that God is love. If this is so, then his character is love, That being the case, when we love him and he loves us then our character will also be one of love. Thus when John the Revelator saw this group of people standing with the Lamb on Mt. Zion, they all had the mark of God written in their foreheads.[18]

Many Christians today, believe that at some point in time, God will put a visible mark on their forehead, similar to branding an animal at round-up time. This idea has spawned a number of songs among western singers, one of which deals with "the round-up in heaven". But what does the Bible say about it? Let's look again at Revelation 7:3 and Revelation 14:1. Both these verses state that the mark, or sign, or seal, or name, all meaning the same thing, would be placed "in" the forehead, not "on" the forehead. At creation, God put a special mass of tissue in our head, which we call the brain or mind, in here we think, reason, remember, have emotions and innumerable other functions take place. It is the control center of our being. It is here that my cousin, John said that God would seal us with his character.

I was still not convinced that he was right. We turned to Ezekiel 20 again, and read verse 12, where it says that he,

---

[16] Genesis 3:20
[17] Genesis 26:26
[18] Revelation 14:1

God gave them the Sabbath to be a sign between him and them, that they would know that he was their God. It was a covenant or a contract between him and all those who claim to love him.

The hour was getting late and we still had not come to a full agreement as to what the seal of God really was. In his mind, it was the character of God, in my mind, it was the Sabbath. Finally at 1 a.m. we put our Bibles away and went to bed.

My mind was in a spin, I didn't know what to believe now. More doubts arose in my mind as to what the real seal of God was. Just before I went to sleep I had my nightly talk with God, and that evening I pled with him, that he would in some way make it plain to me. I did not want to believe anything that was not Biblical, or that would hamper my walk with him, and cause me to lose eternal life. Not only that, but I could be a stumbling stone to someone else, and then I would be accountable if they should be lost eternally.

I fell asleep almost as soon as my head hit the pillow. Because there were so many of us there, sleeping places were at a premium. I was sleeping on the floor between the dining room table and the sofa, straight in from the door at the entryway. My wife was sleeping on the sofa, and across the living room on another sofa slept my daughter. My cousins were sleeping on a bed just to the left of the entryway, so we were basically, all in one large circular room, with stairs in the middle, ascending to the upper floor. The house was a rustic post and beam construction inside. I don't know how long I had slept, the only thing I know is that I was sleeping really soundly, when suddenly I was wide awake. There was a brilliant white light in the room. I raised myself to look at where it was coming from. Over near the door, at the foot of the stairs, stood the tallest, brightest being I had ever seen, clothed totally in a dazzling white garment, his head was up near the beams of the ceiling. He spoke one short sentence to me, "the Sabbath is the outward sign of the inner sealing", and he was gone.

I don't need to tell you that I was awestruck. I realized immediately that God had heard my prayer and had answered it by sending a heavenly messenger to speak directly to me. I felt humbled, yet very honoured to have a visitor such as this. I looked at my watch, it said 4 a.m.. By this time sleep was the last thing on my mind, as I kept reliving again the event that had just taken place. Finally around 5 a.m. I drifted off to sleep again. None of the other members in the household heard or saw anything during the night, and woke the next morning unaware of the heavenly visitor.

The question, "what is the seal of God" had been forever settled in my mind. I knew that God would never forsake me, nor leave me as long as I remained faithful to him. John and I were both right in our views. The problem was that each of us only had half of the seal, we just needed to put them together. Hebrews 8:10, the last part, the Lord says, "I will put my laws into their mind, and write them in their hearts, and I will be to them a God, and they shall be my people". Further on in Revelation we find a blessing pronounced on those that do his commandments.[19] He promises them the right to eat from the Tree of Life, and to enter, through the gates into the New Jerusalem.

So another segment of our journey is completed. God is love, his commandments are a transcript of his character of love, He admonishes us, "if you love me, keep my commandments".[20] If we obey the first four, we show our love to God and by keeping the last six we show our love to our fellow-man. And only by the observance of the seventh day Sabbath, can we show the world, whose side we are on, thus the Sabbath becomes the outward sign of the inner love we have for God and man. This is the seal that the angel in Revelation 7:2 has, when he calls to the other four angels, holding the four winds. Now that we have identified the seal, we can continue on our trip through the remainder of the chapter.

It is so easy to forget where we are, when we spend time digging in God's word. We must not forget that, even though we have entered chapter 7, in reality we are still in the Throne Room in Heaven. The judgement is in it's closing moments, the heavenly tribunal have gone over the names, and are

[19] Revelation 22:14
[20] John 14:15

about to place God's seal of approval on those who love his appearing. The final events of the sixth seal are taking place. Many of God's chosen, have given their lives as a testimony of their love for him. They have followed their brethren in martyrdom, those who gave their lives for his cause back in the dark ages.

The catastrophes that had taken place during this period of earth's history had been blamed on a relatively small group of people, that the world as a whole, looked on as fanatics. These Sabbath keeping Christians dared to be different, just like their fore runners had, that were martyred under the fourth seal.

As John is in vision, he hears the number of those that were to be sealed. He writes that he heard, that 144,000, from all the tribes of the Children of Israel were sealed. Some Bible scholars interpret this to mean that only 144,000 are going to be sealed and taken to heaven. This is what I was taught as a young child in my first four or five grades of school. Many times I felt discouraged about ever having a chance to be among this group. Later on, more study went into this passage and preachers started to teach that the 144,000 were the only ones that were going to be translated without seeing death. The great multitude would all die before Christ's second coming. These, would then be raised from the dead and be caught up in the air[21] with the 144,000, and taken to heaven. Again the prospects didn't look very good to a young teenager like me. What thirteen year old wants to hear that he has to die before he can go to heaven, if he doesn't make the honor roll in the game of life?

It was about this time that I started attending all the evangelistic meetings that came through our district every winter or two. Sometimes I would attend one in our town, then a few months later, I would go to a neighboring church to listen to a different evangelist to see if he could give me any better news, than the last one had. I always came away from these meetings, doubting that I would ever see inside the Pearly Gates. Then came the idea that this numbered group were a special people that were going to give the loud cry

---

[21] 1 Thessalonians 4:16, 17

of Revelation 14, calling everyone to come out of Babylon, and get on the Lord's side. Those who turned their back on the world and accepted Christ as their Saviour at this time, were the great multitude. Still no hope for me. If I wasn't in the 144,000, and I wasn't in Babylon, were was I? About this time I decided to forget all about being in any group and trust the Lord to fit me in wherever he could.

A number of years ago I opened up the book again and turned to Revelation to study it on my own. As I went over this chapter something struck me as being out of place. Theologians were now preaching that the 144,000 were a literal number along with the twelve thousand, but each tribe was symbolic of the leader of that particular group. Thus God would have to put up with twelve thousand people that acted and thought like Rueben, and likewise with each of the other eleven tribes mentioned in verses 5 through 8. Today if you listen to various speakers, whether in church, on TV, or radio, you will hear different interpretations of these verses, even within their own denomination.

It was this sort of conundrum that spurned me on to deeper and more meaningful study of the Word of God, and especially the study of last day events. It was also why I now demand a "thus saith the Lord" when I listen to sermons or Bible studies. So what do I do with this section of chapter 7 that has caused me so much fear and trembling? There was only one thing to do, and that was to turn to the Book itself, and study the texts in light of what the Bible says about the subject.

So lets see if our road map is correct or not. In verse 4, John hears a number that is supposedly literal. He hears the names of the twelve tribes of Israel mentioned, along with the fact that each tribe mentioned includes twelve thousand of its members. Twelve tribes times twelve thousand members equal 144,000 people. It is interesting to note that John didn't see the 144,000, in fact when he went to look at them in verse 9, what did he see? The Bible says he saw a great multitude that no man could number. Interesting.

Lets look at a similar situation in chapter 5, and see if a precedence has been set for us to help us understand more fully the road map that is to guide us through to the Promised

Land. Look at verse 5. Here one of the elders tells John that the Lion of the tribe of Judah could break the seals. John looks around to see if he can see the Lion but instead, all he can see is a Lamb. John heard the elder, he looked, he saw a Lamb. In chapter 7, he heard a number, he looked, and he saw a great multitude which no man could count. The number that he heard, was simply a symbolic number for the great multitude. I know that some feathers may ruffle at this but bare with me, as we continue on with the rest of the chapter.

Let us continue now with verse 9 and see what direction it will take us. This great multitude was comprised of all kinds of nationalities, different, one from the other, people speaking different languages, all stood before the throne. It is interesting to note that while in vision, John is in the court room in heaven, while at the same time and in the same vision, he is shown a future scene of this great multitude that were sealed. Confused? Well lets try and get it sorted out so that even a child may understand it.

While John was in vision he saw the Lamb break open the sixth seal, great calamities fall on the earth, men living in fear of the wrath of God. We know that these people who are fearful, are not on the Lamb's side of the fence. If they had been they would not be trying to hide from him. They would not be afraid. 1 John 4:18, second part says "but perfect love casteth out fear". In other words those who have complete trust in God and the Lamb, and love them with all their hearts, will not be afraid of any calamities or tumult that may fall on the inhabitants of this old world. They will stand up for what they believe even though they may suffer and die for their faith. Their trust is in God. They will have peace of heart and mind, as they live under the shadow of his wings.[22] It is these dear people that John saw sealed, the great multitude. You see how the opening of the sixth seal flows right into the seventh chapter so beautifully.

As we continue with verse 9, we see John in this vision, transported to another time frame in which he sees this great multitude standing before the throne and before the Lamb. I want you to pay close attention to what this group

---

[22] Psalms 91:1-11

of people are wearing. They are clothed in white robes, these robes represent purity. We will be looking at these robes a little further on in the chapter. Another characteristic of this group is that they all carry palm branches in their hands. Throughout the Middle East the palm branch has stood as a symbol of victory. When Jesus rode into Jerusalem on the back of a young donkey, the children went out to meet him with palm branches.[23] I am not aware of any Bible text that verifies this practice, but it was a well known one during the time of Christ and onwards. This great multitude carried the palms, indicating that they had, by the grace of God, gained the victory over sin and Satan.

Just picture in your mind, this great multitude which no man can count, numbering in the millions, and maybe into the billions, all standing there in front of God and the Lamb. They all have glorious white robes on and they are all carrying palms in their hands. It must have been an awe inspiring scene. No wonder this great crowd of people all cry out at the top of their voices, "salvation to our God...and unto the Lamb". No wonder all the angels in the throne room, fall down before God, and worship him in verse 11. Notice what they say in verse 12, "blessing, and glory, and wisdom, and thanksgiving, and honour, and power, and might, be unto our God forever and ever. Amen." This scene was so spectacular and the sound of all the voices so thrilling to hear, it was no wonder that the heavenly hosts proclaim this blessing.

It is interesting to note that John is back in the vision of the Judgement from verse 11 through verse 14. It is still during the period of the sixth seal, notice the question that one of the elders asks John in verse 13. What are these, or who are these people dressed in white robes? Where did they come from? In verse 14, John turns the question around into a statement, telling the elder, "you know who they are". This elder then commenced to tell John about these people. He said that this great throng of people had just come through some very trying times, in fact he used the term "great tribulation". As we saw earlier in this chapter, these dear ones had faced hunger, hardship and death, due to their undying love

---

[23] John 12:13

for Christ. Some may have lost their homes, been separated from loved ones, and may have had to live in the mountains and caves, all because they would not disobey God's holy law. They recognized their need of a Savior who could cleanse them from all unrighteousness, by shedding his blood for them. In fact the elder that was speaking to John in this vision, told him that they had washed their robes, and made them white in the blood of the Lamb, referring to Christ's death on the cross at Calvary.

There are various different trains of thought on the last three verses of this chapter. Probably the most popular one among Bible scholars, is the concept that John is now being shown into the future when the redeemed of all ages are gathered into the Heavenly Kingdom and meet before God's throne, after the Second Coming of Christ has taken place. On a casual reading of these last verses, this is what might appear at first glance, however there is much more here, than we have thought in the past.

We must not forget where we are on our journey, nor the events taking place. I have reminded you, of this fact before, and I will remind you of it again, I am sure. I am doing this so that we can keep in perspective, the sequence of events that God is unfolding to John. This is the only sure road map we have to follow during the closing events of earth's history. Only by studying them and locking them in our minds, can we be assured of a safe passage to the Promised land. Many will have become discouraged and given up hope because they failed to understand this precious book. Many are the preachers, teachers and pastors, who are going to stand before the judgement seat of God and be asked, "why did you not prepare my children for the journey?"

As we are coming to the end of another segment of our trip, the same elder continues to talk to John about these people. In verse 15 he says, "therefore are they before the throne of God". He is continuing the thought from the previous verse. Basically what is being said here is, because they had developed a love for God and man, had come through extremely difficult times and persecution because they would not disobey God's Holy law, they had the right through the blood of the Lamb, to stand there in the presence of God. O, Hallelujah, what a mighty, loving God we serve, to have made this all possible for you and me.

Continuing on in verse 15, the elder talks about the these folks that are being sealed, and says that they serve him, God, day and night in his temple, and he that sits on the throne will dwell among them. Let's look at these last verses from a different angle, and see if we can find more meaning in them than we previously had. This verse says they serve him day and night in his temple. The apostle Paul writing in his first letter to the believers at Corinth, in verse 3, he reminds them, by way of a question that they are the "temple" of God. In 2 Corinthians 6:16 we read...for you are the temple of the living God, as God has said, "I will dwell in them, and walk in them, and I will be their God, and they shall be my people." If it is true that we are the temple of God, then we live in God's temple. This being the case, then the statement that the elder in the throne room, made to John, that these sealed ones served God, day and night in his temple, was one hundred percent correct. They served him in his temple because they were living in his temple. God said "I will dwell in them, and walk in them". The elder told John that the one sitting on the throne would dwell among the folks in the white robes. In other words, he would be with them, and watch over them until he could take them home.

Probation for this world is closing, God's children are now being sealed, but there are still to be some troublous time ahead for this old world. The journey isn't over yet, and those living during this period of earth's history are going to see, to what depths Satan is willing to go, to counteract God's plan for redeeming mankind.

The last two verses of this chapter are really loaded. Up until this time, there have been trials and torment of various kinds, including the lack of food and water as God's chosen ones languished in prisons and in the secret recesses of the mountains. These conditions were the fires that were refining and purifying them for heaven. Through this purifying process they have shown to the world, whose side they are on. There is no more need for them to suffer, as their witness will not change the lives of those who do not have the seal of God. Now God promises them that he will look after all their needs during the coming days when Satan throws this world into utter confusion. He will supply their food as he supplied it to the Children of Israel and to Elijah.[24] He promised to protect them from the scorching sun that was soon to shine down on this old world, as the plagues are poured out on those who follow Satan. In verse 17 it says that the Lamb that is in the midst of the throne, will feed them, and when they are thirsty, he will direct them to fresh fountains of water. They will not live in luxury but He has promised to supply their needs until he comes for them.

He does not leave them with only their needs supplied, He has also promised to wipe away their tears. These dear folks have just recently seen their loved ones tortured to death. They have been saddened by the loss of their loved ones, and many a tear has been shed as they were laid in the graves, to await the call of Christ at his return. It is these tears, that God has promised to wipe away. This earth is about to enter a time of severe turmoil, a time of trouble such as never was, and when God's people see what is happening, they will be glad that their loved ones are safely sleeping in the grave. They will not grieve, but will praise God for watching over them.

We have arrived at the end of another portion of our journey. We have covered a lot of territory in this chapter as we finished up with the events that transpired during and under the opening of the sixth seal. The work in the throne room of Heaven is drawing to a close. All the names of everyone who are living on earth at this time, have been gone over, their destiny is settled. All that remains to be done is for the Judge to make the proclamation, "he that is filthy, let him be filthy still, and he that is righteous, let him be righteous still".[25] We are about to start on another exciting segment of our trip to eternity.

---

[24] 1 Kings 17:3–7
[25] Revelation 22:11

Chapter 8

WHEN ALL HELL BREAKS LOOSE

One night, about the same time as the evangelistic meetings mentioned earlier in chapter six, I had a very vivid dream. Though it has been over fifty years since I had it, the scenes are still clear in my mind. In my dream it seemed that Jesus was coming, the sky was very dark and the clouds were boiling as if a violent thunderstorm was taking place. My father had gathered my mother along with my oldest sister, a brother and I, into the old chicken coop to wait for Him to come get us. We were all perching like the chickens did on their roosts when they went to sleep at night. There was one small window by the door that we could look out, to see what was happening, from where we were perched. As we watched, the clouds became darker, flashes of lightning started to shoot through the sky, the storm seemed to gain momentum. Then through the darkness we could see a small spot of light that seemed to break through the turmoil in the skies. It seemed to get larger and brighter as it came nearer, then it stopped. We could see the angels and Jesus surrounded by a rainbow, suddenly I noticed my mother and father slowly ascending from the roost, then my sister and brother started to go up also. In my dream I tried to jump up after them but my feet seemed to be glued to the perch. My heart ached and I had this sinking feeling in the pit of my stomach, a feeling of utter hopelessness and despair. As my family ascended up through the roof of the old chicken coop, I knew that I had been a bad boy and that Jesus was not going to take me to heaven with him. As I looked out the window and saw them meet Jesus, how I wanted to be with them. Suddenly an angel was standing in the coop, he told me that if I was a good boy from now on, Jesus would take me the next time he came. I woke up just about that time, and was glad to hear my mother making breakfast in the kitchen.

It is funny what five year olds dream about, and which dreams they remember. This particular dream stuck in my mind all these years. At that time I made a decision, that I would be ready for Christ's coming, and not wait for the second chance that I had dreamt about. As I became older and understood the Bible better, I realized that there would be no second chances for mankind, for when Christ finishes his work in the Most Holy place and stands up, it's game over. That's where we find ourselves now, as we begin chapter 8.

Christ now opens the seventh seal, it is the last one to be opened. As he does so, there is an awesome silence in heaven. The greatest court case in all the universes, is drawing to a close, the lawyer and judge is about to make the closing statements which will either clear or condemn the accused. All heaven is silent, waiting for the verdict.

It is interesting to note that as this earth's history is about to close as we know it today, that it follows the same pattern as the creation of the earth. Six days God worked at creating the earth and its inhabitants, then on the seventh day, he ended his work, and rested.[1] Likewise during the judgement, he reviewed the names of all those who were recorded in the books during the opening of the six seals. When he opened the seventh seal, he rested or ended the judgement. Just as he made a declaration on the seventh day of creation, so he will make a declaration upon the opening of the seventh seal.

Let us continue studying our road map now. Many Bible students and scholars want to end the seventh seal with the period that follows the "half an hour". This leaves them free to move the events of the trumpets around as they see fit, placing them in various time frames of ancient history. God knew that there was a possible chance that mankind would do this, so he gave us a warning in Revelation 22:18, 19. If any man shall add unto these things, God shall add unto him the plagues that are written in this book. And if any man shall take away from the words of this prophecy, God shall take away his part out of the book of life...that is a solemn thought, and is why we should not chop up the book and try

---

[1] Genesis 2:2

plugging the pieces into holes in history where they don't belong.

We must not forget that we are still in the throne room with John, and that the opening of the seventh seal involves verses 1 through 6 directly, and most of the rest of Revelation, indirectly. So it is that John ties the 2nd verse to the end of the 1st verse with the word "and". Notice how it goes. In the last part of verse 1, John says, "there was silence in heaven about the space of half an hour. And I saw the seven angels which stood before God, and to them were given seven trumpets." It is important to note that these angels were standing before God in the throne room during the opening of the seventh seal.

In verse 3 John sees another angel come forward, and this angel steps up to the alter which was there in the throne room. In his hand he is carrying a golden censor. Someone gives him a large amount of incense to put in the censer. He is to offer it along with the prayers of the all the saints, on the golden alter that is in front of the throne. As the incense burns, the sweet smell of it mixes with our prayers and rises before God from out of the angel's hand, thus our prayers have a sweet smell to God, no matter how imperfect they may be. Up until this moment the saints have been pleading with God via their prayers, for forgiveness, cleansing, strength and whatever else that they feel they are needy of, or need to change in their lives. It is these prayers that are mixed with the incense and presented before God. At last God is finished going over the books of heaven, the Book of Life has the names of all those who love God in it, while the other books record the names and deeds of those who have turned away from God's love. This is the scene that Daniel saw and recorded for us in Daniel 12:1, where it says "and at that time shall Michael stand up,… and there shall be a time of trouble such as never was since there was a nation". The sheep and the goats have been separated, the declaration goes forth, "he that is unjust, let him be unjust still, and he that is righteous, let him be righteous still". Probation for this old world has closed, just as it did for the people in Noah's day, when the doors of the ark were closed by the angels hand.

But something is happening in the throne room, the angel now takes the censer and filling it with fire from the alter, throws it down to the earth. There is no more need for the censer in heaven, no more need for the fire on the alter. Gods work of redemption is complete as far as going over the books of heaven is concerned. It is just a matter of time now until the wicked have filled up their cup of iniquity and Christ can come and claim us as his own.

When the angel threw the censer to the earth, there were voices and thunder and lightning and an earthquake. The events in these first five verses have taken place fairly rapidly. Notice how all the verses were connected with the word "and". Even within verse 2, 3 and 5 we see the word "and" used to keep things moving right along.

Let's take a quick review of these first six verses. Verse 1 we see Jesus is on the throne beside God the Father. Verse 2, "and I saw seven angels which stand before God". "And to them were given trumpets". Verse 3, "and another angel came". Notice how the term "another angel" ties it in to the angels, in the preceding verse. And there was incense given to him. Verse 4, "and the smoke of the incense" ties this verse into the third one. Verse 5, "and the angel took the censer, and filled it with fire from the alter" ties verse 5 to verses 3 and 4. And last but not least, verse 6, "and the seven angels which had the seven trumpets prepared themselves to sound", ties them into the 2nd verse.

These six verses cannot be separated in any way as they make a complete picture of events which revolve around the closing scenes of the investigative judgment. Also from these verses we can see very plainly that the Bible makes it absolutely clear that the seven trumpets follow the completion of the Judgement and vindication of God's children. It is impossible for them to be placed in past history, as we will find that chapter 9 verifies this beyond any doubt. We must accept the clear Word of God, and put away the traditions of man, if we are to have a safe trip to the heavenly Caanan.

The prophet Daniel was shown some of the events surrounding the close of the judgement. In the last chapter of his book, and the 1st verse, he describes the closing scenes of the judgement. In it he saw Michael, Jesus Christ stand up as the judgment of the world ended. He had just finished showing the rest of the universes and Satan that there was a group of people that could keep his laws and still love him. Then Daniel continues his discourse on the next events that are about to take place by saying that a time of trouble would follow such as never was since there was a nation, even to the time when Christ stands up, ending judgment.

The world had seen a lot of trouble from the very beginning of time. Even in Adam and Eve's time there was trouble, right down through to Noah's day when God was sorry that he had made man.[2] We can read the accounts of each of the great men of God who recorded the troublous times in which they had lived. There were the trials of the Children of Israel in Egypt, and also as they traveled to the Promised Land, they ran into perilous times and situations. Throughout the history of the Jewish nation there had been wars, famines, pestilence, and heartache. The world had gone through thousands of years of trouble, but now Daniel tells us that there is a greater time of trouble coming after the judgement is over.

As in the days of Noah, when God said, I will not always strive with man[3], so it will be when God ceases his work in the heavenly judgement hall. He will lift his protecting hand from those who have turned their backs on him and these folks are the ones that are going to feel the brunt of the trouble that will come when the angels sound the trumpets.

At this point we take another little detour on our journey, and I will tell you why. From my study of this book I find evidence that the events that are about to happen are Satan's counterfeit plagues. Everything that God has done so far, we see Satan countering it with a look alike. A few examples are God's Sabbath, Satan's counterfeit sabbath on the first day of the week, Sunday. God told man that if he ate of the fruit of a certain tree, he would die, Satan said, "you will not surely die". Now Satan knows that God is planning to pour out some plagues on this old world just as he did in Moses and Aaron's day. You will recall when Moses and Aaron went into Pharaoh

---

[2] Genesis 6:6
[3] Genesis 6:3

and showed him the signs that God had instructed them to do, that when Moses told Aaron to throw down his rod, it became a snake.[4] Satan immediately countered by having Pharaoh's servants throw down their rods, which also became snakes, however these fake snakes were not alive and Aaron's snake ate up the snakes of the Egyptians. So what better way to confuse God's children in the end time, than to make up a set of counterfeit plagues to confuse them and try to get them to make a slip and follow him.

Continuing on our detour a bit further and jumping ahead of ourselves in the book of Revelation to the 12th chapter, we read in verse 4, speaking of Satan, that he drew a third part of the stars of heaven with him. In reality what he did was convince a third of the angels in heaven to follow him and in the war that ensued[5], he along with his third of the angels were thrown out of heaven to the earth. What does this have to do with the plagues being Satan's counterfeit plagues? Satan deceived one third of the angels in heaven. A third is not a whole number, but only a fraction of a whole number. From my studies of these texts it appears that a "third" seems to be Satan's number or one of his numbers.

Now that we have finished that detour, let's get back on the road again and get on with our trip. In verse 7 we hear the trumpet of the first angel sound. It is important to note the wording of the verse, first the angel sounds, then follows hail and fire mingled with blood. We must remember that the angels with the trumpets, are heavenly angels but as we will discover a bit further on, the power that is causing this upheaval, is non other than evil angels under Satan's command. Another thing that we must remember is that many of the events that are shown to John in these visions, were beyond his realm of understanding. He recorded what he saw, but was not told what they meant. Whether the events are literal or symbolic is not certain but the effect is always literal. Let me remind you of the image that King Nebuchadnezzar, saw in his dream, the metals and body parts were symbolic

---

[4] Exodus 7:10-12
[5] Revelation 12:7-9

but the nations were real and literal. So it is in this vision that John is seeing.

Many people have speculated as to what this hail and fire mingled with blood is, that John saw. Symbolic, literal ? At this point in time all we can do is guess and speculate as others have in the past. One thing is certain, the results are always literal. We must keep in mind that John was familiar with all these things that he saw in these first four trumpets, blood, fire, hail, etc., so it is not unlikely that they were literal. I hear some saying, "but the hail and blood would put out the fire, and nothing would be burnt up". Don't forget that this is not human lit fire, nor is man in control of the hail and blood. Remember the fire that was sent down on Mt. Carmel in Elijah's day[6], how it burnt up eight barrels of water, and remember how the rods of the wise men of Egypt turned into snakes. It is not at all impossible for this storm to burn up a third of the trees and all the grass. At this point I must remind you of the discussion we had in chapter 1 in regards to interpreting symbols and the use of "is" and "are" along with the words "as" and "like". Many times these words get mixed up in symbolic jargon and chaos results. I am talking about the grass and the trees in particular.

Let's spend a few minutes and see how we are doing. Many theologians and Bible scholars see these trees and grass as men or mankind. They say that grass is symbolic of man, and they usually quote Psalms 90:5,6, to prove their point. But if you look at these verses it is comparing man to the grass, it does not say that man is grass, so we cannot use these verses to prove that grass is a symbol for mankind. Another thing that we must look at is this, if the trees are a symbol for man and grass is a symbol for man, we run into a problem right away in this first trumpet. It says that a third of the trees burnt up, okay so we have lost one third of the human population in the first part of this scene. Now we have the grass representing humans, and it says that all the grass burnt up as well as the trees. So have all the humans on this planet burnt up before the second angel gets to sound his trumpet? That's something to think about. Another

---

[6] 1Kings 18:33-38

problem we have with this way of thinking is this, lets say all the grass burnt up first, that's one hundred percent of the population gone right there. Then we have a third of the trees burnt, there's another thirty percent, how can we have a hundred and thirty percent of the people burnt up? Not to mention that in the third trumpet coming up a great many men die and then in the sixth trumpet another third of the men die. Talk about a conundrum amongst Bible scholars. No my dear reader, when John saw grass and trees burn up, he saw literal grass and trees. He knew what they looked like and he made no mistake when he wrote about them.

Verse 8, John now runs into a problem, he says that when the second angel blew his trumpet, something like a great mountain burning with fire was cast into the sea. Wow what a description, here was something John was not familiar with, he didn't know what in the world was thrown at the world. Here he could only describe this great ball of fire, no it wasn't a ball, it was shaped like a mountain. You see how we have to be so cautious with how we read the Bible. Some say this is just a play on words, but friend, this is serious business, my destiny, your destiny and the destiny of your children may depend on how fully we understand the word of God. This letter was given to John specifically for us in these closing days of earth's history. We dare not mess around with it and rationalize it away in a bundle of obscure symbols.

What result did this burning "likeness to a mountain" have on the sea? The last part of verse 8 says that a third part of the sea became blood, and continuing on into verse 9, it says a third part of the creatures which were in the sea, that were living organisms, died. But it doesn't stop there. Notice, a third part of all the ships sailing on the seven seas, were destroyed. Now you may take me to task over that last sentence, specifically the seven seas as the Bible doesn't mention the number of the seas. Take a moment to meditate as to who the Bible was written for. Take for instance the person in India, when he or she reads this text, what ocean do they think of immediately? The Indian Ocean of course, and what body of water do the Chinese people think of when they read the Bible? The South China Sea. What about the people in Hawaii, do they think of the North Atlantic Ocean when they read this verse? I'm sure you get my point now. This book was written for all people in all countries all around the world and everyone in one way or another will be affected by these catastrophes.

A third part of the sea becomes blood, that's disgusting. I used to hunt when I was younger and on several occasions I shot deer which I had to dress out before hanging it up to air out. Now this may gross you out and I hope to some extent it does, so that you get a picture of what the sea is going to be like. I used to take and slit the abdomen of the deer open so as to be able to remove the entrails of the abdominal cavity as well as the heart and the lungs. Usually the moment that the cut was made into the chest cavity a gush of warm blood would flow into the rest of the cavity and it would get all over my hands and sometimes on my arms and clothes, I can almost smell it now as I write. Do you get a picture of what a third of the sea is going to be like? Add to that, the smell of a third of all the living creatures that died, as a result of this catastrophe, and you will have a pretty good idea of what the conditions of the world will be like when this trumpet sounds.

Twenty short years ago my family and I spent a year and a half in the tropical paradise of the Palau Islands. At a certain time of the year, the trochus season comes along. For those of you who are not familiar with that term, it is the name of a particular sea shell from which mother of pearl buttons are made. The season used to last about a month long. The islanders, man, woman, and children would go out on the reefs and gather up sacks full of the mollusk, which would then be weighed, then dumped in great piles on the wharves where men would sit for hours digging out the mollusk from inside the shell. Many times the meat of these shells would start to decay before they were cleaned. Add to that the decaying portions that had already been dislodged and thrown on the wharf, made one wonder, why they ever went down there to look at it. Now you have a complete picture of the state of affairs that this old world will be when the sea turns to blood and a third of all the billions of fish, sharks, seals, whales, porpoises, and seashells die, bloat, and float to the surface, only to be washed up on the shore. You think there was trouble before, we haven't even scratched the surface yet.

We have another problem with the second trumpet sounding. Many people don't even think of it. It deals with the third part of the ships. SHIPS, not only oil tankers and container ships, what about Cruise ships? Of course if all grass and the trees (people) were burnt up during the first trumpet there would be no one on any of the ships. They would just be sailing around on the ocean with nobody in them. On the other hand, if the grass and the trees were literal in verse 7, then I wouldn't want to be on a cruise in the Caribbean or anywhere else for that matter, as thirty-three plus percent of the ships are destroyed during this time of trouble. Undoubtedly there would be people on these ships, who would die or go down with them into the sea.

Let's see if the next trumpet is better that the last one. I might mention here that many theologians and Bible scholars believe that these trumpets are sounding simultaneously while others believe them to be the seven last plagues of chapters 15 and 16. Still others see them as eras in time overlapping the time of the 7 churches, but we need to stay with a thus saith the Lord and leave them in the order in which God gave them to us.

Verse 10 says that the third angel sounded and there fell a "great" star from heaven. (This star is not to be confused with the star, in the 9th chapter, verse 1.) The Greek word from which this word came from is megas, from which we get the word mega, large or great, enormous, etc. . So John saw this gigantic star, and we have no need to try to symbolize this one away as John knew what stars were. He undoubtedly spent many evenings looking at them while on the island by himself. This star was burning "as it were" or like a lamp. Here John uses the comparison word, he saw a large star falling to the earth and it lighted up the sky like a lamp lights up a room. It caught his attention and he watched it as it fell upon the rivers and the fountains of waters.

Rivers are the life stream of the oceans, but they get their water from the fountains that start back in the mountains.

Many times as I have wandered in the high country of British Columbia, I have been on the top of a mountain, and there only a few feet from the summit flowed a crystal clear stream of water. Where it came from and how it got up to the top of the mountain, only God knows. Some of these places were six and seven thousand feet high with no higher peaks for fifty miles in any direction, yet there was the miracle of good water at the top. It is here that the mighty rivers of the earth are born, it is here that the water is pure and cold, ready to quench the thirst of the hiker. But John sees this star strike not only the rivers, but also the water that is coming from the tops of the mountains. The name of the star is Wormwood or Poison. The springs and fountains of water immediately become bitter, the rivers were poisonous also and verse 11 states that many men died, because of the poisoned water.

What then will happen to God's children? Will they have to suffer along with the rest of the people on this earth, will they die from drinking the poisonous waters from the hills? Many of them will be living in the hills because they won't conform to the laws that Satan has brought into effect. We will study about these laws in chapter 12 and 13. Right now we are concerned for those who have the seal of God, how are they faring during this time of upheaval and destruction? Remember what we read in chapter 7, verse 16 & 17, where John saw the Lamb feeding and leading them to fountains of living or fresh water. God's saints who bear his seal have learned to put their complete trust in him, that's why these verses are so important for us to study and lock in our minds. Psalm 91 is perhaps one of the most precious of the promises that God has given his children, and each one should have these locked in the recesses of their minds, as a weapon against discouragement. We have no fear as long as our trust is in God.

John now hears the fourth trumpet sound, and as he does, a third part of the sun was smitten along with a third of the moon and also a third of the stars. As a result, they cease to shine and everything is in total darkness for half of the day and half of the night. This event is going to strike fear in the hearts of mankind. I saw a sample of this in a small way, back in 1983 while living on the small island of Namu Namu, in the Marshall Islands. It happened in the spring of the year. My son and I liked to go shelling on the reef at night with our flashlights as many shells that weren't visible during the day, came out at night. We also liked to shell, either on the full moon or on the new moon due to the fact, that on those nights, the tide was at its lowest ebb. This exposed more reef, and we could get further out on its edge. This particular night, at about ten o'clock we walked through the village on the way to the north end of the island and a group of our students from the mission school, joined us. We spent several happy hours along the western side of the island, the moon was full and very bright, making walking on the reef quite easy. Being isolated on this tiny atoll, we had no contact with the outside world much so weren't aware that our area was in for a total eclipse of the moon on that particular night. All of a sudden one of the boys spoke up and said "Uncle look at the moon, it is a nana moon, a "no good" moon". We hadn't noticed it getting darker, as we were so engrossed in shelling and fishing, that we had failed to see it. As we stood there on the reef, we watched a compete eclipse take place. I was able to give them a science lesson and explain that God was in control. They were not so sure, as they had never seen one before. They were afraid that it was an evil omen. As we walked back through the village that morning around 12:30 a.m., many of the villagers were sitting around their coconut fires, looking at the night sky. They were discussing the strange event that had taken place, fear was on most faces as we tried to explain it to them.

That eclipse lasted about forty minutes, the next morning the sun rose as usual, this event that takes place when the fourth trumpet sounds is not an eclipse of the heavenly bodies. No one will be able to explain it to the world why it is happening. People en mass will be scared to death that the end of the world has come.

There are some who may try to convince the world that this time period of a half day represents half a year in prophecy. The majority of those who study the prophecies believe that the day for a year rule, ended at the finish of the 2,300 day prophecy that began the start of the judgement in 1844. Another angle to consider is the fact that if the heavenly bodies ceased to give any light for a four month period, life as we know it would cease to exist on this planet. The vegetation would die, including the vegetable farms, orchards, cows would stop milking, more life in the sea, would die. See the problem we have with the day for a year concept. No dear reader, much of what we are studying has to be taken in a literal sense.

As we study God's word, we see a continuity that runs from the book of Genesis right to the end of Revelation. As we travel further on our journey through Revelation, we will find that much of what we are studying right now will have a decided affect on the events further on and visa versa.

Now our trip takes a turn. We have been looking into the future, at what will happen to the physical world when God removes his protection from the earth, but soon that will change as God removes his hand from mankind. John, still in vision, sees, and hears another messenger flying in the midst of heaven, having a message to deliver to the inhabitants of the earth. First of all, we need to identify the messenger.

In the King James Bible, it reads, "And I beheld, and heard an angel flying through the midst of heaven". This angel mentioned here is not the same angel that blew the trumpet, nor is it an angel from heaven. If it is in fact an angel, it will be one of Satan's fallen angels. In the Greek, the word that angel comes from can mean a number of different things. Basically it means messenger, with a wide range of possibilities, including angel from heaven, Satan's angels, church leader, deacon, one in charge of a church, and a number of translations of scripture use "eagle", and I am sure there must be some more as well. So you can see that we have a wide range of choices to pick from when we come to figure out what or who is bringing this message to the inhabitants of the earth. Approaching the problem from the angle that these earth-shaking events are the result of Satan and his evil angels trying to destroy as many people as he can. We can assume that this messenger is either an evil angel or an eagle.

Perhaps we can find some clues to help us pin point it down to one or the other.

It is important to note that this messenger is flying in the midst of heaven and not from heaven. The word that "midst" is translated from means middle heaven, mid sky. John could hear it in his vision giving a most mournful message, and it is this message that provides a clue as to who or what the messenger is. Notice that this messenger said with a loud voice, "Woe, Woe, Woe", to the inhabitants of the earth, by reason of the voices of the trumpet of the three angels that are yet to sound. The message was one of doom. A number of times through out the Bible we read about eagles and it seems that most of the time they are referred to in a negative manner, birds of doom, unclean. An abomination to the people. We will study in the 12th chapter about a woman that flees to the hills on eagles wings. Some Bibles do translate this verse to read "an eagle flying through the midst of heaven"[7], and it does appear to be the appropriate rendition. However which ever way a person wishes to read it, it doesn't change the message any.

It is interesting to note the repetition of the word "Woe" three times, one for each time another angel sounds a trumpet. Each of these next three trumpets are going to have an adverse effect on the human race, each one will cause hardship and misery to mankind, and under each one, men will suffer physical torment, some to the extent that they will wish to die but will not.

Let's do a quick review of the high points during this part of the trip. The seventh and last seal was opened by the Lamb, and seven angels were each given a trumpet. The work of the Lamb as intercessor and judge had ceased in the Most Holy place. Probation for this world came to a close. The prayers of the saints mixed with the smoke of the incense rose up before God. The angel took the fire from the alter and put it in the censor and cast it to the earth. There was lightning, thunder, and an earthquake, after which the seven angels prepared to sound their trumpets. Four angels blew their trumpets in their allotted order, one after the other. As

---

[7] NASB, ASV, NAS, NIV

each one sounded its trumpet Satan was permitted to cause havoc on the earth. He sends three messages of doom to the inhabitants of the earth.

This brings us to the end of this segment of our journey, and more pieces of the puzzle have fit together, soon the puzzle will be complete and we will be able to complete our journey in complete safety, knowing that our God reigns and leads his children by still waters.

Chapter 9

THE PUZZLE

In the winter months, my wife and I enjoy spending a few evenings putting together puzzles as we relax by the fireplace. One year we purchased a particularly pretty puzzle and upon getting home, we proceeded to put it together. We noticed as we worked on it, that many of the pieces were the same shape, though the pattern of course was different. In all, we discovered there were only twenty–two different shapes in the whole puzzle. Being quite a complicated picture with a lot of large areas of one color and various shading into other colors, it took us several days to get it near completion. Finally we had it down to just a few pieces right in the middle of some tree limbs with some mottled background. As my wife went to put the last piece in place we noticed that it didn't correspond to the surrounding pieces. We knew that we had the right amount of pieces for the puzzle but something was dreadfully wrong.

The puzzle was a 1,000 piece one, so it meant that we had about forty–five pieces that were the same shape and size. We started to go up and down the many rows of the puzzle to see if we could find where we had made a mistake. After going over about two thirds of the puzzle we finally found where we had put a piece that looked like it fit, but upon closer scrutiny it was very evident that it was in the wrong location. We removed it and by relocating it to the rightful place, and putting the other piece in its place we had a complete and beautiful picture

The book of Revelation is very similar to a puzzle. There are many different parts to it. Some of the pieces of the puzzle are the same shape, they have been put in place, but the pattern on the piece doesn't match its surroundings. I am afraid that in the past, students of the Word have been in a hurry to get the picture finished, and inadvertently put many of the pieces in the wrong places. It has resulted in a picture that is just as confusing, as before they started putting it together. I will admit that in many places there are texts that have small similarities. These have been placed in vacant spots where they appear to fit, but the picture doesn't match the surroundings. It is these texts that have distorted the beautiful picture that God has painted for us, with the pen of John.

It is not until we start getting close to finishing the puzzle, that the mistakes start showing up. The next seven chapters are going to have some very rough going in them for some of us. I'm sure, if we are patient and take our time, the pieces will fall in place and our journey will be made easier and safer as we see God leading us by the hand through the rough times ahead. It is time to start working on the pieces of the puzzle in chapter 9 as we lay out the road map to guide us as we journey on.

In verse 1 of this chapter, John hears the trumpet sound and he sees a star fall from heaven. This is not the same kind of star as we saw fall in the last chapter, as this one is referred to as a "him". Thus we get the picture that this star is a being or messenger of some sort, because he is given the key to the bottomless pit. The term, "fall from heaven unto the earth" literally means, "to alight on the earth".[1] So this angel, from heaven is given the key to the bottomless pit, then flies from heaven and alights, or lands on the earth. Upon alighting here, he proceeds to unlock the bottomless pit, opening it. As he does this, verse 2 says that a great smoke as of, or from a great furnace came out of it. Many of you readers have seen the smoke of forest fires, how at times the sky is darkened by it, this is what John saw happening here. It is important to note and remember as we travel through this chapter, that John is going to see things taking place that he doesn't understand. Because of this, he will be using a lot of comparisons to things that he is familiar with. I also want to make it very clear that not all of this chapter is as clear cut as the previous four trumpets. I will be honest with you. I do not have all the answers to the questions I know

---

[1] Strong's Concordance Greek index #4098

will come to your mind, as we travel through this portion of Revelation. Christ's disciples asked him when his coming would be. He gave them a list of the events that would take place before he came. Many of the things which he told them, they did not understand or comprehend, then he told them "when you see these things come to pass , know that it is nigh, even at the door".[2] Likewise I believe that many of the events that are about to take place here in chapter 9 will not be revealed to us, but when we see them happen, we will recognize them, and will know where we are in the course of time. This knowledge will sustain us through the troublous times ahead, and give us courage to press on and a greater faith in God's promise to protect and provide for our needs until he comes for us.

As we study the events that are about to take place in this portion of scripture, it is not known if symbols are employed or not. If they are, then God has suddenly switched his method of communications to us. As we have noted in an earlier chapter, when a symbol is used there is generally always an explanation of the symbol. In this chapter, there are no explanations for the hail, fire, and blood nor for the great mountain burning with fire, the star that spreads poison, the locusts, nor for the 200,000 horsemen, that we will be studying about. The Bible is totally silent on all these, there is absolutely no explanation. No statement such as "the hail is" "the blood is" "the fire is "the locusts are" etc., that we have noted in other portions that deal with prophecy in the end time here in the book of Revelation. To my knowledge, there is no scripture in the entire Bible where the locust has been used as a symbol. So we have no Biblical proof, that the cause of these events that take place during the sounding of the trumpets are literal or symbolic. However the effect of these events on the earth and man are literal.

In the early hours of this morning as I was lying in bed meditating on these passages regarding the trumpets, a thought suddenly flashed into my mind. Only the angels sounding the trumpets were from God. The rest of the players in this great drama are evil angels, with Satan as their

---

[2] Mark 13:29

king. He uses things of nature that he has distorted or altered to suit his plan to cast a bad light on the God that created them. God only showed John what Satan would use, he didn't tell, or show him what each thing or player in the saga would be. Of course Satan was not about to reveal all the fine details of what he was doing or going to do. This shows a clear distinction between the character of God and the character of Satan. God always explains to his people what the symbols are or mean, so that we are not left to wonder what he is trying to tell us.

We want to be in control by having all the answers to life's problems. If we don't understand what we read or see, we immediately make a symbol out of the unexplained, and try to attach a meaning to it so that we can now explain the unknown to someone else. In working on this puzzle, man has looked at events in history and said, "from what has happened, I think this Bible text is talking about this event". So they assign different Bible texts to various events that have taken place, that is the first mistake. Next they take all of these events and line them up in a chronological order, that's mistake number two. Now your Bible verses are scattered hither and yon throughout the events of world history, both past, present, and future. But the ultimate is yet to come, all this mumble jumble is now taught as doctrine within the mainline churches of today, that's mistake number three. Instead of this scenario, it would have been much better to take the Bible how it reads, leaving it in its proper order and then take the world events and fit them into the texts in the Bible. Only then will we create a beautiful masterpiece of a puzzle that will guide us on our homeward journey.

As John was looking at the smoke that was coming out of the bottomless pit, something caught his eye. There were locusts or grasshoppers coming out of the smoke, and they were swarming onto the earth. At this point in the vision, John had no trouble in understanding what he was seeing. He was familiar with locusts, and also with smoke. The locusts are then given the power as the scorpions of the earth have power. Living in the regions of the earth where he lived, John was very much aware of the poisonous snakes and insects in the area. It is not unlikely that he had observed scorpion stings and may have even suffered from a few himself.

I can already hear someone say, "who ever heard of a man being stung by a grasshopper"? Maybe not up until this time, but times have changed. When Adam and Eve walked in the garden, they never dreamt that the beautiful rose would ever have thorns on it, nor that some of the fruit on the trees would become poisonous to them. When sin entered this world, things began to change, and the only one that wanted to hurt them was Satan. Is it impossible for him now to alter the locusts and give them the ability to inflict severe pain on the human race?

Remember the story of Job, how Satan accused God of protecting him, and how God said to Satan, you can do anything to him but you can't kill him?[3] God again puts limitations on Satan. In verse 4, the locusts are commanded that they are not to hurt the grass of the earth, neither any green thing, neither any tree. That is a tall order to give to a locust when anything green is their natural diet. It is also interesting to note that a long enough period of time has passed since the grass was all burnt, for it to grow to the point where these locusts are forbidden to hurt it or destroy it.

Probably the most interesting part of verse 4 is this last part. The locusts are not allowed to hurt the physical earth, but only those men who do not have the seal of God in their foreheads. Here again God says, "only so far and no farther" to Satan. He can only afflict those who have chosen to follow him. These men do not have the love of God in them nor the love for God's Holy day, they are the ones that were weighed in the balances and found wanting.[4]

In verse 5, another limitation was placed on the locusts. Lets read it, "and to them (the locusts) it was given that they should not kill them (those without the seal of God) but that they should be tormented five months". Lets stop there for a moment and look more carefully at this part of the verse. Two points stand out very vividly here, first of all whatever these locusts are, they could not kill the inhabitants of the

---

[3] Job 1 & 2
[4] Daniel 5:27

earth, they could only hurt them. This certainly has under-tones of torture, but we must remember that these people have chosen their leader, and God has lifted his protecting hand from them. They are now living under a dictator, and must suffer the consequence of casting their vote for Satan as their king.[5]

The other item of interest involves a period of time. In this verse it says that the inhabitants should be tormented for five months. Now we have two trains of thought on this state-ment, one says that this time period is symbolic time and the other says it is literal time. Symbolic time, a day for a year, this would mean that we would have five months, times thir-ty days, equals 150 days, which would equal 150 years. That seems like a mighty long time to be tormented, that would be like, torment for life. The other alternative would be a literal interpretation of it. This would then give us a figure of five literal months for the length of events under this trumpet.

I've mentioned it before, but I want to cement it in your minds so I will repeat it again, "in prophecy, the cause may be symbolic or literal, but the effect is always literal". We see this in the last part of verse 5. Here it tell us that those who were tormented by the locusts suffered just like they would if a scorpion had stung them. John, saw the agony that these people were going through, he was familiar with the pain and side effects that man suffered. He undoubtedly saw the physician Luke treat victims of these types of insects. That is why he could describe the agony and torment that these people were going through. As we read on into verse 6, we find that these people that are suffering from this plague of Satan's during the five months, seek death, but they can not find it. This almost sounds like they may try to commit suicide, but nothing works. They wish to die but death flees from them. What a sad state to be in. Satan has them in a locked in contract, with no way of escape.

As John continues with verse 7, things really begin to get bizarre. He now tries to explain what the locusts look like, and I am glad that he did, so that we have a faint idea of what we should be looking for along the road to our final destina-

---

[5] Revelation 9:11

tion. John had never seen anything so wild in all his life, it appeared as if nature had created a monster. All he could do was try his best to describe what he saw. In so doing he has used a lot of comparisons to try to make a mental picture for us to lock into our minds for future reference, farther down the road.

Verse 7, wow, have you ever seen a grasshopper as big as a horse? How about a small horse? I have heard that some locusts in Africa and the Middle East reach much bigger sizes than those in North America. I also understand that they range from six to nine inches long but I have never seen a picture nor a specimen of one so I cannot verify that. Whatever size these were that John saw, certainly makes one wonder. Though the size is not as astounding as what they looked like. Now dear reader, I want you to pay careful attention to what he says. The locusts were like horses ready to go into battle. John was familiar with seeing the Roman soldiers on their horses. He may have even seen some soldiers on horses that were going out to war against some uprising in the kingdom. The locusts also had something that looked like crowns of gold on their heads, and they had faces as if they were men. Bible scholars/writers can have a real hey day with this verse. It would be very easy to chop it up, toss it around a bit, see how the pieces fall, add a few symbols for good measure, and come up with a clear cut explanation, "these locusts are...". If John were writing this description today, he may have had something else to compare it to, but he had to settle for things that existed in his day. He never tried to explain what they really were, he only told us what they looked like to him, and left it there. We would be wise to do the same.

But wait a minute, he hasn't finished with his description, verse 8 continues it. These locusts that look like horses prepared for battle, wearing crowns on their heads and having a face like a man, have long flowing hair like a woman. Then to top it off, they have teeth like a lion. The long flowing hair may have been the mane of the horses, not to mention the men who had women's hairdos in the 1970's, but not likely.

John still has some more details that he wants to share with us. In verse 9 he saw some more of the war machine come into play. These locusts wore breastplates, as it were, or like breastplates of iron. Now I am sure that John, like every other boy, when growing up, would run and catch grasshoppers and put them in a little woven basket, to tease the girls with. In handling these little pets, he couldn't help but notice that they had an exoskeleton. He probably never, in his wildest dreams expected to see one wearing a steel coat of mail. The real shocker was when they flew over, and he heard the sound of their wings. He might as well add another "as", and he does. The sound of their wings, were as the sound of chariots of many horses, running to battle.

As I read this narrative, and as I write, I am awestruck at the immensity of what John saw and attempted to describe for us. Even today as I write, I can not fathom the enormity of the thing that John saw, nor can I understand it. John did not understand it, nor was he told what it meant, and that's where we need to leave it. We need to store the event in the recesses of our minds for a later day when we are travelling down that narrow road to the kingdom. When we see events take place that fit the description of these locusts, we will know where we are in the course of time.

We have basically covered verses 10 and 11, but we will run through them quickly again. Here again John reminds us that these horse-like locusts have tails like a scorpion, and that they are going to hurt mankind with those stings. This problem is going to exist for a period of five months, and as mentioned earlier. This must mean literal months, due to the fact, that if it were the 150 years, mentioned earlier, then a saint that was 60 years old when the judgement was finished, would be 210 years old by the time that this trumpet was ended. And there are still two more trumpets to go.

Different writers, both religious and secular, have tried for years to come up with a clear and precise explanation of the events that take place during this time frame. Some have done a "cut and paste" job with it, by cutting it out of its sequence in Revelation and pasting it in the history books back in the time of the rise of the Turkish Empire. Others left it in its rightful place, suggesting that it sounds like John saw helicopters, which sound like horses running, and the stings in their tails are chemicals which inflict a severe disease on mankind, to the extent that men want to die. Both these ideas are questionable.

Verse 11 says that these locusts have a king over them, who is the angel, or messenger of the bottomless pit. This would indicate that they are under his control. This king is also referred to as "the prince of this world".[6] From all this, I think that it is safe to say, the bottomless pit is none other than this earth that you and I live on. Let's look at the second part where it says that the angel of the bottomless pit has a name, which in the Hebrew language is Abaddon, but in the Greek, he is called, Apollyon. The word Apollyon means destroyer or Satan. The first part of the verse says that he is a king. Paul writing to the Corinthian believers, warned them that Satan would come as an angel of light and to watch out for him.[7]

Remember the three woes that we talked about in verse 13 of the last chapter? This verse here is telling us that the first woe is past, finished, over with, but there are two more to come. I don't know if you noticed it or not, but if you look at these first five trumpets, and compare them, you will see that they get progressively worse. The sixth one is even more severe, but wait until the seventh one. The sixth trumpet will be the second woe, and the seventh trumpet or third woe will follow.

I hope you are starting to get a picture of how important it is, that we study this important book in a systematic and consecutive manner. It is laying out a perfect path for our feet to follow, with each signpost in its allotted and proper place.

Many times we read over these verses and never even notice some of the finer details that were recorded for us, to help us have pinpoint accuracy, in identifying the event when it takes place.

With the sounding of the sixth trumpet in verse 13, we hear a voice from the four horns of the golden alter which is

---

[6] John 12:31
[7] 2 Corinthians 11:14

located in the throne room, in front of God. This voice speaks to the angel, which had the sixth trumpet, telling it to release the four angels, that were bound by the river Euphrates. These four angels are likely the ones that we read about in chapter 7:2, that were told not to hurt the earth and the sea until the servants of God are sealed. God's children are now sealed, so it is okay for these angels to be released. These angels have been held in check, by the river Euphrates. John does not elaborate, nor does anywhere else in scripture. All we know is that the Euphrates was to the north of Caanan, and a lot of Israel's enemies lived across the Euphrates River, and from time to time these enemies would cross the river and attack them. It is quite likely that these four angels are some of Satan's forces and that is why the angel with the seal of God cried out and stopped them in chapter 7:2. This angel may have been the "binding of the Euphrates", but there is no scriptural evidence of it.

The four angels are now released, in verse 15. Apparently these angels had been prepared to cause some havoc on the earth. This verse says that they were prepared for an hour, a day, and a month, and a year. There are three possible interpretations of this time period, first, it could just be referring to a point in time. Then it may indicate the actual length of time that they were detained, waiting to be allowed to carry out their destruction. If this is the case, it will be 391 days and 1 hour from the beginning of the sealing until these angels are released. The third and last scenario is that they are prepared to carry out their mission for a period of 391+ days from the time they are released until their job of destruction is complete. The writer favors this last one but any one of them may be right, we will only know which is the right interpretation, when we see it come to pass with our own eyes.

What is the job that these angels have come to do? The last part of verse 15 says that their job is to kill one third of mankind. Remember, this is talking worldwide here, not just North America. At the present population, that would amount to around two billion people destroyed, talk about busy morticians.

John hears that a large army of horsemen numbering 200 million have been marshaled together, arrayed for their job of destruction. As this is brought on by Satan, it is quite likely that these horsemen are evil angels that Satan convinced to join him in the rebellion in heaven. If there are that many horsemen, then there has to be that many horses as well, These riders, whoever they are, have breastplates of fire, and jacinth, and brimstone. Again John is not given any explanation as to who these men are or what their breastplates do, or mean.

John also has problems in describing these horses, as they are not ordinary horses that he is used to. As he tells us what they looked like, he starts off, by saying that the heads of the horses were as the heads of lions. Now we know that John had never seen a horse with a lions head on it before, as such an animal doesn't exist. As he continues to view the scene before him, he sees fire and smoke, and brimstone spewing out of the mouths of the lion-headed horses. Oh how I wish that God had seen fit to reveal to us, the meaning of all these strange things, but I guess in his wisdom he has chosen not to. I remember when some of the evangelists would travel around holding their meetings, that they would have pictures of an army of horses, which were breathing fire and smoke out of their mouths. And they would have elaborate explanations for each of the characteristics of these animals. The breastplates of fire had a meaning, both the jasmine and the brimstone had meanings, as well as the lions head. They could not give a Bible text to backup their explanation or claims, so the listeners had to settle for a lot of "I think it means this", explanations. When we are tempted to do this, we need to read again and heed the council given us in chapter 22, verses 18,19.

We need to keep in mind that Satan, and evil angels are bringing this trouble on the world. God has removed his protecting hand from those who have turned their backs on him. If Satan was able to make a snake talk in the beginning of this worlds history it is not beyond his power to change or mutate these horses, if it is to his advantage.

One thing we do know is the way the men die. Verse 18 makes it very plain that a third part of the men, women, and children, will be destroyed by the fire, smoke, and brimstone, that issue forth from these horses' mouths. Nothing more is said about the horsemen other than the mention of them in verse 16. John must have been impressed with the fact that these animals could cause such destruction, because in verse 19, he again tells us that the power to hurt and destroy was in the mouths. Then he adds a new angle to what he had previously seen, these horses had tails that looked like serpents which had heads on them, and with these snakelike tails with heads they caused suffering. We need to read and reread these last two chapters until we have them locked in our minds and hearts, so that when these events take place, we will recognize them. We will be able to encourage one another to look up for our redemption draws near.

A third of mankind have been destroyed, and one would think that those that are left would take a look at themselves and smarten up, but verse 20 paints a very different picture. It says that the rest of the men, which includes women and children, which were not killed by this plague refused to repent of evil deeds, devil worship, murders, witchcraft, fornication, nor their thefts. These people loved doing what they were doing.

Many mainline theologians have used this text to promote the idea that there is a second probation for mankind. They say that because the term "yet repented not of the works of their hands", indicates that they could have repented if they had wanted to. The word "repented" is a poor translation for a word that means "think differently". Basically what verses 20 and 21 say, is that these people do not want to think differently than the way that they do, or do not choose to think differently.

They did not want to change their lifestyle. That is why, when Christ stood up after opening the seventh seal that he could make the declaration, "he that is unrighteous, let him be unrighteous still". Every one has chosen their own destiny. God is love and in his great love, he gave each one of us the freedom to choose who we want to follow, and what kind of lifestyle we want to live.

The events that fall under the sixth trumpet do not end here. In fact we will be studying the sixth trumpet until we arrive at chapter 11, verse 14, where it ends.

Chapter 10

DETOUR

At this point we have another detour that we have to take. This one will be quite long as we will be going back into the book of Daniel. This will help us understand a little better, where we are in the line of events when we get back on track, in Revelation 10.

When I had originally started studying Revelation, I had not planned on going to the book of Daniel, as I wanted to know what John was talking about without being swayed by another's writings. However there where things that John was shown and wrote about, that were not explained to him in minute detail. All we have is a description of an event that will take place some time before Christ's return so I had to turn to Daniel to help decipher what John saw. The main theme in Revelation 10, revolves around a little book, that John saw in the hand of the mighty angel. He had been told to take the book and eat it, that it would be sweet as honey in his mouth, but would make his stomach bitter or sour. Also a few verses previously, the element of time, was mentioned. With these few clues I turned to the book of Daniel to see what I could find and if they correlated with what was happening or going to happen during the closing events of the earth's history.

In Daniel 8:14, I found a referral to a period of time. Daniel was in vision and he heard a couple of saints, or holy people talking to one another. The one saint asked the other saint how long it would be until the daily sacrifice would be taken away. This conversation was dealing with the previous events of chapter 8, which we will not go into at this time. We will come back to it when dealing with chapter 13. For the time being we will concentrate on verse 14, and then move onto another vision in chapter 9. Eventually we will put all this information together and hopefully it will bring us right back to the 10th chapter of Revelation where we started.

So lets get started by digging right into verse 14, here in Daniel 8. Daniel says, "and he" referring to one of the saints that had spoken in the previous verse, said unto me, "Unto two thousand and three hundred days, and then shall the sanctuary be cleansed". You will recall that we touched briefly on this back in chapter 5, and I promised that we would come back to it again, well here we are.

We are going to be studying about days and weeks and months for the next few minutes, so we need to know if we are talking about literal time or symbolic time. The Bible has a number of instances recorded in it where time was involved. We are going to look at these stories to see if we can find or set a precedence that is scriptural and solid, that we can apply to other references to time. Looking in the Book of Numbers and chapter 13 and 14, we have the story of the ten spies that were sent into Canaan to spy out the country in preparation for conquering and settling the land. If you have not heard the story, you would enjoy reading it. The ten spies had sneaked into the land to see who, and what kind of people lived there. They also wanted to know what the land was like for farming etc.. The spies left the camp of the Israelites, crossed the Jordan River and spent forty days looking over the land. When they returned to camp, eight of the spies gave a negative report of what they saw, while on their travels. Only Joshua and Caleb said, "let us arise and go over and take the land, for God hath given it to us". As usual, majority rules and the eight were able to scare the rest of the Israelites into wanting to go back to Egypt. Here is the clincher in this story, in verse 34 of chapter 14, God told them that for every day that they were spying out the land, they would have to wander in the wilderness for one year. Thus due to their unbelief in God's power, they had to spend forty years wandering in the Sinai Peninsula until all those that had been twenty years of age and upward, had died. Only their children were able to go into Canaan. Here we see that God prophesied that for every day they spied out the land, he gave them a year in the desert. This is one place where we find a day equals a year in prophecy. There are two verses in Ezekiel chapter 4, which mentions it also. In verses 5 and 6, notice how God puts it here, "I have laid upon thee, the years of their iniquity, according to the numbers of the days". Then in verse 6, he says "I have appointed thee each day for a year".

From these stories, we see that in some prophecies, it is appropriate to apply the day/ year principle, however we must be cautious, and look at the context of the scripture, to make sure that it fits the events and time frame. This is where we need the guidance of the Holy Spirit, in opening our eyes to see what the message is really saying. This is why we need to compare verse with verse to see if they conflict with each other. If they match, then the pieces of the puzzle will match and our picture will tell the true story.

Well here we are back at the 2,300 days. From what we have just read, does this mean that we can translate this into 2,300 years? Let's take a look at it a little closer. Verse 14 says, that "unto two thousand three hundred days, then shall the sanctuary be cleansed". Several questions immediately come to mind, the first one is, if the cleansing of the sanctuary is at the end of the 2,300 years, what event is at the beginning of the time span? The second question is, when does the 2,300 days begin and end? If we knew when it ended, then all we would have to do, is work backward, and we would know when it began. However, Daniel was not told the beginning date right away. In fact, a number of days were to go by, before it was revealed to him.

Daniel chapter 9 records a prayer that he prayed to God. While he was praying he says that the man Gabriel came and touched him, and then spoke to him.. Gabriel tells Daniel in verse 22, I am come to give you skill and understanding. Verse 24 states that seventy weeks are determined upon, or given thy people. Seventy more weeks are given to the Jews to straighten up their act. Seventy prophetic weeks would be cut off of the 2,300 days, and then God would turn his attention to saving the Gentiles. He continues by explaining to Daniel in verse 24, that the seventy weeks would include the finishing of the transgression, make an end to sins, make reconciliation for iniquity, and to bring in everlasting righteousness, and to seal up the vision and prophecy, and to anoint the most Holy. This verse states that six things would happen by the end of the seventieth week. It covers a lot of ground.

Let's do a little math for a few moments. Gabriel told Daniel that seventy weeks, would be cut off or decreed against the Jews. These seventy weeks are prophetic weeks as the angel was telling Daniel that these events were in the future. We now have to translate these weeks into actual time. To do that we have to figure out how many days are in seventy weeks, then multiply it by years to arrive at the correct time the event would take place. So lets see how we do, 70 weeks x 7 days in a week = 490 days x 1 year = 490 years. Gabriel was telling Daniel that this prophecy would take 490 years to be fulfilled. Again as in the 2,300 year prophecy, we have an end but no beginning.

The angel continues on in chapter 9, verse 25 through 27, telling Daniel that from the going forth of the command to rebuild Jerusalem completely, including the streets and the walls in troublous times would be seven weeks and sixty-two weeks. After the sixty–second week, the Messiah, would be cut off or killed. Now we have a beginning event to start our calculations from, now there is a beginning and an end. We just have to find out what date the decree was given to rebuild the city of Jerusalem, then we can find when each of these other events would take place. In verse 27, the angel said that the Messiah would confirm the covenant for a week but in the middle of the week, he would cause the sacrifice and oblation to stop. Now we have the seventy weeks chopped up into several smaller segments, namely seven weeks, sixty-two weeks, and one week. That translates into 49 days, 434 days, and 7 days, totaling 490 days times 1 year gives us the 490 years of verse 24.

You who are history buffs, will recall that a Persian King by the name of Artexerxes, issued a decree in the year BC 457, stating that the Jews were to go back to Jerusalem and rebuild the city and the temple. You can also read the account of it in Ezra chapter 6 onward. There, we have the starting date of our prophecy in Daniel. Remember it said "from the going forth of the decree to rebuild Jerusalem". So BC 457 is where we begin our mathematical calculations to see if the events prophesied, came to pass.

I have put a time line chart so that you will be able to visualize the events that we are going to study in the next few paragraphs. We are going to start with the year BC 457, and construct a picture of the history of this earth, spanning from this date down to the year 1844 AD. We must remember as we work with these numbers, that BC and AD are on opposite sides of a center line in time. You might say one is a negative and the other one is a positive number if you like to think in those terms. Consequently the years from BC 457 onwards, count backward until it reaches BC 1, while 1 AD increases in size until we arrive at our current year. Now that you are thoroughly confused we can carry on with our study of the 2,300 day/year prophecy.

On our time line, which has a starting date of BC 457, we will mark off the first segment of time mentioned in Daniel 9:25, that being the 7 weeks or 49 years. Subtracting the 49 years from BC 457 we arrive at the year BC 408, the year the rebuilding of Jerusalem was finished. You will notice that the restoration is the first thing mentioned in this verse. It goes on to say that the streets and the walls would be built in troublous times.[1] The next time period of three score and two weeks, 62 weeks or 434 years reached from BC 408 all the way down to 27 AD. Now if you did your math right, taking –408 BC and adding 434 years to it, you will most likely get the figure 26, and you will be correct. You must remember, when we use numbers on a number line, that it reads -3, -2, -1, 0, 1, 2, 3, etc., however in calculating years there is no 0 year. This being the case, BC 1 is followed by 1 AD, this moves everything on the AD time line back one year, so what appears to be 26 AD is actually 27 AD. The Bible tells us that Jesus was baptized and began his public ministry in 27 AD, right on time, just as the angel in the vision, had told Daniel.

---

[1] Nehemiah ch.4-6

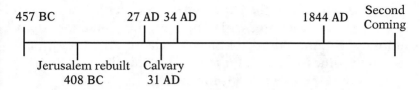

In verse 26 it says that after the 62 weeks or 434 years that the Messiah would be cut off. At some point after 27 AD, Christ would be cut off or in other words, his ministry on earth would cease. Reading on in the next verse we see that it says that he will confirm or continue the covenant with many for one week. When we add one week or 7 days/years to 27 AD we arrive at 34 AD. God had made a covenant with Israel hundreds of years earlier, that if they would follow him and obey his commandments that he would be their God and would look after them. However they had turned away from him so many times and killed his prophets, that he finally gave them a time limit in which to turn from their evil ways. This was the seventy weeks or 490 years, and now we are down to the last week or seven years of the covenant. In the middle of the week he would make or cause the sacrifice and oblation to cease. The middle of the week would translate into 3½ years, adding that on to 27 AD brings us somewhere into 31 AD. It was in this year that Christ was brought before the Roman authorities and accused by the Jews of committing blasphemy and was crucified on Calvary for the sins of the world, for you and me. As Jesus, the Lamb that takes away the sin of the world died on the cross, the veil or curtains of the Temple in Jerusalem, separating the Holy from the Most Holy Place were torn from top to bottom. This revealed the inner chamber where the presence of God had dwelt. God had left the earthly Temple as the sacrifices were no longer needed for mankind, Jesus had given the ultimate sacrifice for us all and his death was right on time according to the prophecy.

What happened during the next 3½ years is history. Jesus ascended to heaven to be with the Father[2] and his disciples continued to preach the good news of a crucified and resurrected Savior. Then in 34 AD, the Jews filled up their cup of iniquity with the stoning of Steven.[3] The seventy year prophecy, had come to an end. From then on, the disciples took the gospel to the gentile nations throughout the world.

In the early 1800's a revival was springing up in America and throughout Europe. In America a group of Christians from several Denominations gathered together to study the prophecies of Daniel and the Revelation. A man by the name of William Miller was preaching that Christ was coming back to gather those who loved him, to take them back to heaven with him. Those who followed him in those years were known as Millerites. In the course of their studies, they came across this 2,300 day prophecy in Daniel. As they studied about the cleansing of the sanctuary, they believed that the sanctuary was the world, thus, God must be going to cleanse the earth in 1844. They interpreted this to mean that Christ would come back that year, to take them home. This coming of Christ was quite widely known as the Second Coming, or Advent, due to the fact that he had come as a babe in the first coming, approximately 1,800 years earlier. These early Millerites, as they were known, believed that Christ would come in the spring of 1844, however the spring came and went and Christ did not come. They did some more study and research and found that the decree went out in the fall. Another date was set in October of that year for the return of Christ. When he failed to show up, on that date there was much heartache and sorrow. This event became known as the great disappointment. Many of those who had followed Miller became discouraged and dropped out of the group, but the remainder turned back to the Bible to see where they had made a mistake. It was at this time that they discovered that the Sanctuary that was to be cleansed was the Heavenly Sanctuary, The Most Holy place where God dwelt. It was the Investigative Judgement with the opening of the seven seals,

---

[2] Acts 1:11
[3] Acts 7:54-60

that we have already covered. So we have come full circle back to the Revelation again. We may have to make a few more detours on our road to our heavenly home, but each one will be worth the effort, as it will strengthen our love for God and our faith in his promises.

We are back on our course again, and we are going to get right into the 10th chapter. It has only eleven verses. It moves along quite quickly from beginning to the end, so let's see what John has for us here.

"And I saw another mighty angel come down from heaven, clothed with a cloud, and a rainbow was upon his head and his face was as it were the sun, and his feet as pillars of fire". John uses much the same language here to describe Christ as Daniel did in his book.[4] John also used similar language when he first saw him in chapter one verses 14 & 15, so we know without a doubt that this mighty angel was non other than the, Alpha and the Omega, Jesus Christ.

The angel is seen with a little book in his hand, that is open. John also notices that he has placed one foot on the sea and the other one on the earth. Whether there are symbols used in this chapter or not is not confirmed by any text. That is to say that the standard procedure has not taken place whereby it is spelled out clearly as in other portions of the book. For instance, no where does it say "the seven thunders are", or "the little book is". This leaves a lot of room for speculation and error, so we must be very cautious as we proceed through the next few chapters.

In Revelation 17:15 it says " the waters which thou sawest, where the whore sitteth, are peoples, and multitudes, and nations, and tongues". So we see here that water is symbolic of great masses of people. Water is a fitting symbol for multitudes of people, because when this world was created, God said let the waters bring forth abundantly. Anyone who scuba dives, snorkels or has anything to do with water, be it rivers, lakes or oceans, know of the masses of living creatures that inhabit them. There are more living creatures in the sea, than live on land. Daniel also uses water as a symbol of nations

---

[4] Daniel 10:6

and people.[5] If the waters and seas are symbolic of masses of people, then we can expect that the earth is symbolic of few people, or the minority. I must tell you that, though this is an accepted view, there is no biblical passage that I know of, or can find to substantiate it. There are two other possible explanations for this 2nd verse. First, it could also indicate that the one standing on them is giving us the message that he is King and Savior of the whole world, including both land and water. The second one, and the one that I favor, due to the nature of the contents of this chapter is this. When Christ was talking to his disciples about the end times he told them that he would put the sheep on his right hand but the goats would be on his left hand.[6] The sheep were invited to inherit the kingdom that had been prepared for them, while the goats on his left hand were told to depart into everlasting fire, prepared for the devil and his angels.

If we are going to use symbols in this verse, then I believe that the right foot standing on the sea symbolizes that there will be great multitudes on Christ's right hand. The left foot symbolizes that the minority are sent into everlasting fire. Now I know that there are some who may not see it the same way that I do. You will notice that John did not say that the angel stood with one foot on the land and the other one on the sea. He made it very clear that the right foot was on the water and the left one was on the land. The message that was shown John here was that a greater number of mankind have chosen to follow Christ than those who choose to follow Satan. We may be discouraged, as we look around us, during the time of trouble that the world will go through. Some of God's children will be in prisons, and all of them will be asking the same question, am I, or are we the only ones that are to be saved, just as the young man in Elisha's time did.[7] When we remember that Christ's right foot was on the sea, we will also remember that there are a great army of believers, out there somewhere wondering the same thing that we are.

---

[5] Daniel 7:2, 3
[6] Matthew 25: 33,34,41
[7] 2 Kings 6:16, 17

This thought will give us great encouragement when we are discouraged.

In verse 3, John hears Christ cry out with a loud voice, like that of a lion when he roars. The Bible doesn't tell us what Christ cried out, but whatever it was, when he cried out, seven thunders uttered their voices. It seems that every time one of the Godhead speaks, there is lightning and thunder. John heard what the seven thunders said. He was going to write it down for us to read, when he heard a voice from heaven instructing him to seal up the things that the seven thunders said, and not to write them down.

There is no further mention of the seven thunders, in fact these are the only two verses in the Bible, that mentions them. There is no record of what they said, however I have heard sermons preached on the seven thunders, and I am not sure where the information came from. I would think that John would have been told at some point in time to write what he heard. Revelation was not a sealed book[8], as it was for the end time. So we will have to leave it at that for the time being, until we understand it more fully.

In verse 5, John sees the angel that was standing on the earth and the sea, lift his hand towards heaven and swear by him that made the heaven and the earth and all the creatures that were created, saying that there should be time, no longer. It appears here, that Jesus the Creator swears by himself that what he is saying is true and trustworthy. There have been several trains of thought on the statement about "time being no linger," and it is quite possible that it has a dual application. The one thought has been that there would be no more reckoning of prophetic time, using the day for a year concept, after the 2,300 days of Daniel 8:14, ended in 1844 AD. While the other concept of this term, "time no longer" translates it to mean that the end of the world is at hand, and time is running out for this old planet and it's inhabitants. This seems to have some merit to it, as the next verse identifies the time frame in which this chapter is taking place.

Here is another signpost for each us to take note of, and lock in our memory bank. The information that John records

---

[8] Revelation 22:10

here in this verse, is of utmost importance to God's saints as they face the events that are just ahead of them. Christ's coming is getting closer and Satan is going to be working harder than ever to discourage and destroy those who have the seal of God in their foreheads. The angel that declared that time should be no longer, continues on in verse 7 saying, "but in the days of the voice of the seventh angel, when he shall begin to sound, the mystery of God should be finished, as he declared to his servants the prophets". Here the angel recognizes that the events following the sixth trumpet are still in progress, that they did not end with verse 21 of chapter 9. The inhabitants are still under the second woe, that is why the angel used the term, "in the days of the seventh angel, when he shall begin to sound". The seventh angel had not blown his trumpet yet, notice the wording, "when he shall" indicates that it is not now, it is in the future, still to come. What was still to come, why was this message given?

The message that the angel gave is meant to buoy up courage among those who are looking for Christ to come. That message was, "the mystery of God should be finished". What is the "mystery of God"? The angel said, that it had been declared, or told to the prophets, and that it would be finished. If the mystery is finished, then it must be revealed to the inhabitants of this world when the seventh angel sounds its trumpet, and the third woe, falls on those who do not have the seal of God in their foreheads. We are nearing home, Hallelujah!, we will only have a short time to wait after the seventh angel sounds.

Remember John saw Jesus standing on the earth and the sea with a book in his hand. We cannot pass by the comment that this little book was "open" in the angel's hand. The fact that the book was open, would indicate that the knowledge that it contained was to be read and understood. Also many commentators looking at this text, translate it to say that, because it is open, it must have been closed at one time, therefore being as it was closed, it must have been sealed. If it was sealed it must be the book that Daniel was told to seal up in Daniel 12:4. You see how supposition can lead one down a road of speculation, and how easy it is, to come to a conclusion other than the one the author intended. We have already seen that the book that Daniel was told to seal up, was the book that the Lamb unsealed in chapters 5, 6, and 7. Others believe this portion of Revelation, refers to the 2,300 day/year prophecy of Daniel 8:14, which we discussed at the beginning of this chapter.

The last four verses of this chapter take us back to, and deals with the issue of the little book that is open in the angels hand. John says, "and the voice which I heard from heaven spake again to me". This is the same voice that spoke to him on earlier occasions mentioned in chapter 1:10 & 11, chapter 4:1 and 10:8. It had to be God the Father's voice that John heard. Anyway this voice from heaven told John to go and take the book from the hand of the angel that was standing on the sea and earth. This angel is the same one we read about in verse 1 and 2, and from the description of him we know beyond a doubt that it is Christ Jesus, but for simplicity's sake, we will use the term "angel". In verse 9, John goes up to the angel and asks him for the book, the angel gives John the book and tells him to take and eat it, that it will be sweet as honey in his mouth. He then continues to tell John that after he eats it, he will experience severe indigestion, his stomach would turn sour, actually the Bible uses the term "bitter" which is probably a better description of what John was going to experience.

John tells us in verse 10, that he took the book and ate it, as he was told to do. The book was sweet just like the angel had said it would be, but, oh boy, when he swallowed it, he knew the angel had told him the truth. Immediately his stomach was just as bitter as his mouth had been sweet. What did all this mean? As far as the little book is concerned, we do not hear anything more in the Bible about it. The meaning of the whole scenario was not explained to John, so he had to leave it at that. The angel; told him that he must prophecy again, before many nations, tongues, people, and kings, what ever that meant. So what do we do with this chapter, and where do we place it in the whole scheme of things? Do we put it in past ages, was it meant for today, does it have any meaning, or application in the future? These are all legitimate questions that are sure to come to the mind of the reader or scholar alike. We will take and look at several possibilities, and see how they may fit into the events of the world both past and future.

Remember in the first part of the chapter we talked about a group called the Millerites, who were looking for Jesus to come in the spring of 1844? Preachers of various faiths, Congregationalists, Baptists, Episcopalians, Presbyterians and Methodists and others, both in America, and Europe, were preaching about the soon coming of Christ. However it was the little group of Millerites that seem to be the prominent players in the drama for the moment. The day came and went. What had been a sweet dream of anticipation and hope, had become a bitter cup of disappointment. They were not the first ones to go through a bittersweet experience. Christ's disciples had anticipated that he would set up an earthly kingdom and overthrow the hated Romans, but their hopes were dashed to pieces on Golgotha's hill. The Sabbath that Jesus spent in the tomb, was spent in bitter disappointment by those in the upper room along with many others who had their hopes vanish with his death on the cross. Little did they realize that it is the darkest just before dawn.

So this episode of John's with the little book seems to indicate a time of disappointment. If we turn to the book of Jeremiah and read chapter 15 verse 16, we read, "Thy words were found; and I did eat them; and thy word was unto me the joy and rejoicing of my heart". Jeremiah ate the word of God and was joyful, John ate the words of the little book and had a bad experience. Quite a bit different reaction than Jeremiah had. This gives us a bit of insight into why this vision, was shown to John. It was to represent an event or an experience that God's people were to go through.

Now we are faced with another question, does this chapter 10 only refer to the Great Disappointment of 1844, or does it have a greater application just before Christ's second coming? We find as we study the Word of God, that many of the prophecies have a dual application. The one that comes to mind the quickest is the one found in Matthew 24, where Christ tells the disciples about the destruction of Jerusalem, and also implies or uses it to describe the events just before his second coming. The first was a minor event pointing to a far greater event in the future. If we were to search some more we would find other like prophecies. Does this same principle apply to the vision in this chapter of Revelation? I believe it does, and here is the reason I say that.

Revelation 10 is part of the road map of our journey to the kingdom of God. Remember that the book was to reveal things which must shortly come to pass. Yes I know that 1844 was still in the future as far as John was concerned but, can we safely cut and paste Revelation 10, on the picture of 1844? What if the disciples had taken Jesus' description of the end of the world and did a cut an paste job on it, assigning it only to the destruction of Jerusalem. Would we then say of the signs that Christ gave them, "oh those were for back then, they don't apply to us today"? Heaven forbid! But sad to say, many scholars, theologians, and preachers are doing that very thing today with the scriptures. I've said it before and I will repeat it again dear reader. We can not, dare not, take a picture of the history of the world, then cut up Revelation, our road map, and paste the verses and the chapters wherever they seem to fit into the world's past and ancient history. True there are some things in the Revelation that we don't understand at this time, but the time will come when we will see and know, what they are.

Chapter 10 is a classic example of the cut and paste scenario. Many Bible scholars have taken the whole chapter, cut it, then pasted it on the map of world history in the mid 1800's. Now we have nothing to encourage us or guide us from the end of chapter 9 to chapter 12. Verse 7 casts some light on the problem we are faced with. Jesus told John, that in the days of the seventh angel, when he shall begin to sound, the mystery of God would be finished. God was the author of the book, Jesus was the bearer of the message and he knew and understood what sequence the events of the world would take, and he gave that message in it's order to John. That's why he told John that in the days of the seventh angel, he knew that the sixth had sounded but the events that were to fall under the sixth were not over yet. The seventh hadn't started yet. Is that Biblical? Yes it is, and there are two verses, that support this concept. The first one is right in verse 7, where Jesus said "when he shall begin to sound". The word "shall" indicates or implies that the sounding of this angel still had not taken place, but when it does, then the mystery of God would be finished. We have to deal with that mystery also but will do it later. Right now we want to look at the other verse that supports the concept that these chapters are in a sequence that we can not tear apart. We have to jump ahead to the 11th chapter, verse 14. Here we read that the second woe is past and the third woe will come quickly. Remember, the second woe is the sixth trumpet. The events that fall under the sixth trumpet do not end in chapter 9 verse 21, but carry right on through to verse 14 of chapter 11. What then does the little book experience of John's have to do with all this? Let's take a look and see.

We have to remember where we are in the chain of events that are transpiring in this time of earth's history. Remember Christ has finished his work in the Most Holy, probation has closed, and Satan has this world all stirred up with turmoil and suffering, and death, while God's children are protected under his wings. How do you think, those who are suffering, feel towards those that aren't suffering?. I'm sure, there are some ill feelings and from what we discovered in the opening of the fifth seal, the saints were told that their brothers would be persecuted and martyred as they were. We can safely say that God's children who have his seal, are going through some very trying times. Satan is not pleased with them and is doing his very best to destroy them. As you remember from chapter 9, approximately eighteen months have gone by since the judgement had finished. It would be safe to say that these people had been persecuted even before the judgement was over. That being the case they may have been living under very difficult situations for several years by this time. They remember the promise of God to come and rescue them from this old world, but time seems to drag on. As they see these signs fulfilling, they take new courage, but still he hasn't come by this 10th chapter.

Another interesting feature of this chapter is the way it is constructed. Did you ever notice that it starts out by telling about the mighty angel with the little book, that was open, in his hand, but doesn't carry on with the little book scenario? Normally verses 3 to 7 would have been at either the beginning of the chapter or at the end of it . Verses 1 and 2 should have been together with verses 8 to 11. God in his infinite wisdom and great love for his children, inserted verse 7 here in the center of the chapter to give them some special encouragement. He knew that what looked like an apparent delay in his coming, was about to take place, and that Satan had one more trick up his sleeve that He was going to let him pull off. God also knew that he had allotted Satan, three and a half years more to finish the second woe. He knew that his children were going to go through a time of exceeding great, disappointment, far greater than the one of 1844. Those in 1844 had not gone through the trials and persecution that these followers of Christ had. It was for this reason that God inserted the promise to them in verse 7, as encouragement, letting them know that only one more trumpet was to sound and then he would take over and bring things to a close.

They have read and studied about the first disappointment, but they didn't think that God would let it drag on so long, hadn't they read somewhere, that he would cut it short in righteousness?[9] It was for this very reason that God gave us this road map, in sequential order, and told us that it would be a blessing to those who read it and understood it. By knowing the events that follow one another, and as we see them being fulfilled or coming to pass, we will take new courage, and our faith in God will grow even stronger. However, those who have failed to study and understand the road map, will find themselves having a much harder time mentally, than those who have locked the knowledge of the book of Revelation in their minds, for just such a time.

In the next chapter the plot thickens and the disappointment deepens.

---

[9] Matthew 24:22

Chapter 11

THE MISSING PIECE

Have you ever been on a journey, and as you drove along, you weren't quite sure what turn to take? Finally after much thought, you make a choice, and drive on, hoping that you are on the right road. The map you are using, seems to have some missing details, because as you drive on, all of a sudden you see what appears to be a dead end. You are tempted to turn around and try an easier route, hoping that it will take you where you want to go, but on second thought, you continue on, to the end of the road. There off to one side you see a narrow little trail, just barely wide enough for your car to pass through. You turn onto it, and after much trouble, you get through the difficult spot and come out on a good road on the other side. This is a perfect description of Revelation 11:1–12.

Many people have tried to decipher it and write commentaries on it, but none have been 100% foolproof. In plain, simple language, there is no clear-cut Bible texts giving us a "thus says the Lord". This has left us with a wide range of ideas from various writers to choose from as to what we want to believe. However this may not be the safest route to go. I believe that this is another one of those passages of scripture where "silence is eloquent", a place where we need to wait on the Lord and let him show us in his own time, what it means. I am not going to try to explain it to you or make any speculations on what I think it says. I am going to point out some very interesting facts that one has to consider if they are going to try to come up with a solution to this passage.

In verse 1, John is given a rod and told to measure the temple of God and the alter and them that worship therein. You will remember that back in chapter 6, we saw a rider with a set of balances in his hand, and how these were used as a standard to judge the people of the world. Likewise this

120

measuring rod that John was given was to be used to see how Gods people measured up to his standard. Don't get me wrong, I don't want you to think for a moment that another judgement is taking place here. I have mentioned it before but I'll mention it again, we are not the only ones on trial, in this Heavenly tribunal that we saw take place, when the Lamb removed the seals from the double-sided scroll. God's character is also on trial before all the universes, due to Satan accusing him of being unfair. The measuring rod was the great standard that God had implemented from time immemorial, his Law of love. These people were to be held up before Satan and the universe, to display what effect this law had on their lives. It not only vindicated those precious sons and daughters of God, but also God himself.

It is interesting to note in the very next verse, that John is told not to measure the outer court, for it was given to the Gentiles. In the temple in Jerusalem there was a section outside the main sanctuary that was allotted to the people that were not Jews. These people could come to worship, but were not allowed inside the temple proper. As John was told not to measure this part of the temple, we see that these people were not being judged. I want to clear something up right here, before I go on any further. When the Bible talks here, about those within the temple it is referring to spiritual Jews of all races, and when it talks about the Gentiles, it is referring to those who have turned their back on God's saving grace, not on literal Gentiles.

The people that John was told to measure were about to go through a time of great disappointment, as we noted in the last chapter. These sealed ones would have to wait until the enemies of God had filled up their cup of iniquity before God could bring things to a close on planet earth. Their cup was just about full but not quite. Verse 2, last part indicates that they will tramp down the holy city, forty–two months. This is a period of three and a half years. Some scholars assign the day/year principle to this text, however we have to look at the context to see if that is feasible and logical. If we translate it to read prophetic time, the sealed ones would have to wait 1,260 years more for this sixth trumpet to be over with, and many of them wouldn't live that long. Remember they are still mortal human beings at this point in time. No, the forty–two literal months or 1,260 literal days will be plenty long enough for the saints to wait for this trumpet to end. I know that many eyebrows are going to raise at all this, but if you dear reader will bear with me over a few more rough spots and detours, everything will fall into place, and we will have a completed puzzle. Our road map will be correct and we will have a safe passage to our heavenly home, and our journey will be over.

Verse 3 talks about two witnesses prophesying for 1,260 days. This time span is exactly the same time as the forty-two months mentioned in verse 2. So it would appear that these two events are covering the same period of this earth's history. Many great thinkers have cut this section out of its allotted place in world events and pasted it in the time slot of 538 AD to 1798 AD, the time period that the Christian Church was persecuted for their faith in God and obedience to his law. However it is interesting to note that the early Christians were persecuted during the 1,260 years known as the Dark Ages, whereas these two witnesses are killed at the end of the 1,260 days after they have finished witnessing. There is a lot more here in these verses than at first meets the eye.

I would like to draw your attention to verse 8. A lot of different ideas have been penned about this verse and others related to it. The Bible is very silent as to giving us an explanation to the vision shown John. In this verse it talks about the great city, called Sodom and Egypt, where our Lord was crucified. This verse seems to use the names of these first two cities in a symbolic sense, for Jerusalem. If we look at verse 2 closely we find that the Gentiles were allowed to run over the holy city, which the Christian world believes to be Jerusalem. Are both these verses talking about the same city? Why are bodies of the two witnesses lying in the streets for three and a half days? Why are they not allowed to be buried if they are actual bodies? Why do the people of the earth have a great party to celebrate the victory over them? And the questions go on and on.

Verse 11 says that after they had lain in the streets for three and a half days, with all the people looking at them, they are raised up. This nearly frightened the people to death, and then John heard a great voice from heaven calling them up to heaven. And they ascended up to heaven, in full view of their enemies.

Now here is the clincher, and I am forever grateful to God for giving this portion of the vision to John. Note how the very next verse ties itself and the rest of the chapter to the first part of the chapter. Reading in verse 13, John writes, "and the same hour was there a great earthquake, and a tenth part of the city fell, and in the earthquake were slain (or killed) seven thousand men". We have several questions that we need to ask ourselves about this passage. The first question we need to ask is, "the same hour as what"? The next question is, what event took place on the same hour, and finally, what were the two results of this event? Before we answer these questions for ourselves, I would like to make a suggestion to each one that reads this book. Some time when you have the time, read Revelation from the back to the front, especially chapters 16–1. As you read them in this format, notice how each one ties to the preceding one just before it. I was amazed at how reading it backwards, helps in understanding it more, than when reading it forwards.

Let us try to answer the questions that came to our minds as we read verse thirteen. The first question basically asked, what had happened on the same hour? To find the answer we have to go backwards to verse 12. Here we find that the same hour included the ascension of the two witnesses. Now read it forwards, and they ascended up into heaven in a cloud, and their enemies beheld or saw them go up to heaven, and the same hour as they went to heaven, there was an earthquake, verse 13. Notice how 12 and 13 tie together. You can go right back through the whole chapter to verse 3 and each verse has a tie to the preceding one. Now we have the earthquake the same hour, we just need to know now what resulted from that earthquake. The verse tells us that a tenth part of the city fell as a result of the quake. This city is the same one that is referred to, as the holy city in verse 2 and the great city in verse 8. Seven thousand men were killed by the quake and the remainder were scared, and gave glory to God of heaven. This all happened right after the two witnesses left this earth.

I want you to look carefully at the structure of this verse for a moment. There are five "ands" used. Each "and" connected the immediate thought to the last thought and the immediate thought was connected to the next or future thought with another "and". The word "and" keeps a thought or a series of thoughts, in line, in a sequential manner, and at the same time ties them all together. I don't know if you have noticed it or not, but "ands" have run all the way through Revelation, right from the 1st chapter to the 11th, and beyond. In fact in chapter 12 every verse except the 12th one begins with "and". The 12th verse starts with "therefore" which is also a connecting word, carrying the one thought on to the next thought.

Now lets continue on our journey. Verse 14 is another of those loaded verses. Remember the three woes from chapter 8:13? We noted that the second woe started in chapter 9:13, and carried right through to verse 13 of this chapter, verse 14 says "the second woe is past". Notice how it came on right after the earthquake and the destruction of the city and the seven thousand men being killed. Then glory is given to God. The second woe is past and behold the third comes quickly. Here we see that all the events, including the death of the two witnesses, the trampling of Jerusalem for 42 months, all these events were part of the sixth trumpet. No wonder God showed John the vision of the open book in the angels hand. No wonder he told John that a bitter experience was coming to God's chosen ones, that they would be disappointed in the apparent delay in his return.

This part of the sixth trumpet (verse 13) is a clear-cut signpost for us to know where we are on the road to heaven. Time will not last too much longer now. Remember what the angel told John in the last chapter? When the seventh angel begins to sound, the mystery of God would be finished. Look at the last part of verse 14 where it says the third woe comes quickly. What a difference from when the first woe ended. It wasn't as dramatic as the ending of the second one. In chapter 9:12 it just said, one woe is past and there are two more to come, but here it says the second woe is past and the third comes quickly. And verse 15 gets right into it.

This trumpet is much different than the former ones were. You may even be surprised when you find out what the third woe is. There is some exciting scenery along our route from here on in. Here we find ourselves back in the throne room in heaven, with the twenty–four elders around the throne, but I am getting ahead of the story. When the seventh angel sounded, there were loud voices heard in heaven shouting, "the kingdoms of this world have become the kingdoms of our God and of his Christ". All heaven knew that the time was just around the corner for the retinue of heavenly hosts to head towards planet earth to get the Lambs bride. The twenty–four elders fell on their faces and worshiped God, and praised him saying "we give you thanks, O, Lord God Almighty, which art, and was, and art to come, because you have taken to yourself your great power, and has reigned". These twenty–four elders have been watching all the events over the past four or five years since the last seal was opened. They have been looking forward to the time when their fellowmen could be rescued from the earth, oh what a day that will be.

If I was to put a title on this chapter, I would have called it, "The Missing Piece". You may wonder why, let me tell you. A number of years ago, the wife and I bought another puzzle to put together. It was a large one, I can't remember if it was 1,000 or 1,500 piece one, but it was a beautiful scenery picture. We labored over this particular puzzle for quite a few days and nights. With each passing day the picture became more perfect and complete. Finally one afternoon we were closing in the last few pieces, when I noticed that there seemed to be more holes than pieces to fill them. We discussed it as we worked and finally we were down to the last piece of the puzzle. Right in the middle there was a piece missing. What a disappointment, after all our work and we couldn't see a finished product. The picture was incomplete.

I found myself in the same situation as I studied the puzzle of the seventh trumpet onwards to the end of the sixteenth chapter. There was a missing piece, nowhere did it say, as it had with the previous two trumpets, that they were over and another event would follow, such as, "and the third woe is past and Christ cometh quickly". I felt that some how the seven last plagues were tied in with the third woe, but I could not find the missing piece that would bring them together. For several years I tried to find the missing link, but I always drew a blank. As I had studied I discovered that the Lamb opened the seals one at a time, right down to the seventh one. When he opened the seventh seal, seven angels were given trumpets to sound. As each angel blew his trumpet, a certain event took place on the earth. When the seventh angel blew his trumpet, and the third woe was to fall on mankind, there was no record of anything happening, the Bible was silent on that subject, or so it seemed. I read the 1st verse of both chapter 15 and 16. In chapter 15, it refers to seven angels having the seven last plagues, for in them is filled up the wrath of God. In chapter 16, the seven angels are told to go and pour out the vials of the wrath of God, but nothing to tie it to the seventh trumpet. Then one morning at worship, my wife asked me to read Revelation 11:18. As I read what the twenty-four elders were saying in that verse, all of a sudden the missing piece to the puzzle, jumped off of the page at me. The twenty-four elders had said, "and the nations were angry, and thy wrath is come". Basically they were saying that the time of God's wrath had come. Here in these verses, namely 15–19 is the description of the seventh trumpet or the third woe, on the inhabitants of the earth. The time has come for God to pour out his wrath on those who have trampled on his Law. It is time for the seven angels, with the seven vials to pour out the wrath of God in the form of the seven last plagues. This is the mystery of God, that John wrote about in chapter 7, verse 10. Here it says that when the seventh angel shall begin to sound, the mystery of God should be finished.

What is the mystery of God? Some Bibles translate the word "mystery" to mean secret act or secret plan. For many years the "mystery of God" was and it still is believed to be the fact that, how can a God of love, destroy the wicked. This is also referred to, as God's strange act. We must remember that it comes from his love for them, and he shows that love, by not forcing them to live in heaven with him where they would be unhappy.

The concept that God was saving his wrath until the end time was not a new idea that originated with John. Job, when he was being tried, says, "O, that thou wouldest hide me in the grave, that thou wouldest keep me secret, until thy wrath be past, that thou wouldest appoint me a set time[1], and remember me!" Here Job knew that a day of reckoning was coming, and he asked God to keep him safe in the grave until the time of His wrath was over. Then he continued by asking God to remember him and resurrect him when He returned. Job also understood the concept of the reward of the unrighteous ones, for he states, that the wicked is reserved to the day of destruction? They shall be brought forth to the day of wrath.[2] David also knew about the final end of the wicked and how God felt towards them. He wrote in Psalms 21:9, "Thou shalt make them as a fiery oven in the time of thine anger: the LORD shall swallow them up in his wrath, and the fire shall devour them". Writing in the book of Proverbs, he recognized that those that did not love God, could not escape his wrath, note how he puts it. In Proverbs 11:4, riches profit not in the day of wrath: but righteousness delivereth from death. Here in this text the stark truth stands out clearly, those that love his appearing will not suffer from his wrath.

Isaiah also knew about the end of the world and what the results would be. There are a couple of verses, we can look at, to see what he says about the subject. Lets read Isaiah 13:9, "Behold, the day of the LORD cometh, cruel both with wrath and fierce anger, to lay the land desolate: and he shall destroy the sinners thereof out of it". The other verse ties right in with this one, "Therefore I will shake the heavens, and the earth shall remove out of her place, in the wrath of the LORD of hosts, and in the day of his fierce anger".[3] You can read many instances in the New Testament about the wrath of God, but the one that really stands out in my mind,

---

[1] Job 14:13
[2] Job 21:30
[3] Isaiah 13:13

is the declaration of those who are scared to death of the events during the opening of the sixth seal. They think the end has come for them because they cry out, "For the great day of his wrath is come; and who shall be able to stand".[4]

A popular concept of the events surrounding the Trumpets is that they are one and the same as the seven last plagues. Most Christians try to super-impose them on top of the plagues. They then have to do a whole lot of juggling around, trying to explain why there appears to be some discrepancies between the corresponding numbers. How much easier it would be, if they would take the Bible as it reads.

Seven Trumpets	Seven Last Plagues Seven vials of the wrath of God
1st—Hail, Fire mingled with blood, Third part of trees burnt up, all grass burnt.	1st—Terrible sores on those who had mark of the Beast. & those who worshiped his image.
2nd—Appearance as a great mountain of fire cast into sea. 1/3 of sea turns to blood. 1/3 of sea life dies. 1/3 of ships destroyed.	2nd—Sea became blood, every living creature in the sea died.
3rd—Star fell on 1/3 of the rivers. Water turned to poison. Many men died.	3rd—Rivers & fountains turned to blood.
4th—1/3 of sun, moon, and stars affected. Ceased to shine for 1/3 part of night & day.	4th—Sun scorches men with fire.
5th—First Woe, Star fell from heaven. Given key to bottomless pit. Locusts come out onto the earth. Sting, and torment men, without seal of God for five months.	5th—Darkness on the seat of the Beast & his kingdom. Gnaw their tongues from pain of sores.

[4] Revelation 6:17

6th—Second Woe. Four angels loosed. Horses breath fire, brimstone and smoke from mouths, kills 1/3 of mankind	6th—Euphrates dries up. Three unclean spirits like frogs appear.
7th—Third Woe. Great voices in heaven, twenty-four elders declare it is time for God's wrath to come. Temple opened in heaven. Lightning, voices, thundering, an earthquake and great hail.	7th—Pour vial into air. Great voice from heaven, saying "it is done". Greatest earthquake ever known to man on earth. Islands and mountains disappear. Great hail about 66 pounds each fall on man.

Notice the above chart, Look at each trumpet and the corresponding plague. At a quick glance there are some similarities, however when one takes a close and careful look at them, we can see that they are unmistakably separate and distinct, one from the other. Lets take a look at them.

In the first trumpet, we see that 1/3 of the trees are burnt up, while in the first plague, every one who has the Mark of the Beast or worships his image, has terrible sores all over them. There is not much similarity between those two. Lets see how we fare with the second set. Here in the trumpets we see that a 1/3 of the sea turns to blood and a 1/3 of the living creatures in the sea, dies. There is a slight comparison in the second plague, in that there is also blood involved. However the entire sea turns to blood and not only 1/3 of the sea life dies, but every living creature in the sea died. So they don't really match up. In the third trumpet we find that a 1/3 of the waters of the rivers and the springs become poisonous. Many people who drink the water get sick and die, while during the third plague the rivers and springs turn to blood. Here we have a slight likeness, one might be able to say that the bloody water would be poisonous, but John doesn't see anybody dying in this plague. He does hear the angel of the waters talking, and we will cover that when we get to that chapter. It is funny, that the angel didn't talk after the trumpet. What about the fourth trumpet and plague? Well 1/3 of the sun, moon and stars ceased to shine during both the day and night, nobody got sunburned there. Now look at the plague, it says the sun scorched men with fire.

I remember back in the spring of '87, my family and I were doing a short stint of mission service in The Gambia, West Africa. When we had a few moments to relax, we would go to the beach and laze around. Due to the intense heat of the sun I would wear a long sleeved shirt, long pants and a hat on my bald head. But I forgot about my feet. I had spent several hours wading in and out and around the tide pools looking for new seashells that I didn't have in my collection. About four o'clock I happened to look down at my feet, they looked a little red. Within a very short time they started to feel uncomfortably warm, and by the next day, I could barely stand on them. For two weeks I laid on the bed with my feet, purple and swollen, I thought I was going to lose them. I have a slight idea of what the general populace are going to feel like during the fourth plague.

The fifth trumpet and plague look somewhat alike when it comes to suffering, but there the likeness ends. Those in the trumpets are suffering from the stings of the locusts while those in the plague are suffering from the terrible sores of the first plague and their sunburns. Let's go on to the sixth set and see if things compare. In the sixth trumpet some weird horses breathing fire and brimstone kill a 1/3 of all mankind that do not have the seal of God. Now the Bible doesn't say that in so many words, but it does say that those who love God will be sheltered under his wings, so I feel safe in making that statement. Now in the sixth plague we have a complete different scenario, absolutely no comparison at all. Here we have three unclean spirits like frogs showing up. so they definitely do not match up. Now for the last set, in the trumpets we hear the twenty–four elders talking, saying that it is time for God's wrath to be poured out, while in the plague we hear God's voice declaring "It is done". In the trumpet men talked, but in the plague, God spoke.

Now if you still believe that the plagues and the trumpets are one and the same, you are on the wrong road to the kingdom and will ultimately wind up, at a dead end. In Proverbs

16:25 it says, " There is a way that seemeth right unto a man, but the end thereof are the ways of death".

Before we close out this chapter, we need to finish looking at the rest of verse 18 and 19. Remember that verse 18, we are listening to the twenty-four elders talking. After they talked about the wrath of God, they went on to say that it was time to judge the dead. This could be taken several ways and they could all be right. It could mean a literal judging of the dead saints, it could mean that it is time for God to come and give the rewards to all those who love him and are waiting for his return. Notice that it does mention giving a reward to his servants the prophets. It seems to imply that they are the ones to be judged, due to the fact that many of the prophets were killed during the history of the Jewish nation, in the Bible.

Then the twenty–four elders go on to include the saints. Those are the ones that are living when Christ returns. But wait a minute, there is another group of people mentioned here in this verse. It says "and them that fear thy name". Who are these people?

As we look at this verse, we see that John saw three groups of people, each group to receive their due reward. We see prophets and saints, but apparently the third group, those that fear his name, do not fit into either of the previous two groups. They are not prophets, nor are they saints. They're only identified as "fearing his name". These could be people who have not known or heard the name of Christ, but who had his law written on their hearts, and had lived a conscientious life, to the best of their ability. Remember that man looks on the outward appearance, but God looks on the heart. What an awesome God.

Finally in verse 19, John sees the temple of God in heaven opened up for all to see. What a show that will be. As all the earth looks up towards the heavens and into that temple, some see the one thing they do not want to see. There sits the Ark of the Covenant, where the Holy Law of God is enshrined, to one group it means salvation, to the other it means condemnation. To one group it means life eternal, to the other group it means eternal death. As this phenomena was taking place, there was lightning, and voices, and thunder, and a great earthquake, and great hail. This hail is not to be confused with the hail of the seventh plague.

God's saints are just about at their journeys end, all heaven is waiting for the last few events to take place, then Christ will sweep through the skies with ten thousand times ten thousand and thousands of thousands of his angels to come and claim his redeemed ones from this old planet and from the torment that Satan has put them through. We will be able to say with Job, "For I know that my redeemer liveth, and that he shall stand at the latter day upon the earth: And though after my skin worms destroy this body, yet in my flesh shall I see God: Whom I shall see for myself, and mine eyes shall behold, and not another; though my reins be consumed within me."[5]

It is interesting to note that when the word seven, or seventh is used, God is in command. When he finished creation, the Bible says that on the seventh day God ended his work, and rested. When we look at the seventh seal, we see that he had finished judgement and stood up. When the seventh trumpet sounded, he ended the work of Satan's destruction, and when the seventh plague falls, he will come and end the reign of sin on this earth. In each instance there is rest involved. At the end of creation, God and all his creation rested. At the opening of the seventh seal, all those involved in the Cleansing of the Sanctuary rested. At the sound of the seventh trumpet, Satan's cohort's have to rest from their reign of terror, and when the seventh plague falls, God's people will rest from the trials and persecution that has plagued them since time began. What a day of rejoicing that will be.

For a quick review, take a moment and look over the following chart:

---

[5] Job 19:25–27

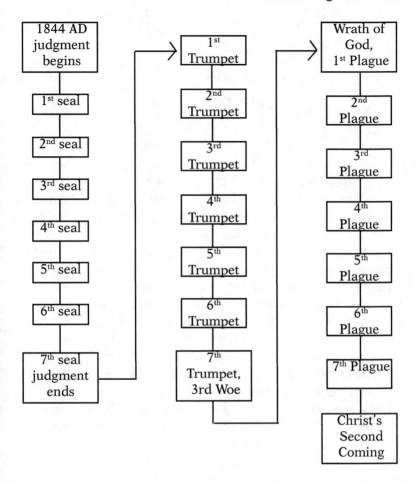

In the above chart, notice the flow of events from the seals to the trumpets, to the plagues. The seventh seal is followed by the first trumpet, and the seventh trumpet is followed by the first plague, while the seventh plague is followed by Christ's Second Coming.

Chapter 12

THE DICTATOR

As we open our Bible to the 12ᵗʰ chapter of the book under consideration, we find that we have to back track on our journey. This is so we can get a clearer picture of why things are happening as they are. It will also show us, beyond a shadow of a doubt, who is at the bottom of all the chaos in the world, and what his plans are.

It is interesting to note that though it will appear that we are going back ward in time, in this chapter, it is equally interesting that the whole chapter is focusing in on the last verse and has it's culmination there. Thus verse 17 is perhaps the key verse of the whole chapter, and without a doubt, all of heaven and the other universes have their eyes fixed on the remnant church. Satan had failed in his efforts to thwart heaven's plan to redeem fallen man previously, and now he concentrates his efforts on destroying God's end time church.

Many who have written on the book of Revelation, use chapters 12–14, as proof that you cannot read it or understand it in a chronological order of events, as these three chapters are out of sequence. Therefore, it must mean that the rest of the book is out of order also. This gives rise to the freedom of moving the seals, trumpets, and plagues around, according to how we think they should be, instead of accepting them the way that God gave them to us. As we continue on our journey, step by step, you will see that, though we will be making several backtracks, each one will put us right back in the proper sequence of events. As an example of that, let me point out that verse 17, places us right back on track in the seventh trumpet, as will chapter 13 and 14. So lets get going and see what insights John is going to share with us.

In verse 1, we read that a great wonder appeared in heaven. From a casual reading of this verse, one would immediately think of something spectacular or amazing that was beyond comprehension, taking place. However, the word, "wonder" also could be translated as "sign" or "miracle", so what John saw in this vision was an amazing sign or event taking place in the heaven. This term heaven, from what we gather in the rest of the chapter, indicates that this panorama was taking place in the sky, between the earth and the heaven where God dwells.

John then sees a woman dressed with the sun, and the moon was under her feet, and on her head was a crown of twelve stars. At first glance in this chapter, it appears that there are two women. The one is literal and bears a son and the other one is persecuted, and must be a church. We are going to take a close look to see if this is really the case here. Lets jump ahead to the 5th and 6th verses, and see if they can shed any light on our problem. Notice that she, the woman bore a son, who was to rule all nations and her child was, caught up to God, and to his throne. This term about "his throne" could be taken two ways, it could be to God the Father's throne or it could mean the son's throne. Now note that the woman, the same one that had the man child, fled into the wilderness and lived there for a period of 1,260 days. There is no record in the Bible that Mary the mother of Jesus fled to the wilderness for three and a half years after he went to heaven, so this must be a symbolic woman. As we travel on through the rest of Revelation, we will find that there are many verses, where the term "woman" alludes to, or refers to a church. This symbolism fits the woman mentioned here, and as we continue on our journey through to the end of the book, this will become very plain to us. From the context of these verses, the woman fled shortly after the Son went to heaven, and spent 1,260 days/years in the wilderness. Remember the day for a year concept that we studied earlier? From all this we can safely say that the woman mentioned in verse one and throughout the rest of the chapter is referring to a church.

Verse 6 is covered in more detail in verses 13 through 16 and we will discuss it when we come to them.

This church was in existence in Israel's day, these were the dedicated followers of God. It did not necessarily include the Scribes and the Pharisees, nor the Priests or leaders of Israel, but there were undoubtedly many of them among it. Remember, this portion of the vision involved the time frame, before the woman's child was born. This was before Christ's first advent, so that puts us back in history a few years previous. This woman was clothed with the sun. Now we have to ask the question, what does the sun represent. Some of the descriptions of things in this chapter have not been spelled out in black and white, like they are in other portions of John's visions. This is one where we have to either be silent, or speculate on it. I am going to suggest that we look at some other texts in the Bible to see if they can shed some light on it for us. First of all, let's consider the sun, what does it give us each day when it comes up? Is the day dark? Or does it shed light all around so we can see? This woman was clothed in the sun, could this mean or signify that she was to shed light around her? Notice what Christ told his disciples," Ye are the light of the world. A city that is set on an hill cannot be hid".[1] Later on, "Then spake Jesus again unto them, saying, I am the light of the world: he that followeth me shall not walk in darkness, but shall have the light of life".[2] So it is not outside the realm of possibility that this woman was clothed with the light of Christ's character, which in turn reflected from the moon under her feet, to the surrounding Nations.

On her head was a crown of twelve stars. As we look at other prophecies we have noted that crowns represent kingdoms. The crown on this woman must then represent a kingdom or a nation, and the nation that Christ came from was that of Israel. This crown had twelve stars on it, the number must have a meaning, or John wouldn't have made mention of it. Some theologians in dealing with this subject assign the twelve stars to the twelve apostles, however it is important to notice that this vision starts before there were any apostles, so the stars must represent something else. As we look at the nation of Israel, we notice that twelve tribes make up the nation. Could these twelve stars then represent the twelve tribes? It is quite likely that they do. Consider another

---

[1] Matthew 5:14
[2] John 8:12

angle, where do stars get their light from? You've got it, they reflect the sunlight just as the moon does. Putting all this together, we see a church prior to the time of Christ, which was made up of twelve tribes of people reflecting his love to those around them.

This woman or the church as we will call her, she being with child cried. You see the early church before Christ's birth was going through some rough times. The hierarchy and corruption in the Jewish religious circles, was causing hardship upon those who were trying to live up to what they had been taught. Satan had crept into the temple ceremonies, influencing greed, theft, and a host of other atrocities against God's true followers in the nation. That is why some thirty or forty years later, we read in Matthew 2, where Christ himself went into the temple and drove the money changers and thieves out of it. The church was wanting to be delivered from this scourge of dishonesty that was plaguing it's advancement and witness to the surrounding nations. The time was ripe for Christ to come and free them from those who had allowed Satan to use them, in suppressing the humble followers of Jehovah.

In verse 3 John now sees another wonder in the vision. A great red dragon that had seven heads, and ten horns, and seven crowns, on its head, appeared on the scene. It is interesting to see that this dragon had these symbols of rulers, or kingdoms, by the presence of the heads, the horns, and the crowns. Perhaps we should try to identify this dragon before we see what these heads, horns, and crowns are. That way we may be able to arrive at a much better conclusion than if we try to figure out who this dragon is from it's characteristics.

To do this lets go ahead to verses 7-9, and read them. Here we have the account of the war that took place in heaven between God and Satan. Satan had not always been a bad angel as some have supposed, he used to have the highest position that any angel could rise to, that of the covering cherub, the one that stood next to God. In Ezekiel 28, is recorded the story of Satan's fall from being the most beautiful of the created beings in God's universe, to a cruel tyrant who tried to take over God's position in heaven. God gave Ezekiel a message to give to Tyrus, comparing him to Satan. Thus we get a picture of what he was before his fall from God's favor.

In verse 12, we see God speaking to Satan, "thou sealest up the sum, full of wisdom, and perfect in beauty". Then God continues on in the next verse to remind him that he had been in the garden of God and had every beautiful stone as a covering. He was reminded that God had given him a perfect voice box, the day that he was created. That he was the anointed cherub, and had the privilege of walking freely throughout the kingdom of God. Then God reminded him that he was perfect in every way, from the day that he was created until sin was found in his heart.

It is really brought home to Satan in the question that Isaiah asks in his book in chapter 14, and verses 12 through 14, How art thou fallen from heaven, O, Lucifer, son of the morning! How art thou cut down to the ground, which didst weaken the nations! For thou hast said in thine heart, I will ascend into heaven, I will exalt my throne above the stars of God: I will sit also upon the mount of the congregation, in the sides of the north: I will ascend above the heights of the clouds; I will be like the most High.

Back in Revelation 12: 7–9 we find that there was a war in heaven, in which God and his angels fought against the dragon and his angels. The dragon and his angels lost the war and were cast out of heaven to the earth. In verse 9 we read that the great dragon was cast out, that old serpent called the devil and Satan, which deceived the whole world. All the angels which followed him were cast out with him. Here then is the answer to the question, who is the dragon of verse four. This verse tell us that he took a third of the stars, or angels also.

So we can see that Satan is the great red dragon. You will recall in the story of Christ's birth, that Israel was ruled by the Romans. It was a decree by Caesar Augustus, that all the Jews were to return to their hometown to be taxed, this is what brought Joseph and Mary to Bethlehem where Jesus was born. It was this nation that the great red dragon gave power to, that stood before the woman to devour her child as soon as it was born. We will talk some more about this great red dragon a little further on in our journey. There it will become a red, or scarlet colored beast with seven heads and ten horns.

As we noted earlier, John saw Satan and his angels cast out of heaven, down to this earth. Then he heard a loud voice saying in heaven, "now is come salvation and strength". What did this mean? If salvation is come, some important event must have taken place, that would have a saving effect on something or some one. The greatest rescue mission ever carried out on this earth, took place when Christ came to this earth as a babe to die on Calvary to save lost mankind. After Christ died on the cross, the rescue mission was complete up to that point. There was no further work that Christ needed to do on this earth for man, that is why he was caught up to God and his throne.

The voice that John hears talking in heaven, refers to Satan as the accuser of the brethren. It then went on to say that he accuses them day and night before God. Now there is a distinct change in the tone of events to what we see in the previous nine verses. There is still persecution but it is of a more intense nature. It has now taken on a more intense feeling as the term woman is dropped and John starts to refer to the church as "they" and "you". It has come down to a more personal matter now. We see this in the 11th verse where it says, "and they overcame him, (Satan) by the blood of the Lamb, and by the word of their testimony". They counted it a little thing to die for what they believed to be the truth.

The voice in heaven was still speaking and John recorded what was said. "Therefore rejoice ye heavens and those that dwell in them." But to the inhabitants of the earth and the sea, the message wasn't that great, they were told that the devil was going to come down to them, full of anger because he knew that he had only a short time. We must remember that what God considers is short, is not necessarily thought of as short by mans standards. These events that were taking place here in verses 13–16, happened back in the Dark Ages, between 538 AD and 1798 AD. In the next chapter we will be looking closer at these dates, and the events surrounding them.

Verse 14 reinforces the events that took place in verse 6. Here John sees the woman given a pair of eagle's wings so that she could escape speedily from the wrath of the devil. These people, who by this time were called Christians, had to leave their homes and farms, to flee into the hills and mountains to escape persecution. However, millions of people did die at the hands of Satan's servants. This is the same time frame that we talked about, when the Lamb opened the fourth seal. And these were the same people who were told that they would have to wait a little longer until their fellow brethren would be killed as they were. In this verse it uses the term, a time, times and a half a time to describe the length of time that the woman or church would be under attack by Satan and his followers. We will discuss these terms, "time, times and a half a time or the dividing of time" in the next chapter. We have seen previously that this refers to the same time frame as verse 6, which uses the 1,260 days/years format.

In verses 15 and 16, we find a scenario with a different twist to it. Up until this point we have always used the term "sea" or "waters" to indicate a large number of people.[3] Here in these verses we see that the serpent casts out of his mouth a flood of water after the women or church. He did this in the hope that the church would be destroyed. This "water" was a great number of people that the serpent or dragon used to try to eradicate Christ's followers. During the period of this earth's history when the Reformers were speaking up against the church of the day, great persecution fell on those who loved God. Satan used human agents to pass laws which forbade the reading of the Bible, and freedom of religion. Millions of Reformers as they were called were killed because they wouldn't bend the knee to the rulers of the time. Many of these Reformers had to flee to the mountains in Switzerland, France, and other nations around there, to escape persecution and death. The ruling church of that day, sent legions of soldiers out into the hills to find the Reformers and kill them. These soldiers were the "waters" that John saw flowing out of the mouth of the dragon.

---

[3] Revelation 17:15

God was not about to let this act of genocide go by unpunished. In verse 16, John saw that the earth helped the woman by opening up her mouth, and swallowed up the flood that the dragon poured out. It is interesting to note that, that is the very thing that happened. In the history books of that period one can read the accounts where the Reformers used the mountain passes to set off avalanches of rocks that wiped out entire battalions of soldiers. God sent in banks of fog, to confuse the would be murderers, causing many to stray from the paths of those steep mountains, to plunge to their death on the rocks below. The vision that John was shown, came to pass with uncanny accuracy, the earth literally opened up her mouth and swallowed up the "waters" that were sent to wreck havoc among God's chosen ones. The dragon was defeated but he wasn't about to give up.

Though most of the reformers were destroyed, God always had a small group of people who remained true to him, down through the ages. It is interesting to note, that in verse 17, it says that the dragon was angry with the woman and went to make war with the remnant of her seed, which keep the commandments of God and have the testimony of Jesus Christ. This term "remnant" often refers to a small piece of cloth, or the left over part. It is exactly like the main piece only smaller, and is at the end. The dragon or Satan, was mad at the church, but he couldn't beat it, so he turned his attention to the remnant of her seed that kept the commandments of God. These were Christ's followers, living at the end of earth's history, who were carbon copies of the early Christians in Christ's day. They obeyed him, loved him, and looked for his second coming, they also had the testimony of Jesus among them. What was this testimony of Jesus? In Revelation 19:10 it says that the testimony of Jesus is the spirit of prophecy. So this remnant that the dragon makes war with, not only keeps God's law but will also have the privilege of having the gift of prophecy among it. These people will have the seal of God in their foreheads and Satan is out to get them. These are the end time church.

As I mentioned earlier, verse 17 puts us right back in line with the world events that have transpired to bring about the sounding of the seventh trumpet. We have seen a beautiful heavenly being, who stood before God's throne, and in his very presence, become jealous of God's position. We have seen how he caused a rebellion and a war that resulted in his expulsion from the heavenly courts. Also how he used human agents to try and kill Jesus as a baby in a manger, how he tried to destroy all those who claim Christ's blood, to cover their sins and cleanse them, and finally he tries to wipe out the last church, just before Christ's second coming. This is the greatest controversy in history, a war between two opposing forces, good and evil, God and Satan, both claiming the earth as their domain. I am so glad that John was shown the outcome of this whole conflict, and that it has a happy ending, but I am getting ahead of myself. The conflict is not over yet, so we will have to wait for the good part of the story until later.

Below is a chart, giving us a picture of the events that took place, and are taking place, in this chapter, along with events taking place from the opening of sixth seal onward.

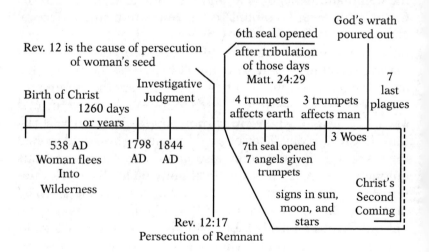

Chapter 13

WHO SAID LAMBS ARE MEEK?

Our journey is half over, and the worst is behind us. Oh there is still going to be some rough road ahead, but it is down hill for God's children from here on. As we continue our journey we will discover some interesting concepts which make our trip a little more exciting as we study the road map.

Before we go any further I want to get a head start on this chapter by sharing something that I discovered in the past few days as I meditated on chapters 12, 13, and 14. Each one of these chapters seemed to be in the wrong sequence, in the picture of Revelation as a whole. As I developed the chart for the last chapter, suddenly the Holy Spirit gave me a some new thoughts. These three chapters which are sandwiched in between the seventh trumpet and the falling of the seven last plagues, basically are all covering the same time span, with a little variance on one end and the other. I will create a chart at the end of the chapter for this so we will be able to see more clearly how it works, then we will understand why John was shown these scenes in his vision. So as not to get things too confusing, we will expand the chart from the last chapter, to include the events in this chapter. Then when we get to the next chapter, we will add some new details to the chart. Then we will have a complete view of the road ahead of us. In the first half of this chapter, we are going to have to backtrack again, as we did in the last chapter. This is so we can set the stage for understanding, what is taking place in the last half of the chapter.

In verse 1, John says, and I stood upon the sand of the sea, and saw a beast rise up out of the sea, having seven heads and ten horns, and upon his horns ten crowns, and upon his heads the name of blasphemy. Verse 2 continues with the description of the beast. John says that it looked like a leopard that had the feet of a bear. His mouth was like the mouth of a lion, and the dragon gave him his power and his seat and great authority. At the time of this vision, John was not aware of a second beast. This is evident from the fact that he did not refer to this one as the "first beast", he just referred to it as, "the beast". It wasn't until the vision continued far enough along, that he saw the second beast, only then does he refer to this beast as the "first beast".

At this point we are going to have to take a long detour in our journey, in fact we are going to have to back track some 2,500 years, to the time of the reign of King Nebuchadnezzar of Babylon. We are with a man called Daniel, better known as Belteshezzar in the Babylonian courts.

One night, King Nebuchadnezzar had a dream[1], which puzzled him greatly. When he woke in the morning, he remembered that he had, had a dream, but try as he might, he could not remember what it was about. Dreams played an important role in the ancient civilizations of the Middle East in those days, and this particular dream was no exception, the only trouble was, his mind had gone blank. He could not remember the details of what he had seen in the dream, and it bothered him greatly. He called in all his wise men, to ask them to interpret the dream, they in turn asked the king to tell them the dream and they would tell him the meaning of it. However the dream was gone from the king and he could not tell them what it was. He wanted them to tell him what he dreamt. Of course no human being was able to do that and they realized it, telling the king that no one on earth could do such a thing. The only one who could know what he dreamed was the gods whose dwelling was not with flesh. They realized that only a super being was able to do what the king demanded.

King Nebuchadnezzar was angry with all his wise men and sent out a decree that they should all be killed, this is where Daniel comes into the picture. He requested an audience with the king, and upon his entry into the palace, asked the king for some time, saying that he would show the king his dream and the meaning of it. The king agreed to his plan, so Daniel immediately went to some of his companions and

---

[1] Daniel 4

they prayed to God to show them the dream and its meaning. God heard their prayers and showed the dream to Daniel, whereupon he went to the king and revealed it to him. Daniel made it very clear to the king that it was not by his wisdom that he was able to reveal the dream. He told the king that his God who lived in heaven had shown him the dream and told him what it meant. Now he said, I will tell you what you dreamed and what is the meaning of it.

Daniel continued, "you dreamt about a large statue or image that looked like a man. This image's head was made of pure gold, it's breast and arms were silver, and it's belly and thighs were brass. The legs were of iron, and the feet were part of iron and part of clay mixed together. Then you saw a stone that came out of nowhere and it struck the image on the feet and the image was broken into pieces and the wind came and blew it all away. The stone that you saw grew into a mountain and filled the whole earth."

The king was absolutely amazed at the accuracy of what Daniel had told him. I can see him leaning forward on his throne waiting to hear more of this incredible dream that he had dreamt. It was all coming back to him now, but the important thing was, what did it all mean? Daniel didn't keep him waiting long, he said "O, king, you are a king of kings". He then went on to say that the God of heaven had given him his kingdom, (Babylon 606 BC–540 BC), and was revealing to him the meaning of the dream. What Daniel said next must have made the kings head swell with pride for he told the king that he was the head of gold. The sad news was that there was going to be another kingdom, (Medo-Persia 540 BC–331 BC), after him that would be inferior to his kingdom. Then a third kingdom of brass, (Greece 331 BC–326 BC), would follow it and rule the whole earth. This kingdom would be followed by yet another kingdom, (Rome 326 BC–351 AD), this fourth kingdom would be strong as iron, and it would break anyone who tried to disobey it. "Then your Majesty, where you saw the feet and toes made of iron mixed with clay, that kingdom shall be partly strong and partly weak." The legs of iron would disintegrate into ten nations represented by the ten toes. The people of this era will try to strengthen the kingdom by intermarrying but as the clay and iron can not join together so the nations will never again be joined together in another world kingdom. You can verify all this from any history book, or a local library.

From this dream that God gave King Nebuchadnezzar, we see that his kingdom was the first of a line of four nations that would rule the then known world. There would never be another nation as glorious or strong as Babylon. As in the dream, each successive nation was inferior to the one before it, until the last one, fell to pieces altogether.

An in-depth study of the Book of Daniel is beyond the scope of this book, however we need to touch on some of the high points so we have an understanding of it, as this will be a great asset in finding out about the beast that John saw in his vision.

Let's go to Daniel 7, and study a little more world history. In this chapter, Daniel is in a night vision. In other words, he had been sleeping and the Lord came to him and gave him this vision. He saw the four winds of heaven blowing on the great sea, and as the waves roared and beat on the shore, he saw four beasts come up out of the ocean, each one was different then the other. The first one was like a lion, the second was like a bear, the third one was like a leopard, and the fourth beast was a nondescript animal. We are not going to go into any discussion on the first three other than to identify what they represented, but we will take a closer look at the fourth beast.

Remember the four kingdoms of the image? Now we have four animals, and each of these animals have their own set of identifying characteristics, just as each part of the great image had. I do want to take a quick look at the second beast for a minute, as we need it for an identification point, a little further on. In verse 5, it says that this bear, Medo–Persia, raised itself up on one side. In other words one side, or one shoulder was higher that the other one. We are going to skip over the third beast for the time being, and go on to the fourth beast, as this is the one that we are interested in.

Rome, the fourth kingdom was the ruling power, at the time of Christ's birth. It ruled from approximately 326 BC to

351 AD. We saw in the vision of King Nebuchadnezzar's, that it was symbolized by the legs of iron, what a fitting metal for that notorious and cruel kingdom. As we read in verse 7, we see the terrible beast had great iron teeth. It devoured, or did away with anyone, who got in its way. It was different from the other beasts that were before it. The other beasts were familiar to Daniel, and he was able to tell us what they were, but this fourth one was not a known animal. It didn't look like anything that Daniel had ever seen before. This beast had ten horns. Going ahead a bit in the chapter to verse 24, Daniel is told that the ten horns are ten kings. These ten horns of this vision stand for the same division of nations as the ten toes of the great image. The vision is true, for Rome was divided up into ten parts, or kingdoms. They were the Franks, Ala-manni, Anglo-Saxon, Suevi, Visigoths, Bergundians, Lombards, Vandals, Ostrogoths, and the Heruli. However, this vision of the terrible beast brings in some more detail that the dream of the image didn't have.

As Daniel looked on this vision he sees something happening, another little horn started to grow up among the ten. It is more stout than its fellow horns, as it grows, three of the first horns are rooted up or destroyed by the little horn. The three horns or kingdoms that were rooted out were the Vandals, Ostrogoths, and the Heruli. Then Daniel sees another wonder, this little horn grew bigger and it had eyes like the eyes of a man, and a mouth speaking great things. This horn was another ruler, or kingdom if you please, that came up among the other ten, out of Rome.

Now we have covered all of the kingdoms that had been shown to Nebuchadnezzar and Daniel, except the last one. In verses 9 and 10, it describes the rock that struck the feet of the image. Daniel says that he was looking at all these events until he saw God sit down in the judgement hall of heaven and open the books. Which we have already discussed in chapters 4 through 6 of Revelation. We need to look a little more closely at the fourth beast.

Daniel says in verse 11, that he looked more closely at this strange horn or kingdom, because he heard it speaking, and then he continued to watch it until he saw it killed and thrown into a fire. Then Daniel is shown some more details about the beast that help us in identifying it. Before we do that we need to do a quick review of events that have taken place on this earth, between God and Satan.

You remember, we studied about the war in heaven, how Satan wanted to be God. When things didn't go his way, he went to the Garden that God had created, and there he used a snake and tempted Eve and caused the fall of man. But God had plan B to go to, giving his Son to die in man's place. Satan was determined not to let that happen so just as he did in the Garden, he looked around to see what or who he could use to foul up Gods plans. Gods time clock was ticking away, the time was right to send his Son to earth to redeem mankind from the death penalty, so Jesus was born in Bethlehem. Satan thought to himself, I've got him where I want now and he can't get away from me. He then used the nation of Rome, just as he used the snake to mess things up. He inspired King Herod to try and find baby Jesus and kill him, but God was looking out for his son. Joseph and Mary took the baby to Egypt for a while until Herod died. Satan was getting desperate, he couldn't trust others to do his work any more so when Christ went into the wilderness after his baptism, Satan personally, tried to conquer him and take the kingdom from him. Jesus met him face on and overcame him again. Outraged, Satan had one more plan left, and that was to destroy all those who loved and followed God, but how could he accomplish such a large project as that? Let us see if this vision holds the answer.

Daniel's thoughts troubled him, as he thought about the vision that he had seen.[2] Someone standing nearby, came and explained the vision to him in verse 17, saying that the four beasts were four kings that would arise out of the earth. In the explanation that Daniel is given, the one explaining it to him, skips over the first three beasts and zeros in on the fourth one. This beast was far different than the others, in that it was described as an exceedingly dreadful beast, one that really threw its weight around. It had teeth of iron and nails of brass, and it stamped on any one who got in its way.

---

[2] Daniel 7:15

Skipping down to verse 24, we find that the little horn would be different than the other ten. What would set it apart from the others, to such an extent that would make it so different from them?

Verse 25 is a real loaded verse. First of all, we see that this "little horn" power or king would speak against God, and would wear out or destroy the saints of God. This power would try to take over the position of God, and would destroy his children. Satan had found an ally, someone that he could use just as he had the snake. The fact that this power spoke against God indicates that it is a religious power. Not only did it persecute God's followers, it also would think or try to change times and laws. Remember Satan has this king under his control, and through this king he sets up a counterfeit time and law. It is interesting to note that he "thinks" he can do it, but God's laws and times are unchangeable. Just what time, and what law would this king try to change?

Let's look at time first. What is time? Well we think of time as in minutes and hours. Sometimes we think of time as, in a day's time, or in a year's time, so time is something that we have or use, and it involves a space between two points, a beginning point and an ending point. It is sort of like a trip, you start at a beginning and you travel until you get to the end of it. The length of your trip was the distance or time between the two points, the beginning and the end. So it is with time. What would involve time, that this powerful king could try to change? As it is also going to work on a law, we need to know what law and who's law is going to be changed.

In the Bible there is only one law that we can find, that runs from Genesis through to Revelation. That law is the Law of God, his Ten Commandments. Originally he wrote it on the hearts of Adam and Eve, and their descendants. However some didn't like it so they chose to forget it, so they could live how they wanted. Then God wrote it on Tables of Stone with his own finger, so we could read it, just in case we were inclined to forget it. He could have written it on a piece of papyrus paper so it could be burnt when man got tired of reading it, but instead he wrote it on stone to show us that he intended it to last forever. Within that Law, there is a time mentioned, that time is the "seventh day". Remember, days can be a segment of time. In fact days are a time segment of weeks, months, and years. In the fourth commandment of the Law, there is a segment of the week mentioned. It is to commemorate creation week, and is the seventh day from the first day, that God started creating this world and our first parents. He asks us to remember the seventh day, and keep it holy, because he ended his work on that particular space in time, and he blessed it and hallowed it. This is the only place that this little horn power can try to change time, as it is the only time that God requires us to keep holy. Satan now uses this little horn to come up with a counterfeit time. Instead of meeting with God on his hallowed day, the seventh day of the week, this power decided that it would worship God on the first day of the week. It made Sunday, the first day of the week sacred by counterfeiting the seventh day with the first day. I am glad that the Bible makes it clear that it only thinks it can change times, you see God's laws are unchangeable and cannot be changed by a mere man. Man only thinks he can do it. You can read in the history books, how the change slowly took place from the time of the Apostles down through history to Constantine's time. It was he that finally gave the head of the Roman Church power over the kingdom by making him head of state. Rome ceased to be a pagan power and became a papal power or kingdom at this time.

I want to make something very clear at this point. I do not want anyone, be them Presbyterian, Anglican, Methodist, Seventh–day Adventist, Mormons or Muslims, or any other of God's children, pointing their fingers at our Catholic brothers and sisters, and saying that they are the beast or little horn power. That is not what the Bible teaches. Christ made it very plain to his disciples, (and to us also) that he has many folds. In these other folds, there are sheep, that belong to him also.[3] He went on to explain to them that a day would come, when there would be one fold and one shepherd. It is not for us to decide which sheep should be in any particular fold.

What Daniel saw, and had explained to him, was about a system, that was under the control of Satan. True there were

---

[3] John 10:16

human beings within the leadership of the system, and these also allowed themselves to be used by Satan just as the serpent did in the garden of Eden. As we study these two books, Daniel and Revelation, and we see how God's saints were and are going to be persecuted, we will also see that the ones who allowed Satan to use them, will eventually stand before the judgement seat of God. Then they will have to answer for the deeds of genocide that they committed just as the Nazi war criminals did, for their misdeeds, after World War II.

What about changing the law? This verse says that he would think to change the laws also. This religious–political power, (remember it is a political power mixed with religion) that tried to change times, will also try to change the law. One of God's laws forbids the bowing down to idols or graven images.[4] In the early Christian Church, idols were forbidden, only the heathen worshiped idols and images, but as time went on this practice crept into the early church. To make Christianity more appealing to the pagans, the use of idols and images began to show up in the local churches. Even back in the Apostles day they had problems with it[5], and it caused no small stir. By the time that Constantine became a "Christian", the use of images and idols was quite prevalent within the church.

The easiest way to sooth the conscience was to get rid of the commandment that forbid the use of images and idols, so the church did away with the second commandment. That left only nine commandments, which didn't look good in the eyes of Christians, so it was decided to split the tenth one in half, making two out of one, thus maintaining ten commandments. Did this really change the law? No, the Bible says "they will think to change times and laws". No matter what they do with them, they can even abolish them, but God's law will still stand. In fact, we will read in Revelation when we get back from our side trip, that one of the last great events before Christ's second coming will be the revealing of his Law in the Heavens.

We have one more item to look at in this verse which will help us identify that the power that came up out of the

---

[4] Exodus 20:4,5
[5] Acts 19: 24-35

Roman nation, was Papal Rome. The last part of verse 25, speaking of the saints that he would wear out or destroy, says that they, the saints would be given into his hand for a time, times and the dividing of time. Let's look at what this means. A "time", was a term which referred to a year. So what we have is as follows.

Time = 1 year = 360 days
Times = 2 years = 720 days
½ Time = ½ year = 180 days
1,260 days/years

This is the same event as we studied about when the Lamb opened the fourth seal back in Revelation the 6th chapter. It is the same 1,260 years that began in 538 AD when Constantine gave the pope the authority to rule the nation, and ran until 1798 AD, when General Berthier marched into the Vatican and took the pope prisoner. Thus ended a rule of tyranny and bloodshed. The great and dreadful beast that Daniel had seen in vision over 2,000 years earlier, had come to it's end. No longer did it have power over the earth, or it's inhabitants. The pope died in exile and the church never regained the power which it formerly had.

Now we have come right back to Revelation 13:1, to John's vision of the beast that arose up out of the sea. Daniel's beast had ten horns, and now we see that John's beast also has ten horns. Just a little note of interest in comparing the vision of Daniel's to that of John's is this. In Daniel's vision, he was looking from his day forward towards the end of time. In so doing he saw the four beasts in their order, the lion, the bear the leopard, and then the great beast. John on the other hand was shown the beasts, from a standpoint of looking backward, due to the fact that in his vision he was looking backwards from the end of the world. It is interesting to notice that this beast that John sees is only one beast, but look at it's characteristics. This beast that has risen out of the sea, looked like a leopard, and his feet like that of a bear, and it's mouth was like the mouth of a lion. Daniel saw a lion, bear, leopard and a beast, John saw the beast, leopard, bear, and lion. Why did John see only one beast, yet it had all these similarities to the other three animals. The Bible doesn't say, in so many words, but the fact remains that there was a lot of influence in religion, and culture passed on from one nation to another. Thus, this beast that John sees, has customs and religious beliefs from the Babylonians, the Medes, and the Persians, along with Greek mythology, all mixed up with pagan Rome's ideologies, as well as Papal Rome's power. This beast of John's has every possible evil that it could have, all wrapped up in one ball.

Now John saw that the dragon gave the beast his power and great authority, verse 2. In verse 3, he was shown that the beast had some kind of problem earlier on, for he says that he saw one of his heads wounded to death. We must remember that we are dealing with a system or a church here, when we use the term beast. Remember the beast had seven heads, and now John sees one of them was wounded to the point that it died. When General Berthier took the pope captive and took away the churches land, a great wound was inflicted upon the church. But notice, this same verse says that his deadly wound was healed. If taking the land, and the Vatican City away from the church created a wound, then giving the land and city back would heal the wound. That is exactly what happened, the wound was healed when on February 11, 1929, Mussolini gave back to the church, the Vatican City, along with power to the pope to rule over the nations of the earth. That is exactly what has happened, almost every world leader goes to the pope for council and advice. Is that what the Bible said would happen? Exactly, notice the last part of verse 3, where it says "and all the world wondered after the beast". It is because of the accuracy of the Bible that we can put our faith and trust in God's Holy Word. It is why we can know what is before us as we journey down the road on our way to the Heavenly Kingdom. It is because of the Bible that we do not need to fear the future, it is the sure word of God, and he will see us safely through the troublous days ahead.

Verses 4 to 7 are a repeat of all that we have already covered back in the book of Daniel. Just going over it quickly, people worshiped the beast; no one could make war against him; he had power for forty–two months, which works out to the 1,260 years; he blasphemes the name of God; he made war with the saints, and last but not least, all that dwell on the earth shall worship him, whose names are not written in the Book of Life of the Lamb. All of God's true children who follow him, will not worship the beast.

And so ends the first part of this vision that John is having. Why did God repeat this vision to John, when he had given it to Daniel first? God did not want any of his children to be lost because of any misunderstanding of the scriptures. Had God just given John a vision of the second beast, he along with all of God's children would not have had a clue as to what verses 11 onward, was talking about, especially when it came to "the image of the beast". But we are getting ahead of ourselves again.

John now continues the narration of his vision for us. In verse 11, he tells about seeing another beast, but this one comes up from out of the earth. Quite the opposite from the first beast, which came up out of the sea. What is the difference between the sea and the earth? It is sort of like an algebra equation, you have to do some deductions first before you can arrive at a solution. In this case we have a number of "known" and one "unknown" to deal with. The "known" are the two beasts, and the sea. The unknown is the earth. The two beasts represent nations or powers if you like, and both are religious-political powers. The sea is well known, it represents people or populated areas, remember chapter 17:15, where we read that water were symbolic of peoples and multitudes and nations. So the first beast came from a heavily populated area of the world. So what can we conclude then, that the earth represents? Well if seas are symbolic for "many people", then the earth must mean the opposite, or "sparsely settled area". So we see the second beast coming from a place where there are fewer people than from where the first beast came from.

This second beast had two horns like a lamb, and he spoke like a dragon. This beast was very much lamb like. Everyone loves gentle little lambs in the spring of the year, they are so cute and adorable. Some years ago a neighbor of mine who raised a few sheep each year, had a sweet little lamb. It was fed and pampered with much loving care, but after a time it grew up into a ram. When it became four or five years old it decided that it should be the boss of the farm, so he started getting "pushy" and if you weren't watching carefully, you could find yourself flat on the ground from a quick bunt from the ram. Eventually he had to be gotten rid of because of his aggressive nature. Does that sound like our lamb here in verse 11? This lamb like power came, or rose up, as the first beast was losing it's power, which was in the mid 1700's. The only nation on earth that fits the description of the lamb like beast would be the United Sates of America. In fact it had it's roots in the persecution of the first beast. It was because of all the trials that the Pilgrims were going through in England and Europe, that they set sail for a land that was basically uninhabited as far as European standards were concerned. They wanted to get away from the religious persecution that they had been subjected to, so they came to a new land, where they could live according to the dictates of their conscience, and worship God freely, without being harassed, and imprisoned. Their Constitution, promised every man the freedom to worship as he saw fit. Somewhere something went wrong.

We read in the 12th verse that this lamb like beast, when he spoke like a dragon, he made all the inhabitants of the earth, to worship the first beast. Here we see the first usage of the term "first beast". Just to make sure that we do not make any mistake as to the first beast John inserts the identifying feature "whose deadly wound was healed". There is no mistaking who the USA is going to force the world to worship. Remember what we learned about the first beast, he wanted to be god, he thought that he could change God's law and day of worship, and he does make laws to that effect.

This lamb beast does great wonders for the people to see. It almost sounds like a giant fireworks display in verse 13. Here it says that he does great wonders and causes fire to come down from heaven to the earth in full view of the inhabitants of the earth. Verse 14 says that he deceives them that dwell on the earth, by the miracles that he performs. Now some theologians read verses 13 and 14 as if it is Satan that is doing the miracles. However, as we look closely at it, there is no doubt that it is United States governmental laws that have been passed to make all men surrender their allegiance to the first beast power. He then goes on to tell the people of the nation and the world that they should make an image to the beast. When one makes or has an image of something, the image is not the original, it is a copy of the original. It looks like the original, but it is separate from the original. Let me give you a simple example.

When you get up in the morning, you usually go into the washroom and take a look at yourself in the mirror, just to see if you made it through the night all right. The question is, who do you see in the looking glass? Do you see yourself, or is it an image of you? I am sure you will agree with me that it is not you in the mirror. Some of us do not want to even be related to the one we see in the mirror, in the morning. The one in the mirror is only a likeness to the one standing before it.

This is not an idol that John is talking about, but rather that of, copying or making an image to the ideals of the first beast. At the end of verse 14, John again identifies this beast, but this time he uses the idea that the beast was wounded by a sword but still lives. This is the first clue as to how the beast received the wound. A sword is a weapon of war. Berthier performed an act of war when he went into the Vatican and arrested the pope on that fateful day, but he unknowingly fulfilled Bible prophecy. From this we are able to link it up with history, which helps to confirm, the Bible's record of events.

It is extremely important at this point, to have it straight in our minds as to where we are, in the sequence of events that have taken place, and those that are taking place, as well as events that are yet, to take place. Remember these events are the mile markers that tell us, not only how far we have come, but also how much farther we have to go, on our journey home.

In verse 15, we see just how far the second beast will go, in forcing the inhabitants of the world to worship the image of the first beast. Let's look at it a little closer. It says that he, the second beast representing the United States, had power to give life unto the image of the beast, the church of Rome. Wow! Notice that the Bible says that the second beast, namely the United States of America, has the power to give life to the first beast. What does this all mean? Just another little example to try to make it easier to understand. If you are at a party, and it is going rather slow, then someone comes in and livens it up a bit, we say that he added a little life to the party, he made something happen. So it is when the United States of America gives life to the first beast, it makes something happen.

Recently, we watched on TV, the grand opening of the John Paul II Cultural Center, in Washington D.C.. What really caught our attention was the speech made by President George Bush at that momentous event. During the opening ceremonies, the President of the United States of America, made a statement something to the effect, that he was honored that the pope chose the Capitol to build his edifice in. He then went on to say that he hoped the whole world would listen to what this great man had to say, referring to the pope. This is the beginning of giving life to the image of the beast, that John saw in his vision.

Continuing on with verse 15, we find some more shocking news. He gives this life to the image of the beast, so that the image of the beast should both speak, and cause, that as many as would not worship the image of the beast, should be killed. At some point in time a decree will go out from Washington, that everyone who does not conform to the laws in regards to worship shall be put to death. This decree will be world wide, notice how it is put back in the 12th verse. That causeth the earth and them that dwell therein to worship the first beast. This involves the whole world.

Let's go on and see what that law is that is so important to the church of Rome and the United States. In verse 16 there is a clue. And he, the second beast, causes all, both small and great, rich and poor, free and bond, to receive a "mark" in their right hand, or in their foreheads. We have heard about marks and seals, etc., before. We read about those who had the seal of God in their forehead and now we are dealing with a mark that the beast places on people. Using a bit more algebra, it doesn't take long to find out what that mark is. If the seal of God in the forehead is the development of his character in us, with the observance of the seventh day Sabbath, as an outward sign of that seal, then Satan will have a counterfeit mark also. If God's seal, is his character and the Sabbath, then Satan's counterfeit will be his character and Sunday observance.

There is one difference between the seal of God and the mark of the beast, God's seal is only in the forehead, whereas the mark of the beast is either in the hand or in the forehead. What does all this mean, being in the forehead or being in the hand? First of all we have to ask ourselves, where is the forehead? The answer is pretty obvious, it is the area of the head just above ones eyes. It is most important to note the terminology of these scriptures, notice it says in the forehead, not on the forehead. Many writers and theologians make a big issue of the mark of the beast being as some visible stamp or brand that is placed on the skin where everyone can see it when you walk past. Wrong, wrong, wrong. These seals and marks are in the forehead. What is in our foreheads? Why our brains of course. There is the key to the whole issue of the marks and the seal, they are implanted in our minds, they are a decision, a choice, that each and every person will make. These choices are not the type like where you wake up in the morning and say, "today I am going to town". You will not, just out of the blue, say, "I am going to go and get the seal of God today," or "I want the mark of the beast". These choices are sometimes spread over the course of a lifetime, it is how we live our life that will determine which seal we receive.

Then there is the issue of "in the hand". Of course this only applies to those who receive the mark of the beast. If the mark in the forehead indicates that it is a case of choice or belief, and that decision is made in the mind, then the mark in the hand can not be the same thing, for the hand cannot think, it does what the mind tells it to do. If the mind sends a signal to the hand saying, pick up the pencil, the hand reaches out and picks up the pencil. The hand did what it was told, not what it believed, for the hand had no belief. It simply performed a task. So those who choose to obey the beast from fear of retribution, even though they do not believe its doctrine, will receive the mark for their works. The hand stands as a symbol for works, whereas the mind is a symbol for choice, or belief.

Remember, everyone in this world will have either the seal of God in their foreheads or the mark of the beast in the forehead or the hand. So everyone will have a mark. You will either be on God's side, or Satan's side, you will receive the stamp of approval from one or the other.

The clincher in this great drama is the fact that no one will be able to buy or sell, trade or hire or get a job unless they have the mark, or the name of the beast, or the number of his name. This means that those who have the seal of God will not be able to carry on any commerce for gain or sustenance. They will not need to for they have built up a relationship of trust in him, for he has promised that all the needs of his children will be supplied. Psalm 23:5 says, "Thou preparest a table before me in the presence of mine enemies: thou anointest my head with oil; my cup runneth over". If God could provide the needs for the Children of Israel in the wilderness, he will be able to do the same for his children in the closing scenes of this worlds history. We have nothing to fear.

The last verse of chapter 13 has caused much concern among the populace of the world. Many different theories have come up over the years, and many different formulas have been used to try to pin down an exact meaning to the number 666. Most have used the Roman numerals to arrive at the magic number, and all of the formulas that I have seen, point to the head of the Roman church. The Bible makes it very clear in verse 17, that it is the number of the name of the beast. I will leave it there for the time being. Whatever it means, we can be assured that God will reveal it to us when the time is right.

We have covered a lot of ground on our journey through this chapter, and I hope it has made your earthly journey a little less stressful for you. We have seen the rise and fall of four world empires, the rise to dominance of a small horn that came out of an exceeding grotesque beast. We saw how this small horn rooted out three of its bedfellows and destroyed them to the point that they no longer exist. Today we say that they are extinct. We saw the little horn power rise to dominance and rule the world during the Dark Ages. How it tried to be God, even to the extent of claiming to forgive sins, which only the God of heaven can do. Then it took upon itself the job of exterminating all those who did not follow its doctrines. We saw all the world wondering after the beast. Then we saw another beast arise that looked like a lamb but was very powerful. We saw it join with the first beast and between them they resurrected persecution of God's chosen ones. We had a fantastic side trip, and it brought us right back to the period between the opening of the fifth seal and the pouring out of the seven last plagues. This is a period of turmoil and persecution, a period of great anticipation for God's children as they read the road signs and know that they are almost home. There is a surprise for us in the next chapter.

Before we do the chart, we need to make a few mental notes, as to what is happening. First, in chapter 12 we were shown who the perpetrator of sin was and is. It revealed Satan's plot to overthrow God's rulership, destroy his Son, the church and finally the remnant of her seed, who keep the commandments of God. In this chapter, we saw Satan's agents who he used and is using to make war with the remnant of the woman's seed, as he tries to attain his goal as supreme ruler of this earth. Now let's see if we can put all this information together on the chart so that it makes a perfect picture, or map if you please, of the events that have happened on our journey thus far, or are to happen somewhere further down the road.

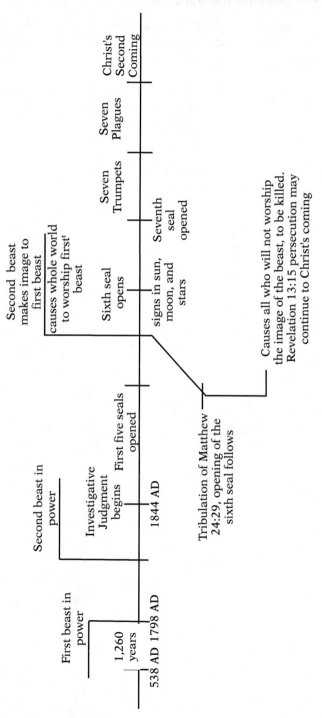

We will be looking at another chart in the next chapter that will parallel this same time period, but will have different players taking the lamp light.

Chapter 14

THE SPECIAL INVITATION

As we embark on our journey through this chapter, there will be some rough going as this one doesn't follow any set pattern as the previous chapters have. This one seems to jump all over the place, back and forwards without any rhyme or reason. However we will look at it, to see if we can find out, the message that John was trying to get across to us.

The key to understanding the first five verses of this chapter, lay in the last chapter. In fact, these verses belong in the last chapter, they are the climax of the vision of the second beast. When the Bible was divided up into chapters and verses by the men of those days, they did not notice that the tie, "and I looked", of verse 1, shows a continuation of the scenario of chapter 13. It is the climax of that chapter. Chapter 14 should have started at verse 6, where a whole new scene takes place, dealing with a special message to the world. As we will find, it has it's own ending as well, but for the time being we need to finish the scene of the last chapter, by continuing with these first five verses of this chapter.

John has just finished viewing the panoramic scenes of the time of persecution that was and is to fall on God's chosen ones, chapter 13, verses 11–18. As he continues this scene, he says "and I looked", it is like he is in the middle of time, he looked behind him and saw the persecution of God's people, then turning around and looking the other direction he sees the end result. Those who had gone through the trying times of the last days, were standing with their Savior on Mt. Zion. They had overcome the beast by remaining true to God and his laws and putting their trust in him. Those who had survived the persecution and the death sentence imposed by the United States government in partnership with the papal powers of Rome, are those that John sees standing with the Lamb here in the 1st verse.

Just what or where is Mt. Sion, that John saw in the first verse? This term "Sion" or "Zion" seems to have several different applications or meanings, it can mean a mountain near Jerusalem[1], or Jerusalem itself[2], or the dwelling place of God.[3] This last one is what John was describing , for we read in Hebrews 12:22, "But ye are come unto Mt. Sion, and unto the city of the living God, the heavenly Jerusalem, and to an innumerable company of angels". Here it is referred to as the city of the living God, the heavenly Jerusalem, it is here that John sees the 144,000 that have the name of the Lamb's Father written on their foreheads.

It must be noted here, that John does not see all the redeemed from all ages standing in heaven at this time. These are only those who have overcome the beast in this last great conflict between Christ and Satan. They are the great multitude that no man could number, that John saw back in chapter 7, verse 9. These are they that came through the great tribulation and were victorious over the beast. Now John sees them again in this vision, and he is shown a few more details that he didn't see back in chapter 7.

In verse 2, he hears a great orchestra playing on their harps and a large choir singing a song. It is interesting to notice how he describes the voices of the singers. He says that he heard a voice from heaven as the voice of many waters. Remember that water is symbolic of a great multitude of people, what John is saying here is that he heard many multitudes of people playing their harps and singing. We read in verse 3, that these people are singing a new song that no one can learn except they themselves. These saints have gone through an experience that no other beings have ever gone through, they have been tried and tested, and have been redeemed or bought back from the world.

John was shown that these redeemed ones are not contaminated with any false doctrines of any other religions. They follow the Lamb wherever he goes. These are the sheep of his pasture that he spoke about to the disciples while he

---

[1] Dueteronomy 4:48
[2] Zechariah 9:9
[3] Hebrews 12:12

was here on earth with them. He said, "And other sheep I have, which are not of this fold: them also I must bring, and they shall hear my voice; and there shall be one fold, and one shepherd".[4] When laws are passed by governments, to force their citizens to worship a false god on a false sabbath, there will be a great awakening of all the sincere followers of God, from all denominations and persuasions around the world. When these laws are enacted, then people will have to make a choice of who they are going to follow. They will either choose the beast and receive his mark or they will choose to follow Christ and receive the seal of approval from God. It is at this time that the one "fold" that Christ talked to his disciples about, becomes a reality, it is at this time that there will only be one shepherd. People by the tens of thousands will stand up and say, "I want to be counted among the sheep of God's fold". They will leave the mainline churches of today and give their hearts fully to the Lord, embracing the seventh day Sabbath of God and receiving his seal in their foreheads.

Finishing off with this segment of his vision, John records that these were redeemed from among men and that they are the "first fruits" unto God and to the Lamb. This is not to say that they will go to heaven before the redeemed of all ages are resurrected from their graves, it simply means that they are presented as living proof of their devotion to him. They overcame the beast, as Christ overcame Satan in the wilderness and are thus called the first fruits. Notice the testimony that John gives of them in verse 5, "in their mouth was found no guile or deceit, for they stand without fault before the throne of God". Oh that each one of us might be in that group.

Thus ends the vision that started in chapter 13. As we continue on our journey, we now have to take another detour so that we can add some more details to the road map. We won't go back quite so far in history or quite so far into the future as we have just done. However we will get a fuller understanding of the call to join the last fold of the good Shepherd.

In this chapter, a new term is incorporated for the beast, that we have not seen used previously, it is the word Babylon. This word comes from an ancient city that was being

---

[4] John 10:16

built some time after the great flood of Noah's day. Man had begun to increase on the earth, and of course, Satan was right in there, trying to thwart God's plans by twisting the minds of the people. Consequently, the people decided that they couldn't trust the God of old man Noah, so they decided to build a very special city. This city would have a tower so tall that if another flood were to come along they could climb up in the tower and would not be swept away as the antediluvians were. Plans were laid and the work was begun on this great undertaking, little did they know that their creator was watching them from heaven[5]. It was their plan to develop a city so large that they would not be scattered all over the earth. Remember, these are all relatives, cousins, uncles, aunts, brothers, sisters, and parents. All descendents of great, great, great grandfather Noah, so they did not want to be separated from one another. However as God looked at this scene he saw that it wasn't a good thing, so he went down and changed their language to many different languages. This caused a lot of discord amongst the workers, and confusion was the order of the day. Because of the trouble this caused, by the workers not being able to understand each other, it became known as Babel. Finally the people of each language group packed up their tools and moved away from the city, to other parts of the earth. This is where we get the word Babylon from.

Remember back in the book of Daniel, we read about King Nebuchadnezzar, and the kingdom of Babylon. It supposedly was in the same area as the Tower of Babel. This name meant "gate of the gods", in the Babylonian language, however the Hebrews associated it with the word *balal* which meant "to confuse".[6] As the various kingdoms rose and fell, there were different forms of religion all mixed together, and finally we find ourselves down in the feet and toes of the great image with hundred's of different religions and persuasions. When the beasts that John sees, arise to power, and laws are passed which conflict with the law of God, he shows John, in vision, all the confusion amongst those who claim to be holy, but are

---

[5] Genesis 11:5
[6] Seventh-day Adventist Bible Commentary, pg.829

not, this is spiritual Babylon, or in plain language, it is a false religion. As we continue on our journey through the next 5 or 6 chapters we will see just why God used the term. With this information to help us, we can now begin our trip and get this detour behind us.

In verse 6 John tells us that he saw another angel fly in the midst of heaven, having the everlasting gospel to preach unto them that dwell on the earth, and to every nation, and kindred, and tongue, and people. This angel, as were many of the other ones that he saw, was flying in the midst of heaven. Remember that the "midst" means the middle of the heavens or in the air. This angel has a special message that it must give to the inhabitants of the world. This message was the everlasting gospel, that Jesus loves the world and that he had come and died for all mankind, that whoever believed in him would have everlasting life.[7] This message was to be carried to all the world. Was this angel to do this all by itself? Remember what we learned back in the beginning of the book of Revelation, that the word "angel" can mean messenger as well as a heavenly being. So this angel could mean people with a message from God, going out into the word telling everyone about the gospel of Jesus Christ. Jesus, himself gave the gospel commission to his followers, telling them to go out into all the world. They were to teach all nations and baptize them in the name of the Father and of the Son, and of the Holy Spirit.[8] So this messenger represented God's followers, who would go out preaching and teaching the message of God's love and of Christ's soon return, to get his followers.

This messenger also had another message to deliver to the inhabitants of this world. Looking at verse 7, this messenger uses a "loud" voice, in other words it speaks out very strongly, so that everyone can hear it. The first part of the message was, "fear God and give glory to him for the hour of his judgement is come". This message was to be given just before the judgement began, that we studied about in chapter 4. At some time just prior to the year 1844, a group of God's followers were to give a message to the world that his

---

[7] John 3:16
[8] Matthew 28:19

judgement was about to begin. These same people were also to tell the world to worship him who made the heaven and the earth, and the sea, and the fountains of water. One might think that it was not necessary to include this message, but God knew from past experience that the world would turn away from worshiping him as their Creator, and would worship a human being in the form of a pope, instead of him. This was the message that the first angel was to deliver to the world and it's inhabitants.

The second angel's message is a real short one, Babylon is fallen, is fallen, that great city, why? Because she made all nations drink of the wine of the wrath of her fornication. Here we have a scene of a great city called Babylon. This cannot be the Babylon that Nebuchadnezzar had built because John knew that it lay in ruins, and had not been rebuilt for centuries, and is still in ruins today. Peter, writing a letter to another church signed off his letter with "the church at Babylon salute you".[9] This may or may not have been the church in Rome. There has been much controversy over this, however there is a reference in the 17th chapter of Revelation to Babylon the great city, and it implies that it is speaking of Rome. We will cover it in more detail when we arrive there on our journey. Notice that here in this verse it refers to Babylon as being "that great city" the same as in chapter 17.

We cannot go on to the next message until we have covered the last part of verse 8. Here it tells us why the great city fell, because she made all nations drink of the wine of the wrath, of her fornication. Babylon, the medieval Roman Church had forced her doctrines and dogmas on the entire known world at that time. Any who opposed her were beaten down and destroyed, just as the early Reformers were. They tasted her wrath on the guillotine, at the stake, were torn apart by horses, and tied to posts in the ocean, where they drowned as the tides came in, all because they would not accept the fornication of her doctrines. Like the three Hebrew youth who would not bow down to the Golden Image made by King Nebuchadnezzar, so these faithful ones would not bend the knee to a counterfeit god. Because of their stead-

---

[9] 1 Peter 5:13

fastness in what they believed, they gave up their lives just as Stephen did[10], rather than go against the God of the Universe.

The "Babylon" that John sees here in these verses is a religious-political system that arises near the end of this earth's history, and as we saw in the last chapter will involve more than just the Vatican.

The vision now takes on a new angle. We are looking at the same time frame as the opening of the fifth and sixth seals. This is a warning to the whole world, to sit up and take notice while there is still an opportunity to make the choice for eternal life. This call goes out to all mankind before Christ's intercession in the Most Holy place in heaven comes to an end, at the opening of the seventh seal. Again the messenger, in a clear, loud voice, proclaims his message to the world, "If any man worship the beast and his image, and receive his mark in his forehead, or in his hand, the same shall drink of the wine of the wrath of God". This warning comes before the laws are enforced, which demands the death penalty for those who choose to follow the true God and worship him on his Holy day, the seventh day Sabbath, or Saturday. It gives everyone a chance to look at the options, either follow God and receive eternal life, and a home in heaven forever, or follow the beast power and be destroyed eternally. In fact as we read further on in verse 10, we see that those who choose to follow the beast or his image, will be tormented with fire and brimstone. In other words they will be burned up before God and the angels. Many people, at first glance will immediately ask "how can a God of love do such a horrible thing"? It is because of his love for them, that he does not force them to live with him in heaven where they would not be happy, so in that great love, honoring the choice they have made, he destroys them eternally. Those who choose to worship the beast and his image or receive the mark of his name, at some point in time will cease to exist.

John now points to or is shown another group of people, in verse 12. He says, "here is the patience of the saints, here are they that keep the commandments of God and the faith

---

[10] Acts 7:59

of Jesus". This last part is better translated "faith in Jesus", it is only through faith in Jesus shed blood on Calvary[11] that we can claim his character as our own. It is only through faith in his promise that he will come back and take us home[12], that will see us through the trying times ahead. Verse 13 gives hope to those who die in the Lord from this time forward. A voice from heaven speaks to John, telling him to write a message to them. The message was, "Blessed are the dead which die in the Lord, (believing in him) from now on, that they may rest from their labours". This seems to indicate all those who died during the time covered by the three angels messages, as well as those who will be martyred for their faith during the fifth and sixth seals. There is no mention in the Bible that anyone will die after Christ's declaration that judgement is finished. When the sealing angel seals his children, then the promise, "I will never leave thee nor forsake thee", will be fulfilled.[13] It is then that God's children will fully understand the meaning of the 91st Psalm.

Now John sees another picture come into view as he continues describing the vision that he had. In verse 14, he sees a white cloud and on it sat someone who looked like Jesus. He was wearing a golden crown, and in his hand was a sharp sickle. It appeared that he was going to harvest something. An angel came out of the temple in heaven and spoke to him in a loud voice saying, thrust in your sickle and reap the earth for it is ripe. Then Jesus did as the angel said, he garnered in the crop that was ripe. Here we have a quick rundown of the coming of Christ to redeem man from the earth. On several occasions Christ used the gathering in of the harvest, as an object lesson for his disciples as he taught them by the seaside. He had talked about the wheat and the tares growing together, and how it was unwise to try to pull up the tares until all the grain was ripe. In that example he pointed out that when the grain was ready for harvest the farmer would gather the wheat into the barn and bundle up the tares to be burnt.[14] In this parable that he used, he told

---

[11] John 3:16
[12] John 14:1-3
[13] Hebrews 13:5
[14] Matthew 13:30

them that the kingdom of heaven was like the farmer and his field. John heard Jesus tell this parable and he had firsthand knowledge of the farming practices of his day. When he saw in vision, the Son of Man on the cloud, with the sickle, and he heard the angel give the command to harvest the earth, he knew what was happening. He did not need to use any symbols to describe what was going on, as it was very plain for him to understand.

Verses 17–20 tell about the harvest of those who do not have the seal of God in their forehead. However in this scene it is not a wheat field that is being harvested, but a vineyard. The angel doing the harvesting here is told to gather the clusters of the vine of the earth because they were ripe. Remember back in verse 8, where Babylon, referred to as "she", made all nations drink the wine of the wrath of her fornication. The term "she and her" indicate that this is a woman that John is seeing here. A woman is symbolic of a church, this being the case there is no doubt that Babylon is a religious-political power that has forced the nations of the world to do what she commands. The angel in verse 19, gathers the vine of the earth and throws it into the great winepress of the wrath of God. The harvest is complete and finished.

Verse 20 has always posed a lot of questions, and I am not in the position to try and explain it at this point in time. The gathering of the grapes, the pressing out of the wine, and the blood coming out of the winepress seem to be symbols of the reward that the beast powers receive for their part in the treading down of God's law and the murder of his saints. When we go ahead a few chapters to the 17th chapter we see that church of Babylon is drunk with the blood of the saints and with the blood of the martyrs. This is why, when the grapes are placed into the winepress and the pressure is applied, that blood comes out of the press, showing that the death of God's people has been avenged.

I am sure that some that read this, are hoping that there is an explanation of the length, of the river of blood, mentioned in verse 20. I have never heard of such an explanation, though I am sure some have tried. None of these latter visions were explained to John so we have just had to compare verse with verse to arrive at a solution, so we can get a picture of what God wants us to know. Later on, we will see where visions are explained to John. That will make our trip a bit easier as we will have some more mileage signs to show us where we are in regards to the end of the journey, and our final destination.

Now for a quick review of this chapter. We saw the completion of the previous chapter, how John saw the redeemed that had the seal of God in their foreheads, standing with the Lamb on Mt. Sion.

In the next vision, he was shown the three angels that each had a special message to give to the world. These messages were in regards to the state of those who had the mark of the beast in their forehead or in their hand. Then he was given a quick preview of the harvest of the world and how the two harvests would end up. So ends this chapter.

Chapters 12, 13, and 14 have taken us on side trips to give us a better understanding of scenes that are about to take place. All of them went back in time or history, to different starting points. Chapter 12 went back in time to before Christ's birth, while chapter 13 and the first part of 14 began in or around the year 538 BC, and carried us forward to the 144,000 being seen in heaven with Jesus. Chapter 14, verse 6 and onwards, had its beginning just prior to the beginning of the heavenly judgement in 1844, and it brought us down to the scene of the harvest of the earth. Though all the beginnings were at different points in time, the endings all culminated right around the closing scenes of this earth's history. They set the stage for the next five chapters. Exciting things are ahead for God's people, our destination is in sight and our journey is almost over.

Across the page is another chart which covers the events that John was shown in this chapter. You will see how they correspond to the previous charts in chapter 12 and 13.

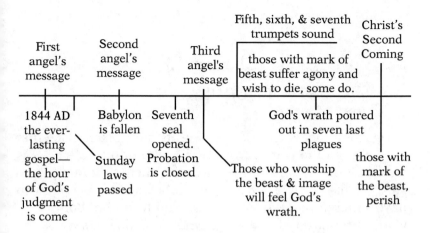

From these 3 chapters, we see three different scenarios that cover the same general time span. Chapter 12, pin pointed the power behind the second beast powers in chapter 13, and in chapter 14, God's messengers pointed out what would happen to those who worship the beast and his image.

In our next chapter we are back on course as we journey into time.

Chapter 15

ENCOURAGED

Our journey is almost over, events have taken place that have shaken the world. Now God is about to turn loose his wrath on the nations of the earth, for their continual disregard for his law. He is also going to avenge his people who have suffered persecution for their faith in him, both those who were martyred and those who were able to survive the onslaught of the beast power. We see here in the 1st verse of this chapter, that John is shown another scene in the great controversy between God and Satan. He says, "and I saw another sign in the heaven, great and marvelous, seven angels having the seven last plagues, for in them is filled up the wrath of God".

As he beheld these seven angels standing in the courts of heaven, John was filled with excitement and anticipation. He had seen all the events that had taken place so far, in his previous visions, and he knew something momentous was about to happen. He portrays the feelings of a child, as it is sitting under the Big Top at a circus, as it waits for the act to begin. With bated breath, the youngster watches the doors intently to see the first of the animals, or acrobats to enter the arena. With these same feelings, John is watching these "great and marvelous" events unfold, and as the curtain in the arena lifts he sees seven angels having the seven last plagues of God's wrath. Then suddenly the curtain falls on the scene, blocking out the events that were about to happen.

As the curtain is lifted again, John sees another act in the drama, taking place. He sees something that looks like a sea of glass, mingled with fire. It is hard for us to envision, what he is describing here. A number of years ago, while on the Island of Truk, I stood on the beach as the sun was setting in the west. The lagoon was almost dead calm with only the slightest ripple on it. As that great shining disk touched the horizon, the entire sky turned orange. There was a golden pathway from the sun to the shore, as the sun sank over the edge of the ocean. The lagoon appeared to be on fire, it was an awe-inspiring sight. However the view of the sea that John saw was even more spectacular. There was no ripple on it, for it looked like a pane of glass, absolutely smooth, and it was mixed with fire. It is hard for us to imagine in our minds, just how beautiful this scene must have been. This sounds like the description of the New Jerusalem that we find in chapter 21, verse 21. He is undoubtedly, being shown, the future at this point.

Why did the vision suddenly change at this time? Why did John switch from the issue of the plagues, to the scene of the sea of glass? The Bible gives no explanation, for this sudden change in scenery. I have tried to refrain from inserting speculation into this study, but at this point I will share an idea that came to me as I read this verse.

God's children have been living under very trying circumstances up until this time. He knows that they are getting tired, waiting for him to come and take them home, so he gives John this quick little look into the future, to encourage the waiting ones. We don't know what is going through their minds, but it could be that those with the seal of God in their foreheads, remember the sign posts that they have studied about and locked in their memory. They will be comforted with the thought that as soon as the plagues are over, God will come for them.

Now let us get back to verse 2 and see what else that John was shown. As he continues with the description of this sea of glass, he sees all those who have gained the victory over the beast, and over the image of the beast, and over the number of his name, standing on this sea of glass. These, then are the saints that have gone through the persecution, facing the death penalty for refusing to worship, or refrain from working on Sunday, the first day of the week. They have been faithful to God's Ten Commandment Law and have been translated without seeing death. These are those, that Paul saw caught up into the air at Christ's Second Coming.[1]

---

[1] 1 Thessalonians 4:17

This group of people that are standing on the sea of glass are the same ones that he saw standing with the Lamb on Mt. Sion in the last chapter, the 144,000. They are the great multitude that he saw sealed back in chapter 7, when he turned around to look at the 144,000 that he had heard about. Here in the last part of verse 2 we see that these dear ones who are on the sea of glass in heaven, have harps, just as the ones in chapter 14 have. Going on to verse 3 we see another similarity, these on the sea of glass are singing a song of Moses and the Lamb, praising the great and marvelous works of the God saying, "Just and true are thy ways, thou King of saints". Interestingly, the 144,000 also sing a song before God in the 14th chapter. Both groups have been redeemed from the earth, and had to gain the victory, over the beast and his image, and over the number of his name. As the Bible doesn't mention a special coming of Christ to pick up the 144,000, to take to heaven by themselves, we have to assume that they are part and the same as all those who are alive when Christ comes the second time to take us all home to heaven with him, along with the resurrected saints.

After this portion of the vision was finished, in verse 4, John then says that he looked and behold the temple of the tabernacle of the testimony in heaven was opened. As the temple opened, he saw the seven angels mentioned in verse 1, that had the seven plagues, come out of it. These were dressed in white linen, symbolic of Christ's purity and righteousness which he gives to all those who love him and keep his commandments.

Some may question whether the white linen stands for Christ's righteousness or not. If we jump ahead to chapter 19, verse 8, we read that the "fine linen" clean and white, is the righteousness of the saints. The Bible tells us that God wants to give us good gifts. He covers us with the robe of righteousness[2], he has a crown of righteousness to give us when we get to heaven[3], and there are many more texts scattered throughout the Bible about righteous people and how they became righteous.

[2] Isaiah 61:10
[3] 2 Timothy 4:8

As the angels leave the temple, one of the four beasts that stood around the throne of God and the Lamb, handed each one a vial, full of the wrath of God. This wrath is the same wrath that is mentioned in chapter 11, verse 18, when the seventh trumpet sounded, and the twenty–four elders declared that it was time for the wrath of God to come. Remember that the seventh trumpet was also the third "woe on the inhabitants of the earth"[4], with the exception of those who have the seal of approval from God.

After the angels leave the temple in heaven, John saw that the temple filled up with smoke from the glory of God and from his power. There is an interesting side note that John puts in at the close of the verse. He says that "no man" was able to enter into the temple until the seven angels had finished their task of pouring out the plagues. When we get to heaven, it will be interesting to find out if the four beasts and the twenty–four elders had to leave the temple during this time, or if this term "no man" had some other meaning .

This chapter has been a short one, but it gives us two things. First of all it sets the stage for the pouring out of the seven last plagues, and secondly, it gives encouragement to those who are waiting and looking for the Second Coming of Christ. I cannot stress enough, the importance of reading and studying the book of Revelation, by God's children in these last days of earth's, history. Remember what we read in the 3rd verse of the 1st chapter, "blessed is he that reads, hears and keeps the things written herein". By studying this book over and over again, we will lock each milepost in the recesses of our mind. When the events written in this book take place, we will know exactly where we are on our journey into the future. Those who have failed to study the map, will have a hard time as they face the unfamiliar road ahead of them. When we feel discouraged or disheartened, all we will have to do is look at the road signs, see how many we have passed and how many are still ahead, and we will know that we are almost home.

---

[4] chapter 8:13

Chapter 16

THE GRAPES OF WRATH

This chapter is a continuation of chapter 15, for in it we will see the pouring out of the plagues that the seven angels received from one of the four beasts as they left the temple. As the seven angels departed from the temple, John heard a great voice coming from it, telling the group of angels, to go their ways and pour out the vials of the wrath of God, upon the earth. These vials were probably more like soup bowls so that they could be emptied rapidly.

As the angels emptied their bowls, this earth was plunged into the most terrifying and devastating events that have ever occurred. Even the destruction of the earth in Noah's day did not come close to what was awaiting the inhabitants of earth in these closing scenes, of the last days of this worlds history. For in Noah's day the people were swept away and drowned fairly quickly, in the floodwaters. In the last days before the return of Christ, those who have chosen to follow the beast, or have accepted his mark in the hand, will suffer literal, physical and mental torment, just like they had inflicted on the faithful followers of Christ.

I must mention again, the difference between the counterfeit plagues of chapters 8 to 11, and these plagues, that they are the wrath of God. The counterfeit ones only affected one third of the population. These plagues will be universal as they fall on all who have the mark of the beast. Remember back in chapter 13 verse 12, where it said that the second beast that came up out of the earth, caused the whole world to worship the first beast. From this we know that there will be people all over the entire globe, in every country of the world, who will have the mark of the beast for one reason or another. Thus it is reasonable to believe that these plagues will fall on the entire planet, the only ones who will not be affected directly will be those who have the seal of the living

God. He will have them covered under his shadow[1], he will cover them as a hen covers her chicks. All others will feel the effects of the wrath of God.

So let's get into the chapter and see what is going to happen to those who have turned their back on God and his love. There has been a train of thought over the years, that the plagues of God will not be universal. One writer stated that if these plagues were universal, all life, would be destroyed on planet earth. On our journey through this segment of out trip, we will discover that during the pouring out of God's wrath, there is no record or mention of anyone dying. This chapter only records instances of the suffering that mankind go through, who have the mark of the beast, or worship his image.

The 2nd verse starts with the first angel pouring out his bowl on the earth, notice how all-inclusive, that statement is. It didn't say "on a third of the earth" or any other portion of the earth, it just stated "the earth. From this, we can conclude that the whole world was involved in this plague.

Continuing on to the last part of verse 2, we notice that this plague caused terrible sores to break out on those who had the mark of the beast. Again, it is important to note that it doesn't specify a "percentage" of those who had the mark of the beast, it simply says that it fell on the men, who have the mark of the beast, and worship his image. These men, and that includes all mankind, come down with terrible sores, that John describes as noisome and grievous. One dictionary describes the word "noisome" as a disgusting, offensive odor. So these men have a sore that is causing them a lot of pain and discomfort, and on top of all that, they smell so bad that they can't even stand themselves. Can you imagine how these people will feel when they look around the country and see a group of people whom they hate, without any sores or discomfort. Worse still, when the news breaks that there is a group of people all around the world who will not bow down to the wishes of popular church, and they are unaffected by the plague, animosity will run high. The pressure of persecu-

---

[1] Psalms 91:1,4

tion will begin to increase, causing more hardship on those who are following God's precepts.

Something to make note of here in the pouring out of the plagues is, that there is no mention of any time spans such as in the latter of the trumpets. These plagues seem to fall very rapidly, as John does not go into much detail as to the effect they have on mankind. He just gives a quick rundown of the cause and just as short, report on its effect.

John sees the second angel pour out his bowl on the sea, and it immediately turned into blood. This was not blood like you and I normally think of or see. Look closely at verse 3, here it says that it became as, or was like the blood of a dead man. John was probably familiar with the death of men, and certainly that of animals, but for some reason he chose to use dead men's blood for his comparison. Now I have never seen dead men's blood but I have seen the blood of dead animals. When blood ceases to be pumped through the veins, and it gets cold, it becomes clotted and jelly like. This is exactly what John saw happen in the second plague, the oceans and seas turned into one large jellied blood pudding.

This blood pudding had a severe reaction on the inhabitants of the seas. The fish couldn't swim through it very well and certainly couldn't get it to pass through their gills, so they all died. The sharks that are normally attracted to food by the smell of blood, were smothered in it and couldn't see where it was all coming from, so they died too. The great whales of the sea that live on the krill died because the krill had died in the pudding, and so the whales wound up dead in the pudding also. If you have a hard time trying to imagine just what it will look like, go to the next church pot luck and look at the jellied salad with the fruit cocktail mixed into it. Next imagine that all the pineapple pieces are fish, the sliced peaches as whales, the maraschino cherries as sharks or some other form of sea life. Hopefully this is put in raspberry Jello. Now you know exactly what John was shown, when that second plague was poured out. Not a pretty sight nor will it smell like roses on a spring day.

Now it is time for the third angel to deliver the contents of his bowl to the earth. This angel poured his bowl of God's wrath out on the rivers and the fountains of waters. These also turned to blood, but unlike the still water of the seas, this blood remained liquid, probably due to the fact that the rivers and fountains were running water, and didn't have time to coagulate. John hears the angel of the waters say, "thou art righteous oh Lord, because you have done this thing". Then in verse 6 he continues, "because they", speaking of those who worship the beast, "have shed the blood of the saints, you have given them blood to drink because they deserve it". Is it coming clear to you now, how these bowls of God's wrath can be the "third woe" on the inhabitants of the earth?[2] Then a voice out of the alter or heaven declares "even so Lord God Almighty, true and righteous are thy judgements. You have avenged the blood of the martyrs."

The sealed servants of God have seen a terrible grievous smelly sore develop on those who have the mark of the beast. They have seen and probably smelled all the dead creatures of the sea as the odor sweeps inland on the air currents. They hear about the bloody putrid water that the people are drinking, and now they are about to be observers of the forth plague.

Some years ago, I drove my daughter down to medical school at Loma Linda, California. There was no air conditioner in our little car, as we don't usually need it where we live, but driving across the Mojave Desert, was another story. The temperature at Kramer Junction was 114 degrees, and we had to drive behind a pilot car from the junction nearly to San Bernardino, at around 20 miles per hour. We thought that we would die from the heat. The next day we drove out to Desert Hotsprings on an errand, and on the return, going down hill, the car ran hot. The thermometer read 117 degrees in the shade. We had a taste of the next plague that day.

Another angel comes into the picture now and pours our yet another bowl, this one on the sun. Power was given to the sun to scorch men with fire. There was a special reason why God used the sun in the closing scenes of the earth's history. Men had worshiped the sun on the first day of the week, so it became known as Sunday. As man liked the sun so much, God said, I'll give you more. John records in verse

---

[2] Revelation 8:13

nine that the men were scorched with great heat, and they blasphemed the name of God, who had the power over these plagues. Yet after all they had gone through, they still would not give glory to God by acknowledging that he was in control of the events that were taking place.

Now the fifth angel comes on the scene to pour out the bowl that he is carrying. This plague is poured on the seat of the beast, and his kingdom was full of darkness. Here we see again, part of the retribution that is to fall upon the church of Rome. As we see in verse 10, this plague is to fall on the "seat of the beast". He does go on to say that the beast's kingdom was full of darkness. This can also be taken several ways, it can mean that the Vatican city is in a literal blackout, as was Egypt in the time of Moses[3], or it could be referring to a time of spiritual darkness. We must also ask "what is encompassed in the kingdom"? Does this mean the Vatican, or the city of Rome, or does it cover the entire jurisdiction of the Roman Church, including all it's adherents? Let's read on and see if we can find an answer to these, and other questions that arise in our minds, from this text.

Verse 10 finishes by saying, "and they gnawed their tongues for pain", and actually verse 11 is the continuation of verse 10, as it finishes the thought, or plague, spoken of there. By continuing on, with the rest of the plague we see the final results of it. Let's put it together and see what we come up with. Speaking of those who are of the kingdom of the beast, John says, "and they gnawed their tongues for pain, and blasphemed the God of heaven because of their pains and their sores, and repented not of their deeds". Wow! What a scenario, now we are beginning to get somewhere, in identifying the seat of the beast and his kingdom, and who is affected by this plague of darkness. We will deal with the issue of darkness in a few moments, but first we must find out who are involved in the suffering from this plague. The clue is found in verse 11. Speaking of those who gnawed their tongues, it says they did that because of their pains and their sores. These sores are a carry over from the first plague back in verse 2, so there hasn't been a whole lot of time elapsed,

---

[3] Exodus 10:21-23

since the plagues began to be poured out. We now have an I.D. on those who suffer from the darkness, they are those men who have the mark of the beast, and those who worship his image.

These inhabitants of the earth have a reason to gnaw their tongues. They have these nasty smelling sores all over their bodies. Their food has died in the sea, so many of them are suffering from hunger, from the loss of the fish in the sea. Their bodies are dehydrating from the loss of body fluids oozing out of the open sores, and the only thing they have to drink is that terrible bloody water that reminds them of all the servants of God, that they have killed, spilling their blood on the ground. To top this all off, their skin is peeling off their bodies from the terrible burns they have received from the scorching sun.

A few years ago we lived in The Gambia, West Africa. While there we saw the effects of what the sun can do to the human body. During the winter months of November through to May, thousands of European tourists converge on The Gambia to relax on the beach and soak in the sunshine. A great many of the female tourists swim topless, and had not had a great amount of exposure to the effects of the sun on their tender skin before they arrived in paradise. By the second day there, they looked like they had just got out of the roasting pan. They would have to spend a day or two in their motel rooms to recuperate, by this time they had started to peel and decided to get back out doors for some more sun before heading back home. They would come out of the hotels looking like they had leprosy, from all that peeling skin, and of course there was lots of new pink tender skin for the sun to shine on. By the end of the day many of the people had burn on top of burn and oh how they suffered. That sun in Africa was only a sneak preview of the strength it would attain when God's wrath was poured out in the fourth plague, on the inhabitants of the earth, and now this darkness has come upon them. With all the suffering and discomfort they are going through, and now to have darkness cover them so they cannot see where they are going, just puts the icing on the cake. Every time they try to move, they bump into furniture, or some other object, hurting their sores and sunburn even more. Curses pour out of their mouths, but yet they will not admit that they have brought all this on themselves, by the choices they made in life.

As a youngster growing up in the 50's and 60's, attending church, parochial school, and the various evangelistic meetings that came our way, it seemed like this next plague, was every pastors and evangelists favorite one. I also believe with all my heart that this one probably struck more fear in the hearts of more people, than any of the other six. It quite likely has had more interpretations than any of the others have, as well. Let's take a look at it.

As the sixth angel pours out his bowl on the earth, we see the waters of the great river Euphrates, dry up, preparing the way for the kings of the east to come and do battle. There have been many speculations, over the years as to what the "drying up" was referring to. Years ago, the popular thought among theologians, was that the literal river would become dry, so that the armies east of there could march through the riverbed, to do battle with the forces on the other side. Then came the missiles and rockets of the late 50's and early 60's. It was then realized that the river didn't need to dry up any more as the rockets and missiles could be fired over it, so another interpretation was in order. I can't remember how many different explanations I have heard about this text, and I am not going to add to them in this book. I believe that it is one of those things that will be revealed to us when it happens.

After the Euphrates has dried up, we see three unclean spirits like frogs, coming out of the mouth of the dragon, and out of the mouth of the beast, and out of the mouth of the false prophet. It is interesting that these unclean spirits, are likened to frogs. The Bible doesn't expound on this likeness, so we have to look to nature and how frogs live, to try to understand how these unclean spirits operate. Many frogs have an ingenious method of catching their food. They have long tongues that they can extend very rapidly to catch flies and bugs that venture too close to them. In light of this, we can conclude that these three unclean spirits are going to use their tongues to deceive the kings of the earth and the whole world in general.

Perhaps we should identify the three unclean spirits. There is no question as to who the dragon is. The Bible is very plain on that one, for we read in chapter 12, verse 9, where it tells us that the great dragon is non other than that old serpent called the Devil and Satan. That's very plain. Then we have the beast to deal with. As we have been going through the book of Revelation, we have discovered that the beast is the Antichrist power of the church of Rome. We will be looking more closely at that in the next two chapters. But the false prophet has not been mentioned before, in the book of Revelation. In fact it is only mentioned four times in the Bible, and three of those times are here in the last few chapters of our road map.

The term "false prophet" indicates that there is also a true prophet. In the book of Acts, chapter 13 and verse 6 , we read an account where there was a certain Jew, at a place called Paphos, who was a sorcerer. He was with the deputy of the country, who was interested in what Paul and Barnabas were preaching about. However the sorcerer, whose name was Elymus, tried to discourage the deputy from listening to them, whereupon Paul looked at Elymus, and the Holy Ghost came upon Paul and he told him that the hand of the Lord would fall on him, blinding him for a season.

Here we get a glimpse of what a false prophet is, and how one works. First of all, he appears to be on the side of right, just like Elymus, who was a Jew. No one suspected him of sorcery, he was on the right side. So it is with the false prophet here in this chapter, he appears to be a prophet of God, but he has turned people away from the saving grace of a loving God, by the use of his tongue, speaking smooth sayings.

Can we pin down, who this false prophet is? I believe we can by the simple method of elimination. We have here the dragon, (Satan), also the beast, (Papal Rome). Then we have a prophet who has apostatized and become a false prophet, which has joined ranks with Satan and Rome. The true church of God had been persecuted for hundreds of years, until the people were able to escape to the New World and set up a nation where religious freedom would reign supreme. And so the United States of America became a haven for the Protestants of the medieval Catholic Church. Here in the New World, they were free to worship God as they saw fit. That was nearly 300 years ago. Protestantism has grown, and now is slowly changing its face. It never did break all its ties with the Vatican, for it kept the Vatican's Sunday as a day to worship God on. When the Protestant Churches join hands with the government that has linked up with the Vatican, embracing doctrines that they had formerly left it for, they will then become Apostate Protestantism. This means that they have turned their back on what they had formerly believed, they have become traitors to the cause they once died for. This then is the false prophet of Revelation 16:13, they used to be God's children, just as Elymus was, only to turn against him, so they can gain favor with the beast.

What about the evil spirits that come out of the mouths of the Devil, beast and Apostate Protestantism, what are they? Verse 14 tells us that they are the spirits of devils, working miracles, which go out to the kings of the earth, and to all the people of the whole world, to rise up against the God of heaven and fight for their rights. The Bible doesn't really say it in so many words, but that is the intent of Satan as we will find later on.

John was told in verse 15, that Christ would come as a thief in the night, when no one was expecting him. Christ pronounced a blessing on him who watches and keeps his garments lest he walk naked, and others see his shame. Here again is a blessing pronounced on those who watch and are ready for Christ's return. They are ready because they are not only wearing the robe of Christ's righteousness, but they have studied the road map, and will not be caught unawares.

Much discussion has gone into the meaning of verse 16, where it says that God will gather them together at a place called Armageddon. We hear many preachers pounding the pulpits today, terrifying their parishioners with hideous stories of this impending battle. Many of them, along with the gossip magazine at the grocery checkouts, suggest that this great battle will be fought in the Middle East between the

Jews and the Arabs. However the Bible doesn't even say that it is fought.

There are some who believe that this is a mental battle which takes place in the mind. This may not be far off, when one looks carefully at these verses. In them we see that these three unclean spirits of devils use the beast, and the false prophet along with Satan himself to stir up the general population of the earth. Their minds are in turmoil as they see and suffer physically from the previous plagues. Now they suffer a mental anguish as they struggle with problems around them. We will leave it there and wait and see what transpires as time goes on.

Moving on to, the seventh angel with the bowl of God's wrath, we find that he pours it out into the air. At the same time a great voice sounds out of the temple in heaven, from the throne, saying, "It is done". The last plague is about to fall on planet earth. It is going to be a real shaker. John heard voices, and thunders, and saw lightning, and then he saw a great earthquake such as had never been since man was created, it was the BIG ONE. As a result of this mighty earthquake, the great city was broken into three pieces. The other cities of the world collapsed and great Babylon suffered her share of the plague. Verses 18 through 20, shows us a word picture of the destruction that takes place during this time. Islands and mountains disappear from sight, if ever there was a time in this earth's history when things looked black, it was now.

Of course, we must remember that those with the seal of God, are under his protecting care through all of this turmoil. As we view these events, we know that truly our redemption draws near. There are just two events standing between God's children and heaven. First, the seventh plague has to finish, and it does so with fierce vengeance, great hail falls out of heaven on mankind. Each of the hailstones weigh between 40 and 62 pounds, depending on how one translates the word "talent". The last verse of this chapter says that the men blasphemed God because the plague was so great. I have heard of 10 and 15 pound hail, from time to time. As a youngster I remember seeing a picture of a 12 pound hailstone that went through the roof of a house in Alberta, Canada, back in the 50's. It not only went through the roof, but struck the sofa, breaking it in half. What will hail, the weight of a talent, do?

We have passed the last signpost of our trip, our journey into time is almost over. The next event we see, will be the coming of our Lord and Savior on the clouds of glory, with all the heavenly hosts with him. However, we have to wait a few more chapters before we can cover that event in full.

Let's take a quick review of the events of this chapter. First of all we do not know how long the pouring out of the plagues will take. It appears that it will be a very short time, seeing as those who suffer from the smelly sores, suffer in each of the next four plagues at least, and probably go through the last two as well. As we went through these verses in this chapter, there was no indication that the plagues fell on different sections of the earth, missing some places and hitting others. It just said that it fell on the men which had the mark of the beast and on those who worshiped his image, period. The Bible does not mention any exceptions.

Now just a quick review of where the angels poured out their bowls of wrath. The first one poured his out upon the earth, the second was poured out upon the sea, the third was poured upon the rivers and fountains, the forth upon the sun, the fifth upon the seat of the beast, and the sixth upon the river Euphrates, and the last one was poured into the air.

The events that were started when the seventh angel sounded his trumpet, heralding in, the third woe on the inhabitants of the earth, is over. In the next few chapters, one of the angels that poured out one of the bowls, takes John on another little side trip, but I am getting ahead of the story, and that's another chapter.

Chapter 17

TWO WOMEN, A DRAGON, AND A BEAST

Our journey now takes a side trip. John has had a view of the seven churches, then he was invited up to heaven to observe the Investigative Judgement. As the judgement ended he heard the seven trumpets sound, one after another. As the last trumpet sounded the seven last plagues began to fall on the earth. These were the last events to take place before Christ's appearing in the clouds of heaven. Now here in this chapter, we see John, transported back in time, back somewhere between the opening of the fifth seal, and the sounding of the seventh trumpet.

John opens this phase of his vision by recording, that one of the angels which had been given a bowl of the wrath of God, came by to talk to him. As they talked the angel invited John to come, and he would show him what would happen to the great whore that sat upon the waters. That is strange language for the Bible, but it's there, so we have to deal with it. Who is this woman that the angel is showing John, and what does it all mean? Why is she referred to as "the great whore"? We will discover the answers to these and many other questions that will come into our minds as we travel through this, and the next chapter.

Because this entire chapter is going to be talking about this infamous woman, we might as well find out who she is right from the start and that will make it easier in the long run. Let's go right to the end of the chapter to verse 18, for an explanation of who the woman represents. Here in this verse it tells us that the woman that John saw, was that great city which controls all the leaders of the world. In short, it is the Roman Church, or system that we have seen in previous chapters and also back in the book of Daniel. It is the little horn power that rooted out three of the ten horns in Daniel 7. You will also remember that here in the Revelation we are looking at two women, the virgin who is the true church and the whore who is the false church. With this in mind let's get back to verse 1.

We have covered just about all of verse 1, but there is one more item that we need to deal with, that is, the place on which the whore is sitting. At this point in the vision, John sees her sitting on many waters, what a strange place to sit. Again we will jump ahead a bit to find out the meaning of the term "many waters". Looking at verse 15 we find that the water where the whore sits represents people, multitudes, and nations, and tongues or those of different languages. This term "many waters" is telling us that what John saw was not just multitudes of people or nations, but many multitudes, and many nations. There we have it, this whore, in sitting on all these people and nations etc., shows that she is actually in control of the major portion of the inhabitants of the earth. Let us carry this thought a bit further. If this woman is in control of all the people and world leaders, and she is symbolic of the great city of Rome, and all it stands for, then it is reasonable to say, that it is really the church of Rome that is controlling the world. This woman is under the control of Satan, doing his bidding in trying to rid the world of God's chosen and faithful children.

Verse 2 confirms everything we have discovered so far about the great whore. Here the angel shows John, that the kings of the earth have committed fornication with her. How would obeying her, be considered fornication? If she is a false church, then she has a false doctrine. It is by accepting these false teachings, or going along with them, that the leaders of the world commit fornication with her. That's not all we have here in this verse, for it says that even the inhabitants of the world are made drunk with the intoxicating effect of her doctrines. People who are not grounded in the Word of God, will be easily led astray by these false teachings, to the point where they will do whatever she commands. If she decides that those who do not worship on the day she says, should be destroyed, they will do whatever she tells them to do, even killing God's faithful ones.

In verse 3, a whole new terminology takes over, but basically covers the same information, only in greater detail. The reason for this is, that in verse 1 the angel said, "come hither and I will show thee...", but in verse 3, John says, "so he carried me away in the spirit". In other words, the angel took him out into the wilderness. There is no explanation for this term "wilderness", whether it is referring to spiritual darkness or sin, or if it is a literal wilderness, the Bible doesn't say. In this case, he heard the angel talk about a whore, but when he was taken to the wilderness, he sees a woman, sitting on a scarlet colored beast. It is interesting to note here again, that John, first was told something, and then he saw something. This scarlet colored beast, full of names of blasphemies, claims to be God. This beast that has seven heads and ten horns is the same as the great red dragon of chapter 12. However in this vision, the seven crowns are missing for some reason. We will come back to these heads and horns a little later on, and also discuss the seven crowns.

At this point we need to clear up a possible misunderstanding. We have been reading about the four beasts, the first beast, another beast, image of the beast, mark of the beast, and now we have a scarlet colored beast. Are these all the same animal or nation? We know that the four beasts are earthly nations, and that the first beast of chapter 13, is the last one, of the four beasts that Daniel saw. We have discovered that the second beast, also referred to as another beast, is the United States, while the mark of the beast is Sunday observance in place of the Sabbath. So all we have left is to deal with the scarlet colored beast that the woman sits on. Sometimes Bible scholars, and theologians get this scarlet colored beast mixed up with the other beasts, and talk about it as "the beast". They consider it to be the apostate church of Rome, but it is not. The apostate church or the papacy is the woman sitting on the back of the scarlet colored beast. This beast is the same as the great red dragon of chapter 12, none other than that old serpent the Devil and Satan. The fact that the woman is sitting on his back shows that it is he, who gives the woman the power to rule. It is Satan that is behind the papacy, for it is his counterfeit church instituting, and enforcing his counterfeit day of worship.

John continues in verse 4, to describe the woman that he saw. She was all dressed up in fine clothes of purple and scarlet, and wore a great array of jewelry made from gold and precious stones and pearls. This array of splendor is seen in her churches, and edifices, to this day. She held a golden cup or goblet in her hand which contained all sorts of evil abominations and filthiness of her fornication. Some years ago, while visiting my brother in southern California, I had the privilege of accompanying him on an errand that took us to Sunset Boulevard in Hollywood. While there I saw just about every form evil walking the streets, that one could imagine. Some of the ladies were dressed exactly as the one John saw in his vision. He probably felt the same way that I did in Hollywood, uncomfortable. However John was in the presence of an angel and he must continue on, with what he was viewing,

Next he sees that the woman has something written on her forehead. As he looks closer he sees that her name is MYS-TERY, BABYLON THE GREAT, THE MOTHER OF HAR-LOTS, AND ABOMINATIONS OF THE EARTH. These names depicted her character. She was shrouded in mysterious religious rights that were far from Christian. The name Mother of Harlots and Abominations, has a lot more to it, than first meets the eye. This whore or prostitute if you please, is the mother of a number of daughters, who are also prostitutes. She has populated the world with other women, that think, and act, just like her, and also hold the same ideals, as she does. Who are they and how did they become like her?

First of all we know that this woman is a religious organization, a church, a religious system, that has promoted her doctrines throughout the world. I must point out again, that this woman becomes prominent on the earth at the end of time, and in no way represents the members of her congregation. As we have seen earlier, the church of Rome instituted the observance of Sunday as the day of worship in the Middle or Dark Ages. Along with this, she declared that she had the right to forgive sins, and institute the sale of indulgences, and the doctrine of purgatory. These are all contrary to what the Bible teaches, from this was born the Protestant movement or what is better known as the Reformation. The followers of the Reformers such as Luther, Jerome, Huss, Zwingli, and others were targeted by the church, and persecuted for speaking out against it. It is interesting to note, that even though these Protestants left the mother church, the church of Rome, they took with them some of the doctrines that she taught, such as infant baptism, immortality of the soul, Sunday observance etc., however from all outward appearances they made a complete break with her, even condemning her for her actions during the Dark Ages. A change is slowly taking place today among the mainline Protestant churches, to reunite with the church of Rome, forgiving her for what she did to them in ages past. When they unite with her in forcing the observance of Sunday in place of God's seventh day Sabbath, Saturday, and take an active part in persecuting those who worship on the Sabbath, they will become the harlots mentioned in verse 5. It is when governments and leaders of nations commit fornication with them, in the act of passing legislation, enforcing their dogmas on the inhabitants of the earth, that she becomes the great whore and they, the harlots. I must add that those who remain within her shroud when the call goes forth from God to "come out of her my people", will also be included in her punishment, as we will see later.

Through various chapters, I have mentioned that God's people are going to go through a time of trouble with some giving up their lives in martyrdom, for the Lord. I am sure that some of you have wondered where I got my information from, as I haven't given any concrete evidence from scripture to this effect. We did study back in the fourth seal, about the people who had been killed for their faith.[1] Then in the fifth seal, they were told that they had to wait until their brethren and fellow servants "should be killed as they were", before their blood was avenged. Jesus, in talking to his disciples on the mount, told them that they would be delivered up to be

---

[1] chapter 6

afflicted and killed, and hated for his name sake.[2] So we see that persecution is to arise again just before Christ's return. Did John see any persecution in his vision? Let's read on in verse 6, and see what he has to say. He records that he saw the woman drunk with the blood of the saints, and with the blood of the martyrs, of Jesus. Ah, there we have it, this end time church and her daughters, are going to be involved in trying to force Sabbath keepers to worship on their false sabbath under penalty of death.

Another question now comes to mind, why does God allow his children to go through this persecution if he loves them so much? The answer is not a simple one, but we will try to discover what God's plan is, in allowing it. First of all, we must remember man's fall in the Garden of Eden. From a perfect sinless world, through one mistake, Adam and Eve along with all their descendents, lost their sinless state. God in his great love for his creation provided a way that he could buy them back from sin, by dying for them. However he must let Satan try them as Job was tried, to see if they are faithful and true to his precepts. This time of trial will be a time of soul searching, a time of shaking out the chaff from the grain. Those who are faithful to God, through the trials and tribulations, even to the point of giving up their lives for their belief in him, can be trusted in heaven. Sin will not arise a second time. This is why God allows these things to happen.

The vision is over, and as John is contemplating it, the angel asked him why he was so amazed at what he saw. He then continued by telling John that he was going to tell him about the woman and about the beast that she was sitting on, that had the seven heads and ten horns.

In verse 8, the angel begins his explanation of the vision. He starts out by telling John that the beast he saw, was and is not, and he shall come up out of the bottomless pit. Ultimately, this scarlet colored beast will go into perdition. Those who live on the earth, whose names are not written in the book of life, will wonder or marvel, when they see the beast that was, and is not, and yet is. This word "perdition" is a big word and though most will have a vague idea as to what it refers to, it is

---

[2] Matthew 24:9

has a deeper meaning. One dictionary describes it as a state of final spiritual ruin, hell, which will result in non-existence. God wanted his people to be dead sure in their reckoning as to who the beast was so that they should not be deceived by it.

We need to spend a moment looking at the term, "was, is not, and yet is". As this is referring to Satan, we need to see just how it relates to his actions and circumstances. In the first part of verse 8, it doesn't say "yet is". You will notice that it only refers to "was and is not". The "yet is" doesn't happen until he comes up out of the bottomless pit. There are several explanations of what this could mean, we will look at two of them. The first concept is that the "was" could be referring to his rule over the earth from the Garden of Eden until the cross and Christ's death. The "was not", dealing with the span of time from the death of Jesus, until the end of the judgement scene in chapter 8, and verse 7, when the trumpets begin to sound. That would leave the "yet is" to cover the time from the sounding of the first trumpet to the return of Jesus at his Second Coming. Remember we studied about the fact that the trumpets were Satan's counterfeit plagues. Also remember that locusts had a king over them, who was the "angel of the bottomless pit".[3]

The second possible explanation could go this way. Though God is ultimately in control of the world, Satan has held sway, over the earth and its population thus he "was". Jumping ahead to chapter 20, we read about Satan being bound for 1,000 years, and cast into the bottomless pit. There he will not have anyone to deceive or control, as all his followers are dead and those who have the seal of God in their foreheads are in heaven with Jesus. Thus he is unable to tempt or control anyone, he "is not" in the drivers seat any more. At the end of the 1,000 years, he is released for a short time, this being the "and yet is".

I personally lean towards the first scenario, as it appears to take place within the time frame of this woman that sits on his back. Also because in verse 11 we read that the beast that was, and is not, is the eighth beast, and is of the seven, and he goes into perdition. This verse seems to indicate that

[3] Revelation 9:11

Satan himself, may sit as a pope or ruler in the papacy. That may be why those who have the mark of the beast, on their forehead, or in the hand, are amazed with him.

In verse 9, he points out to John that those who use their mind wisely will understand the meaning of this verse. He explained that the seven heads are seven mountains on which the woman sits. If you ask any history teacher, what city sets on seven hills, they will immediately tell you that it is Rome, for it is known as the City of Seven Hills. Now we have this feature to add to the rest, in helping us identify, who and where, this woman is located.

Next, the angel tells John that there are seven kings. Five of these kings are fallen. This could indicate that they have died, as the next part of the verse says that one is, indicating that he is in existence in the time frame that encompasses this scene. That makes up six kings, so there is another one that is still to come. When the seventh one comes the Bible says that he will continue or reign for only a short time. There is no Bible explanation as to who the kings are. There are a number of different ideas that have floated around the circles of Protestant thought, and any one of them may be correct. These kings may represent popes or they may represent time periods within the period of the Papal rule. It may be that these kings, are the popes that rule in the Vatican after the healing of the wound in 1929. If this is the correct interpretation then it would mean that five of the popes have ruled and died, one is now ruling and there is one more to come. Whatever it means we will soon know. We mustn't forget that the Vatican is in Rome, so both terms are synonymous when dealing with the Church, and this woman that John has been shown.

It is interesting to note that there is no symbol for the seven kings given in this scene of the scarlet colored beast. When we look at chapter 12, the red dragon not only had the seven heads and ten horns, he also had seven crowns on his heads. If the seven heads on the dragon of chapter 12 also represent seven mountains, and each mountain had a crown on it, then it would be safe to say that those seven crowns represented the seven kings in this chapter that have no symbol for them. Let me make it plain at this point, there is no Biblical proof that this is the proper explanation for the problem of no symbol for the seven kings.

There is some thought that the seventh king that is "not yet come", could be the beast that was, and "is not". When the beast that "is not" becomes the beast that "yet is", he will be the eighth king, and somehow be of the seven. It is not absolutely clear how the seven kings and the beast that was, and is not, get together. We must not lose sight of the fact that this beast is Satan. The other possibility is that he will rule along with the seventh king, time will tell.

In verse 12, the angel explains to John that the ten horns that he saw on the scarlet colored beast, are ten kings. These are not to be confused with the seven kings that we have already covered, but are separate and distinct, in that they have not received a kingdom yet. They will however, be given power to rule as kings for a short period of time with the beast. This statement, seems to imply, that the beast that the woman was sitting on, is going to be reigning as a king, or at least ruling or controlling events. All ten of these kings, whoever they are have one purpose in mind, and that is to support the beast. Verse 14 states that ten kings will make war with the Lamb, but the Lamb will overcome them, because he is Lord of lords, and King of kings. I like the next statement that the angel made to John, when he said that those that are with the Lamb, are called, and chosen and faithful. I pray that I am in this group, and I hope you are too.

We have discussed verse 15, on several other occasions so there is no need to go into any more detail at this point.

It is interesting to note in verse 16, that the ten horns on the beast, who are kings, turn on the whore that had been sitting on the back of the beast. They hate her, and in their hate they make her desolate by destroying the faith that her adherents had in her. Then they make her naked by exposing her for what she really is, a used woman, a whore, who let Satan use her against the children of God, just as he used the snake in the Garden of Eden, against our first parents. Though Satan was successful the first time, in the Garden, he fails the second time due to the shed blood of the Lamb on Calvary.

It is not clear, as to what happens next. There is no clear cut explanation, and we have the choice of passing over it, or speculating as to what "eating her flesh, and burning her with fire" means. As I don't approve of speculation, I will pass over it and wait until I see it fulfilled, if the Lord preserves my life, until that day. It definitely is a mile post along the route to our heavenly home, so we need to lock it, in the recesses of our minds for future reference. Whatever it is or means, the angel told John that God had put it in the hearts of the kings, to fulfil his will. They also were impressed to give their kingdom to the beast and let him reign, until the words of God, are all fulfilled.

We covered the description of the woman at the beginning so won't go over verse 18 again.

It has been an interesting journey through this chapter. We have seen how the scarlet colored beast used the woman to deceive the world and to oppress the saints of the Most High God, even to the point of killing them. We have seen her rise to prominence in the world, only to be brought down to destruction by those that she thought were faithful and true to her.

These events have taken place, probably during the later part of the fifth seal, or the first part of the sixth seal. This is evident from events that transpire in the next chapter, but I am getting ahead of myself again. It promises to be as exciting, or more so, than this chapter was.

Chapter 18

THE EQUALIZER REIGNS

This chapter, like the last one, is a filler, by that, I mean that it fills in details that were not included in the main body of the story. In this case, it is going to fill in some more route signs for us to follow, showing us more clearly, just where we are in relation to Christ's second coming. It is an explanation of the things, and events, that John was shown in the last chapter.

I want you to notice how John ties this chapter into the last one. He says, "and after these things I saw another angel come down from heaven". He had just witnessed the scene of the woman on the scarlet colored beast, and saw her demise, then he continues describing more scenes of the vision with the phrase "and after these things". One thing that is different in this chapter, is that John does not have a personal tour guide, like he did in the last chapter. As he writes this, he seems to be standing on the sidelines as an onlooker, describing what he sees taking place.

In this chapter we will again be using the term "Babylon" in referring to the woman of ill repute, along with her daughters, the harlots. John hears this angel that he saw come down from heaven, cry out with a strong voice, saying, "Babylon the great is fallen, is fallen, and is become the habitation of devils, and the hold of every foul spirit, and a cage of every unclean and hateful bird". This is quite a description for a church that had attained popularity among the nations of the world. As we look at these characteristics, we get a crystal clear picture of how low this organization has sunk. As it was in Christ's time, the leaders of the church are the downfall of it. It was the leaders in the temple at Jerusalem, that were involved with extortion, cheating, and stealing from the members of the congregation.[1] They did

---

[1] Matthew 21:12

this by charging unfair prices for the sacrificial animals that they sold to the people, who came to worship at the temple. The leaders in Babylon are guilty of the same crimes as the money changers were. They are condemned and will be punished for the selling of indulgences, and charging their parishioners money to get loved ones out of purgatory, a place that only exists in the minds of misinformed members. No wonder that John describes it as a dwelling place of devils, a container full of every foul spirit. To get a living glimpse of what John saw here, stop by the vulture pen, the next time you visit a zoo and take a look at these detestable birds, and smell the stench that comes from the fecal matter that is all over the enclosure. Then you will have a fuller understanding of how God views Babylon the great, and why she fell out of favor with the world.

The angel continues with his dialogue in verse 3, by giving John the reason, why the popularity of the church began to wane. He tells that it is because all nations drank or partook of the wine of the wrath of her fornication. Wine has an intoxicating effect on those who partake of it, and so the world became intoxicated with the wine of her false doctrines such as infant baptism, purgatory, a false day of worship and her claim to be able to forgive sins. As the world leaders bowed to the demands of the pope, they committed fornication with her. What were the demands that were made on world leaders and kings? That everyone should cease from work on the first day of the week. When the worlds nations bow to the demands or wishes of the papacy, passing laws that force their citizens to worship or honor the popes wishes, then this prophecy will have been fulfilled.

Not only have the leaders of the earth found favor in her sight, but also the merchants of the world have become wealthy because of their association with her. Whether that is from direct dealing with her or from the fact that she has given them permission to carry on trade if they fall into line with her demands, is not made clear here in this text. We will take a deeper look into these merchants and their wares, a little further on in the chapter, but right now, we must see what is happening in verse 4.

It is at this point that John hears another voice from heaven calling, come out of her, my people. This call to come out of Babylon may not be a literal, audible voice that will boom forth from heaven at a given time, although if God chose to use that format, he could. The call could come from the Bible, as a person spends time in His word studying the prophecies of Daniel and the Revelation, finding out the will of God from that angle. The call could come from listening to a radio broadcast or viewing a television evangelist giving a study on the end times. It could be from a friend who has a desire to share his love for God with a neighbor, encouraging them to surrender their lives to God's service. The call to "come out of her my people" may even come to some, from the reading of this book. God has many ways that he can use to get this message out to humanity, before the door of his mercy closes.

The Bible does not verify who this voice is, it just says "another voice from heaven". Looking ahead in verses 5 and 20, we see that the term God is used by the speaker, while in verse 8 it says that, the Lord God is the one who judges her. It appears that the voice that John hears speaking, is God the Father, as the reference to the Lord God implies that this is Jesus. These people that he refers to as "my people" are all those who have a sincere love for him even though they have been mislead by their leaders. They have had doubts in their minds, as to the legality of the church, in it's demands on their loyalty to its authority. They have read in the Bible, or heard from friends or on the news, that there are many who defy the demands of Babylon, and worship on the seventh day Sabbath, of the Bible. They have not seen the importance of this day until now. When the call is given to come out of her, my people, there will be a mass exodus of those who are dedicated believers in the saving grace of the blood of Jesus Christ. These people will come out from the Catholic Church, the Presbyterian, Anglican, Methodist, Episcopalian, Jehovah's Witness, Lutheran, and United Churches, as well as the Latter Day Saints, and any other churches or religions that have made an alliance with Babylon. When the Holy Spirit makes the call, they will stand up and say, "we will follow you". These dedicated Christians, will leave Babylon behind to become the sheep in the Masters fold, that Jesus talked to his disciples about, when he said, "other sheep have I, that are not of this fold, but the day will come when there will be one fold and one shepherd.[2]

This call to come out of her "my people", is given before probation closes. The invitation to "come out of her", indicates that people will still be in the valley of decision, as they weigh the pros and cons of the events that are taking place on the earth. They have seen the earth shaking events that have taken place under the opening of the fifth and sixth seals. They have beheld the children of God as they stood fast for their faith, and suffered at the hands of so called Christians, for keeping God's Holy Sabbath day. They have witnessed the persecutions and possibly the deaths of martyrs who would not bow down to the demands of a false religious system. When they see these things, they will step forward and say, "we want to be counted among the worthies". They will receive the seal of God's approval in their forehead, and thus will not be partakers of Babylon's sins, nor receive her plagues.

The voice from heaven continues speaking to those who are called out of Babylon, right through to the 20th verse. In verse 5 it tells them that her sins have reached up to heaven and that God will remember her iniquities. He has been watching his children and how they have been treated by those professing to be his advocates on earth, and it grieves his heart beyond all measure. These dear ones that have left Babylon, have been on a journey also, but have been on a different route up until this time. Now they join up with all those who John saw back in chapter 7, helping to make up the great multitude that are sealed just before Christ stands up and casts the censor to the earth in chapter 8.

It is important for God's children today, to understand the road map and memorize it, so that they can share it with these new fellow travellers who may not have had the privilege of having it explained to them. They will have to be nurtured and encouraged, as they too will face the trials and

---

[2] John 10:16

torments of the evil one during the sounding of the seven trumpets and the falling of the seven last plagues.

The voice from heaven continues to speak to those who have just come out of Babylon, in verse 6. Though it sounds like the people are supposed to reward Babylon for her misdeeds, what it really says is that God will do the rewarding, for in verse 5 we read, that God has remembered her iniquities. Thus he will reward her with a double portion according to her works. She will receive twice as much punishment as she meted out to His children.

Not only had she been cruel to the saints, but she also had a very bad case of self-esteem. As we read in the next verse, she glorified herself, and lived extravagantly. When one views the cathedrals and churches, and sees the extravagance that has gone into them at the expense of it's parishioners, no wonder God says that an equal amount of torment and sorrow will fall on her. She looks upon herself as a queen, with the whole world as her footstool. She claims to be no widow, and will not see any sorrow. She has a very high opinion of herself. It is because of this attitude problem that she has, that God says that her plagues will come in one day, death and morning and famine, and she will be burned completely with fire.

Some may ask if this day mentioned here in verse 8, stands for a year, as this appears to be a prophecy. If we look further on in both verse 10 and 17, we see the effects of her demise, but here it says that in one hour, her riches have become nothing. From this we can conclude that the term "day" and "one hour" both describe either a short, period of time, or a designated time, that will be allotted for her destruction. Verse 8 concludes with a confirmation of what John saw in chapter 17, verse 16, by reaffirming that Babylon, that great city, the mother of harlots, would be utterly burned with fire. There will be death, and mourning, and famine. What an infamous end to such a pompous establishment, the Lord God has judged her and allowed her utter destruction.

The aftermath of the demise of Babylon, is felt worldwide, kings of the earth who have committed spiritual fornication with her, having lived in harmony with her wishes, shall mourn and lament for her when they see the smoke from the fire, as it devours her. From these verses, it appears that the destruction of Babylon the great by fire, is to be taken as literal, though I am sure that there are those who look at this fire and destruction from a symbolic standpoint. As John was not shown or told what all this talk about fire was about, we have to conclude that it is literal fire and literal burning, resulting in the total destruction of the great city. It would be much easier to understand, if the voice from heaven had given such an explanation. We must bare in mind that this is the explanation of the vision of the great whore, the mother of harlots and abominations, that John was shown in the last chapter.

When we look back at previous dreams and visions, both in the book of Daniel, and here in the Revelation, we see that symbols were used, within these dreams and visions. However when they were being explained to both Daniel and John, they were told what the symbols stood for and at the same time were given the interpretation of these visions and dreams, using non-symbolic language. Remember we discovered earlier, that in prophecy, symbols are often used to describe an event or problem while the result or punishment is always literal. From this, I feel we are safe in saying that due to the nature of these verses, Babylon the great, the mother of harlots, that great city, the religious-political structure known as the papacy, the anti-Christ, will be literally destroyed by fire. This event will take place at some point in time, before the return of our Lord and Savior in the clouds of heaven, at his Second Coming.

Just why the description of all the merchandise is mentioned in verses 11 through 19, is not clear. There are various trains of thought on this portion of the chapter. Some Bible scholars look at the gold, silver, fine linen, wine, oil, fine flour, and various other merchandise mentioned in these verses, are referring to spiritual things, such as doctrines. They compare the gold to that which Christ spoke of, when he said "buy of me, gold tried in the fire". The fine linen is compared to the righteousness of the saints, mentioned in chapter 19, verse 8, and the list goes on and on. It is interesting to note that it is not the preachers or priests, or the great city, that is selling these items of merchandise. It is the merchants, and the owners of ships, and factories, that are aghast, at the fall of Babylon. Now the Bible doesn't use those exact terms, we have to remember that John was writing about things that were familiar to him. If he were shown this vision today and was writing in the 21st century, to the church, he would probably talk about gas, lumber, commodities, investments, and the stock market. He would talk about air transportation, and those who owned airlines would be the ones standing afar off, for the fear of her torment, weeping, and wailing due to loss of revenue.

When the World Trade Center fell on September 11, 2001, the whole world came to a standstill momentarily. Stock markets closed as stocks plummeted around the world, within the first twenty-four hours after it happened. People asked the question, "how can this be happening to us"? Stockbrokers and shareholders looked on with amazement as they saw the markets drop, but the markets, unlike the fall of Babylon, recovered after a few days. Babylon is finished for ever, never more to rise again. Is it any wonder, that the voice from heaven tells John, that all the merchants, and ship masters, and sailors, stand a long way off, and lament the loss of this great city? Is it any wonder that they cast dust on their heads, and cry, weeping and wailing, because the great city is no more, and they have lost their source of income? The fall of the papacy, and all it stands for, collapses just as suddenly and unexpectedly as the World Trade Center did on that fateful day. However, it will have a much greater and far reaching effect on the world than did the Trade Center catastrophe.

A completely opposite picture of the fall of Babylon, is presented in verse 20. Here heaven and the holy apostles and prophets are told to rejoice over her fall, as God is avenging them, for the way they were treated by her. Then John saw a mighty angel in verse 21, take up a heavy stone and throw it into the sea. As the angel did so, he said that Babylon would be thrown down with violence, just as the stone was. Then the angel declared that she, Babylon would not be found anymore, that no one would dwell inside her gates again. This declaration came as a result of the deception she used on the merchants of the earth, and also due to the fact, that she was responsible for the deaths of the prophets, saints, and all that were slain upon the earth. Thus ends this chapter.

Now for a quick review. This chapter is an explanation of the things that John was shown in the previous chapter. He was shown the fall of Babylon, and why she fell. He heard the voice of God from heaven, calling his people to come out of her, so that they would not be responsible for her sins, nor receive her plagues. Then he saw her destroyed with fire, and all the businessmen of the world upset when they saw the smoke of her destruction. Finally he heard the joy in heaven over her destruction, as the martyrs and saints are avenged by God. Thus ends the anti-Christ that Satan set up to try and thwart God's plan to redeem sinners. Once again Satan is defeated in his effort to overcome God, and set up his own kingdom on this earth.

What new road signs will we see in the next segment of our journey? What exciting things will the next chapter hold for us? We will have to wait until we arrive there, to find out.

Chapter 19

A BANQUET FIT FOR A BIRD

Our journey is almost over. We have been watching the road signs as we travel along, taking care to look for any new developments that may give us a clue as to how close our destination is. It is at this stage of the trip that we, like John the Baptist, may have questions arise in our minds. Our question won't be whether Jesus is the Messiah or not. It will be, how long must we wait until Jesus comes to free us. It may have seemed like such a long time since the laws went into effect, forcing us to flee from our homes and villages. It may seem a long time since we saw the results of the sounding of the first trumpet. It may seem like a long time since our stomach last felt like it was full. God's mercy and grace, has sustained us thus far, and if we have locked this road map in our minds, we will know beyond a shadow of a doubt, that we shall soon see him, and the most exciting part of our trip will begin.

As John has just finished watching the events unfold in the previous chapter, a whole new scenario, begins to unfold before him. The atmosphere changes, there is a more relaxed feeling as he picks up on the story of our journey, here in the 19th chapter. He hears a loud sound, that of a great multitude, in heaven, praising God, saying Alleluia, Salvation, and Glory, and honor, and power to our God.

It is important to note that this great multitude is heard in heaven. Many times one reads over these portions of scripture and either misses, these details or the significance of the situation or occasion that is taking place. Here is a large group of beings, giving praise to God. This is not just a multitude of beings, but a great multitude, denoting that it is much larger than a mere multitude. One dictionary describes a multitude as a great number, not just a few, or a couple, or a dozen or so, it says a great number. When John said he heard a great multitude, he was really saying, "I heard a great, great group of beings" in heaven. That is like multiplying great x great = great multitude. Or you might multiply it this way, a multitude x a multitude = a great multitude. It is not a multitude that is doubled or tripled in size, whatever the size that the multitude is, multiplied by its own number, is what the great multitude is comprised of. Now we begin to get an idea of how many voices that John heard singing and praising God.

The Bible does not say who these beings are. The King James Bible calls them "people", which seems to imply that these are redeemed from the earth. At first glance we might be inclined to think that they are either those who were resurrected at Christ's death, or that this scene is after Christ has come the second time and taken his children home. However in the Greek, it only says a "great multitude", but it doesn't say a multitude of what. It uses the very same vernacular as in verse 6. The translators assumed that "multitude" automatically implied "people", so they interjected this word into the scriptures. I would like to believe that these are fellow human beings. However, they are probably heavenly beings such as angels or beings of other universes, who have been watching the events unfold on earth, and were visiting in heaven, who sing these praises to God.

In this song of praise, they sing that his judgements are true and righteous. And that he judged the great whore, which corrupted the whole earth, with fairness and avenged the blood of his servants who had been slain by her. In verse 3, this great multitude, sing again, Alleluia, and her smoke arose up for ever and ever. These two verses tie this song to the preceding events in chapter 18.

As this song is sung, the twenty-four elders and the four beasts fall down and worship God, saying, "Amen, Alleluia". It is interesting to note that no mention is made of the great multitude falling down and worshiping him. This is another reason why I believe that the word "people" in verse 1 should not have been used there, as that word implies that it is speaking of human beings. If this were the case then, they too, would fall down along with the twenty–four elders and the four beasts.

In verse 5 we hear another voice from out of the throne saying, "Praise our God all you servants, and all that fear him, both small and great". This voice is probably that of Gabriel, who stands next to God, as it says, "our God". This term shows that the voice recognizes that God is also his God. Then John hears all heaven break out in song as they sing, Alleluia, for the Lord God omnipotent reigns. The song continues on into the next verse as they sing, "Let us be glad and rejoice, and give honor to him, for the marriage of the Lamb is come, and his wife has made herself ready". This portion of the song shows us that the redeemed of the earth, are not the multitude that John hears singing, as the wife hasn't been brought home yet.

This wife or bride that John is referring to, are all the saved from all ages, from the time Adam and Eve were created in the garden, down through the years, to the present time. And of course there will be all those who have gone through the time of trouble, in the last days who have been faithful to him, even in diversity with the world. They have put their faith in him and have accepted his robe of righteousness, which has now become their righteousness. Through him, they have become perfect. Notice in verse 8, speaking of the bride (church) that permission was given that she was to be dressed up in fine linen, clean and white, for the fine linen are the righteous acts of the saints. Isn't that beautiful, permission is given, or granted, that God's people can be dressed up for the wedding. Actually, it was commanded that they be dressed up for the occasion. This robe is symbolic of their character, the character that they have developed by beholding Christ, by living day by day on the word of God, by accepting his shed blood on Calvary, by complete surrender of their will to his. They have allowed themselves to be changed into his image and thus are considered sinless and perfect, capable of living in peace and harmony throughout the endless ages of eternity, with God and their fellow men

I don't mean to discourage you, but as I wrote that last sentence, the magnitude of what I had written, struck me like a bolt of lightning. I asked myself, how is it with me? If Christ were passing out the robes of righteousness, would one be given to me? Do I live in peace and harmony with my neighbors? Do I have any hard feelings against anyone? Am I truly committed to Jesus? Could God take me today, to live in heaven forever, and know that I would not stir up any trouble with any one? I would certainly need his robe of righteousness to cover up my imperfections. These are solemn thought provoking questions that's God's children will be faced with, in the last days.

As I read verses 9 and 10, a number of questions came to my mind. The first one was, who is telling John to write? Was it the voice from the throne, was it the voice from heaven saying, come out of her my people, or perhaps was it the angel declaring that Babylon had fallen? As I studied backwards in Revelation, I discovered that John is still in the presence of one of the angels that had the seven bowls.[1] This angel was guiding him through the last two chapters and now he tells John to write, "Blessed are they which are called to the marriage supper of the Lamb". This is one wedding in which only the most elite are invited. Only royalty are invited to this celebration, the princes and the princesses of God, his sons and daughters. That is you and me, and everyone else who follows him wherever he leads. How important it is that we remember today, that we are royalty and as such, we are ambassadors for the King of kings.

The angel then goes on to tell John that everything he has told him is the true word of God. At this John immediately falls at the angels feet to worship him, whereupon the angel commands him not to do it. The angel continued by saying, "I am your fellow servant and of your brothers that have the testimony of Jesus". He then went on to tell John to, worship only God. Then the angel slipped in a wee bit of insight into the verse by adding that the "testimony of Jesus" is the spirit of prophecy. This gift of prophecy has been given to God's children from very early in the history of the world, right down to our day, and from what we read in the Bible, we will probably see this gift poured out again in a mighty manner before Christ's Second Coming.[2]

---

[1] Revelation 17:1
[2] Acts 2:17

When the angel had finished speaking to him, John is shown more scenes revolving around the final events of this earth's history. We are nearing the end of our journey on this earth. In verse 11 we see heaven opened and a rider on a white horse comes forth. This riders name is Faithful and True and in verse 13 we find that he has another name. Here he is called the Word of God. As he rides out of heaven on his white horse, the armies of heaven follow him on white horses. These armies are the multitudes of angels that have been watching this great controversy for centuries. The rider on the white horse also has a name written on his clothes, King of kings and Lord of lords.

This is the extent of the description of Christ's Second Coming, in the book of Revelation. As a youngster I had always heard that he was coming in clouds of angels and a rainbow was around his head. That there would be a great earthquake, and the lightning would be flashing and the thunder would be rolling through the heavens, and terror would rule supreme. Somehow, somewhere I got the idea that all this was in the book of Revelation, but as I was preparing to write this book, I discovered that I had been mistaken all these years. I knew I had read or heard these ideas somewhere, so I spent some time putting together the final scenes of Christ's coming, from other writers of the Bible.

In Acts 1:9 we read that Jesus was taken up in a cloud into heaven, after he had spent forty days with his disciples after his crucifixion. As the disciples stood there looking up into the air, trying to catch a final glimpse of their beloved Master, a couple of men clothed in white asked them why they were standing there.[3] They, then went on to say that this same Jesus would come back to earth in the same manner as the disciples had seen him go to heaven. It would be a visible coming, as I had read that he would come in the clouds of heaven and every eye would see him come.[4] Another picture I had in my mind of his coming was that there would a lot of thunder and lightning, but as I looked it up[5], I discovered

---

[3] Acts 1:11
[4] Revelation 1:7
[5] Matthew 24:27

that it was only comparing his coming to that of lightning as it flashes from east to west. One thing I wasn't wrong on, and that was the noise of his coming. I knew that there was going to be shouting and trumpets[6], as he descends in the clouds of angels that come with him. One other picture that I have had in my mind was that of all the righteous dead, arising out of their graves. John didn't record much on this subject, but Paul in his letter to the Thessalonians made mention of it.[7] He said that as the trumpets sound, and at the call of the archangel, those who died loving God, would come out of their graves to meet him. I can just imagine the earthquake that will take place as billions of graves open at the same time all over the world. This is the picture that is in my mind, of Christ's Second Coming.

Those who have died, loving the Lord will rise first, then we who are alive and remain on the earth will caught up with them in the clouds to meet Jesus in the air.[8] And so we will always be with Jesus from then on, for ever and ever through out eternal ages. Jesus has told us that there are many mansions in heaven and that he was going to go there and prepare a place for us.[9] If I go and prepare a place for you, I will come again to get you, and take you home. Now as we have met Jesus in the air, we start out on the last and most exciting part of our journey, a REAL TRIP INTO THE FUTURE, a trip that will take us through the heavens and past the planets and galaxies that we have only dreamed about. A trip, out and beyond where the greatest telescopes can see, a trip to that home where there will be no more September 11[ths], no more parting, no more broken homes or death. No more hunger or financial problems, just everlasting peace with our heavenly Father, and our Savior, Jesus Christ.

From here, on to the end of the book of Revelation, events that are recorded, do not always fall into a sequential pattern. In other words, things appear to be mixed up a bit. We will try to get everything sorted out as we go along, but from time to time we will find verses that refer either backwards

[6] 1 Thessalonians 4:16
[7] 1 Thessalonians 4:17
[8] 1 Thessalonians 4:17
[9] John 14:1-3

to a previous event, or forward to a future event. We will try to get them all in the right perspective with the guidance of the Holy Spirit. And if I make a mistake do not blame anyone else for my error.

In verse 17, John sees an angel standing in the sun. Why this angel is seen as standing in the sun is not explained in the Bible. There have been various theories brought forth by different authors, but they have not presented scriptural evidence as proof, that what they say is the truth. It is probably not of great importance or the angel would have explained the significance of it to John. The interesting part of this text is the invitation to the fowls of the air to come to the banquet of God. The angel is so kind as to read out the menu to the birds so that they can take their pick of what they want to eat, and who they want to eat on.

In verse 19, John sees the beast, and the kings of the earth along with their armies, all gathered together to make war with Jesus and the heavenly host. It is interesting to note that this battle seems to be a bit one sided. Though the beast and the kings of the earth gather together to make war with Jesus, there is no mention of a battle ever taking place, for the next words simply say, "and the beast was taken" and cast into the lake of fire burning with brimstone.

Now we have run into a tough one. As we studied previously, there are a number of beasts scattered throughout the book of Revelation. It has not been easy to keep them all in their proper cages, so that we don't get them all mixed up. So far it has not been too great a problem, but I am not sure just what cage this beast belongs in. As we look back in chapter 17, we see in verse 12- 14, that the kings of the earth give their power or allegiance, to the beast and they make war with the Lamb, and the Lamb overcomes them. The beast of Revelation 17 is, or appears to be Satan, verse 8, as it ascends out of the bottomless pit. The problem we run into here is, that this beast in chapter 19 is taken, along with the false prophet, and cast into the lake of fire, while the armies are fed to the birds. In chapter 20, verse 10, we see the devil, Satan being thrown into the fire where the beast and the false prophet are. From this it appears that the beast and the false prophet are cast into a fire at Christ's Second Coming and Satan is then thrown into the same fire at the end of his 1,000 years of solitary confinement. This is not to say that the fire has burnt for a 1,000 years, but that it is the same kind of fire, that gives the same kind of results, eternal destruction.

I am glad that God is a good zoo keeper, and has all these beasts under his control, as I have an extra beast that I do not have a cage for, unless...the extra beast is the same as the other beast, or second beast of chapter 13. Yes it is the same one, this beast here in chapter 19 is none other than the United States of America, the lamb like beast that deceived those that live on the earth. Compare Revelation 13:11–14 with verse 20 of this chapter, the beast in both instances is the same one, performing miracles and deceiving those who received the mark of the beast and those who worshiped his image. It is the lamb like beast and the false prophet that are cast into the lake of fire at Christ's Second Coming, while Satan is cast into the same fire at the end of the 1,000 years.

Now we come to the last verse of this chapter. John sees the remnant, those of the armies, the captains, mighty men, free and bondmen, both small and great, along with the horses, all destroyed by the sword that proceeded out of the mouth of the Lord. This sword is compared to the words that come from the mouth of God.[10] It is possible that the remnant of the attempted battle are slain by a command from the mouth of Jesus. The chapter ends with a sad epitaph, "And all the fowls were filled with their flesh".

---

[10] Hebrews 14:12, Revelation 1:16

Chapter 20

JUDGED BY THE SAINTS

In the last three chapters of Revelation, the pace changes as the final climax draws near. There is not the continuity that we have seen in the previous chapters. These last ones are basically fillers, shedding more light on areas that have already been covered in some instances, while in others, new thoughts are brought out which shed more knowledge on other passages. There is counsel for all those living in the final end, of this earth's history. We will find one, maybe two, descriptions of the Second Coming of Jesus. More scenarios of the bride, and the Lamb's wife. Another judgement that takes place at the very end of time just before all the unrighteous are destroyed, and the list goes on and on.

Some might ask, "why is all this necessary", seeing as we have covered a lot of it already. The bottom line is that God thought that we needed it, or he wouldn't have shown John these scenes and told him to record it for us, and who are we to argue with God.

Chapter 20 starts out with an angel coming down from heaven with the key to the bottomless pit, and carrying a great chain in his hand. Here we come in contact again with the word "bottomless pit". We have read about it back in the 9th and 11th chapters of this book. In chapter 9, we read about the angel of the bottomless pit while in chapter 11 it talks about the beast of the bottomless pit. Now here in this chapter we see another angel from heaven, having the key, come down and lay hold on Satan, throwing him into the bottomless pit.

We must keep these angels from heaven and the angel of the bottomless pit, sorted out and separate. You will remember back in chapter 9, where we talked about the "star" or angel that fell from heaven, or was sent from heaven and alighted on the earth. He was given the key to the bottomless pit. When he opened the bottomless pit, smoke came out, and out of the smoke, came the locusts, who had a king over them. This king was the angel of the bottomless pit. It is important to note that he did not come from heaven, nor was he given a key. He, and the smoke, and locusts, were released only when the heavenly angel gave him his freedom. Here in this chapter, the angel wasn't given the key, because he already had it from before. That is why John said that he saw an angel come down from heaven having the key to the bottomless pit.

The term "pit" has a number of different meanings, covering everything from the pit of the stomach to a fruit pit, such as a cherry pit, however the pit that John is describing here, is a pit that holds something. In Bible times, pits were used to hold water, as in the case of a well. Sometimes, pits were used to hold animals in, such as lions. In the Strong's Concordance, the word "pit" is translated as a prison. You may remember the story of Joseph, how his brothers threw him into a pit, to get rid of him.[1] That pit became a prison to Joseph, as he was unable to get out of it on his own. From all of this, it is safe to say that this "bottomless pit" that John is talking about, is some sort of a prison, in which to hold someone.

In verse 2, John sees the angel with the key, lay hold on the dragon or Satan, and bind him for 1,000 years. Just how could Satan, be bound? When someone is bound up, say with a rope, he is unable to move or do anything. The bound person can not function in his normal fashion. Thus it is with Satan, but his binding is not with ropes or chains, even though a chain is mentioned here in these verses. Many times we hear someone refer to "a chain of circumstances". This chain in reality, is a series of events that take place as a result of existing conditions or state of affairs. So it is with Satan, he is bound, or tied up with the "chain of events" that have taken place just previously, when all those who had the mark of the beast were destroyed and fed to the birds. Now he has no one to deceive anymore, as we read in the 3rd verse. Here the angel casts him into the bottomless pit and puts a

---

[1] Genesis 37:24

seal on him, that he should not deceive the nations (people) any more until the 1,000 years are up.

With everyone gone from the earth, those with the seal of God taken to heaven, and those who had the mark of the beast, all dead, this earth will be desolate. It has become the "bottomless pit", which Satan is bound to, with no one to tempt or torment, no one to cause affliction on, but verse 3 does not end on that note. The last sentence of the verse states that Satan must be loosed, from his prison for a little while at the end of the 1,000 years. We will pick up that part of the story, a little later on.

The scene changes now as John continues with the record of his vision. He sees a lot of thrones set up in heaven. Although the Bible doesn't specifically mention the word heaven at this point, it is implied in the latter part of verse 4. As the verse continues, it uses the term "they", and they sat on them. Here it is saying that someone was sitting on the thrones that John saw in heaven, but who are they, and what are they doing, sitting on the thrones? John is using a different style of writing here, as everything is backward. It would be much easier to understand by reading forward from the end of the verse. That way we would know who was sitting on the thrones without having to make any assumptions. Due to the fact, that he used this format, we have to leave a number of blanks in the interpretation, and then fill them in as we continue. John then goes on to say that judgement is given to these people, who are sitting on the thrones. Now we are getting somewhere. This is another courtroom scene that is taking place, but at a different time than the judgement when the Lamb opened the seven seals. This is not the investigative judgement of chapters 5–8. That one we will call the first judgement, while the one we are presently reading about, we will call it the second judgement, as there is another, a third judgement to take place before God closes the books forever.

We need to know who is involved in sitting on this judgement. John continues here in verse 4 by saying "and I saw the souls of them that were beheaded for the witness of Jesus, and for the word of God. And which had not worshiped the beast, neither his image, neither had received his mark upon their foreheads or in their hands." Ah, there it is, the answer to who is sitting on the thrones. It is all those who had been martyred for their faith in Christ, along with all those who would not bend the knee to the beast or his image. At first glance, this appears to include only those who had died at the hand of evil men for their belief in God, and those who had gone through the last great time of trouble, refusing to worship the beast, and his image. What about the billions of God's faithful children, down through the ages, who had been faithful to him? Are they not included in this judgement? Are they not given the privilege to go over the books along with the martyred ones, and the remnant who came through the last great conflict?

The answer to the above questions lies in the last part of verse 4 through 6. John saw that these people who were setting on the thrones, would live and reign with Christ for a period of 1,000 years. Paul, in writing to the Corinthian believers, asked them if they didn't know that they were going to be judging the world. Not only that, but that they would also judge angels.[2] If the saints are going to judge the world and angels then they are going to have to sit in a judgement. The only place that they can do this is in heaven, after they have been taken there by Christ. This judgement of the world and the angels, by the saints, will take place during the thousand years that Satan is bound to this world.

The judgment that the saints will set in, is not of the same nature as the investigative judgment, making a decision for, or against those that are being judged. They will be going over the names that have been removed out of the Book of Life, to see for themselves, the justice of God, in removing those names. Many will have questions as to why a certain loved one or a brother or sister in the church is not with them in heaven. On the other hand, they may be surprised to see someone, that they didn't expect to be there. By going over the records, they will be judging God's decisions in the investigative judgment, and declaring them just and good. This is

---

[2] 1 Corinthians 6:2,3

the second judgement. It was this judgement that John saw taking place in verses 4 to 6.

In verse 5, he specifically states that the rest of the dead did not live again until the end of the 1,000 years. By using the term "rest of the dead" implies that there were more dead ones, and that some had been resurrected, or raised up, while the "rest of the dead" remained dead. The resurrected ones had been raised in what John calls, the first resurrection. This was described for us back in 1 Thessalonians 4:16, where it says that the dead in Christ shall rise first, and then we shall be caught up with them, to meet the Lord in the air. This resurrection takes place at the beginning of the 1,000 years, while the second resurrection happens at the end of the 1,000 years.

At the end of the 1,000 years, John saw Satan released from his prison, verse 7. It is interesting to note how this release takes place. Remember that Satan had been bound and cast into the bottomless pit right after all those who followed the beast were destroyed by the voice of Jesus, at his second coming. Satan had no one to tempt or control. That was at the beginning of the 1,000 years. Verse 5 says that the rest of the dead, (those who were not raised at Christ's coming, and those who died at his coming), would be resurrected at the end of the 1,000 years. Here we see both the resurrection of the wicked and the release of Satan, happening at the same time. It is the resurrection of these people that release him from his prison, as now he has people who he can again control and deceive. In fact, in the very next verse we are told by John that Satan immediately goes out to the nations or peoples of the earth, into all corners of it, to gather the people together for a great battle. These wicked people from all down through the ages from Adam's time to the present will be there. Mighty men of war such as Goliath, the Midianites, Ammorites, and Hittites, will be there. Men like Mussolini, Stalin, Hitler, gang leaders with their members, along with other great minds, will all be gathered together under one leader, General Satan himself. John saw a vast army, as the sands of the sea in number, billions of people, all rallying around their fearless leader.

As this great multitude of humanity, listen to Satan as he lays out his plan, a new hope springs up in their hearts as he promises them victory over God and the saints, the very ones that they hate so much. Though we haven't read or studied about the New Jerusalem coming down to this earth, we see indications in verse 9 that the events of chapter 21, verse 2, have already taken place. In the first part of verse 9, John saw this great militia, with Satan as their leader. He sees them, go up on the breadth of the earth, surround the camp of the saints, and the beloved city, with the intent to overthrow Christ and his saints, and set up their own eternal kingdom.

As this great multitude is gathered there to do battle, fire comes down from God out of heaven, and devours them. Sin, sinners, and the instigator of sin, Satan himself, are finished forever.

John is shown different scenarios of the same event. This is probably to help us have a fuller understanding of the last day events, and how things will turn out. In the previous chapter, we saw the beast and the false prophet taken and thrown in the lake of fire, prior to the 1,000 year period, when all the men of the earth were slain. Here in this chapter, in verse 10, we see the devil or Satan, who deceived this great army of people, thrown into the lake of fire where the beast and the false prophet are. There he is tormented by the fire, or literally burned up, never more to exist. This is the same event, with the same results as the fire coming down from God in the last verse, burning everyone up. It has added the terminology of a "lake of fire", to correspond to the same terminology of verse 20, of the last chapter. Both the fire that comes down from God, and the lake of fire, have the same effect on the beast, false prophet, and Satan, and whoever is not written in the Book of Life. It totally destroys them.

John is shown another segment of the judgement take place. Here we have to back up to a period just prior the 2nd resurrection, before the 1,000 years has ended. This judgement does not involve Satan, the beast or the false prophet, only those who allowed themselves to be deceived by these three. Here John sees a great white throne with God setting on it. In verse 12, he saw that everyone who had died, from

Cain, right down to those who were killed at Christ's Second Coming, stand as it were, before him. In reality it is saying that God and the saints were going over the books, for we read in this verse that the books were opened. The term "books", tells us that this word means more than one book, so we have at least two books here that are being opened before God and the saints. Then the verse talks about another book, which is the Book of Life. No question on that one, as we all know what it contains. Here we have at least three books that are being gone over. It is very important to understand this next sentence. It says "and the dead" were judged out of those things that were written in the books, plural, according to their works. Notice that it says the "dead" were judged. This does not mean the resurrected dead, but the dead before the second resurrection.

God cannot leave any loop holes for sin to arise again, he cannot leave any stones unturned, so he allows the saints to view his judgements. What a fair God we serve. One of the books, is the book of Remembrance[3], and may also be called the Book of Deeds. The Bible doesn't mention such a book by that name, but there are a number of texts that imply that such a book exists. We read in Jeremiah that God will pay back, every nation according to their deeds.[4] In Romans, it says, in regards to the judgement, that God will render to every man according to his deeds[5], while Jude says that God will execute judgement on all their ungodly deeds.[6] One thing is certain, their works have a lot to do with why they are dead. The last part of verse 12 states that "the dead were judged out of those things which were written in the books, according to their works".

The other book may be the Book of Death, although the Bible doesn't mention such a one by name. The only indication of this is the fact that there is a Book of Life, and those whose names are written in it will be saved. When one's name is removed out of the Book of Life, it has to be put

---

[3] Malachi 3:16
[4] Jeremiah 25:14
[5] Romans 2:6
[6] Jude 1:15

somewhere. However, the Bible is silent on this topic and this idea borders on speculation.

Verses 13 to 15 tie everything together. It covers the time from the second resurrection to the cleansing of the earth with fire. Verse 13 describes the resurrection of those whose names are not in the Book of Life. It says that every person that was dead, whether they were in the sea or in the grave, were raised up. Each one was judged according to their works. This is the third judgement. God would not have anyone going into eternal destruction without showing them why he was allowing them to die eternally. In his love for them, he shows them the record of their life, how they would not be happy living in a sinless world with him and the saints. Then and only then, is death and the grave cast into the lake of fire, along with all who are not found in the book of life. Sin is forever gone, the redeemed will now live in perfect peace and harmony with their Savior, God, and their fellow saints and angels. The great controversy between God and Satan is over.

Our journey has been an eventful and an exciting one, true some have taken different routes to get there. Some were laid to rest peacefully while others had to give their lives as a testimony of their love and faith in Jesus. Still others had to suffer persecution, both physical and mental, others lived in privation, in prisons and the mountain recesses, but all had one thing in common, their faith in the promise that Jesus would come back and take them to live with him forever.

Chapter 21

AND THERE WILL BE NO MORE DEATH

This chapter is going to give us several different views of the New Jerusalem. To start off, John begins by saying that he saw a new heaven and a new earth. That was because the old heaven and the old earth had passed away, it had been destroyed, or cleansed by the lake of fire, that we talked about in the last chapter. Now as John looks out over the scene before him, he cannot help but be amazed at the transformation of the earth. Things have changed so much, in fact the first thing that catches his attention, is that there is no more sea. The great seas of the world, as we know them today, came about as a result of sin. Now that the sin problem has been done away with, the seas that separated people have been done away with also. This is not to say that there won't be some large bodies of water, for those of us who enjoy looking at, and studying the mysteries of the marine world in. Even though the sins of the antediluvian world had brought about the flood that cleansed the world the first time, thus creating the great oceans, God made something beautiful out of it. He had created seas in the first place[1], and put an abundant amount of whales and living creatures in it.[2] We can expect to have seas in the new earth, along with the wonders of nature, that God placed in the first sea. The sea that John was talking about was the sea that separates people. Remember that he is in exile on that rocky island in the Mediterranean. As he is writing this book to the churches, that great body of water was separating him from the church members that he so loved, and longed to be with. It is this kind of sea, that will not be on the earth when made new again.

As John writes verse 2, a question immediately comes to the mind of the casual reader of the Bible. He had just writ-

[1] Genesis 1:10
[2] Genesis 1:21

ten in chapter 20 verse 9, that the saints and the "beloved city", which is understood to be the New Jerusalem, was surrounded by all the wicked people along with Satan. Now he sees it coming down from God out of heaven, prepared as a bride adorned for her husband. At first glance, this seems to be contradictory with chapter 20, until we realize that we still have to deal with, "meanwhile back on the farm" scenarios. This is one of those cases, and we will be seeing more of them in this chapter and quite a number of them, in the last chapter. In actuality, John is viewing the New Jerusalem coming down to earth prior to the destruction of the wicked, but in this vision all the traces of sin is removed from the earth, so that we are not distracted by it.

Just for curiosity sake, let's take and put it in it's proper sequence so that we get an idea of how it would be perceived, had John written it in the order of events. This is how it would look. "And I John saw the holy city, new Jerusalem, coming down from God out of heaven, prepared as a bride adorned for her husband. And I saw Satan go out, and deceive those who had the mark of the beast, in their forehead, who had been resurrected. He gathered them together to battle, the number of them was as the sands of the sea. And they went up on the breadth of the earth, and compassed the camp of the saints, and the beloved city. Then fire came down out of heaven, and devoured them. And the Devil was cast into the lake of fire and brimstone, where the beast and the false prophet are." Now do you see why John separated it? The destruction of Satan and the wicked detract from the beauty of the new Jerusalem. It takes the away the joy of the earth made new. That is why John appears to repeat himself here in this chapter, so that we have a fresh view of things. We will see a similar case in verse 8 when we get there, and you will experience some negative feelings as we deal with it.

As John is standing there looking on the scene, he hears a great voice from heaven. He has heard this voice on several other occasions, in other visions, as it drew attention to some event. This voice was probably that of Gabriel saying, "look, the tabernacle of God is with mankind. He is going to live with them, and they are going to be his people. God , himself is going to be there with them and will be their God." What good news that is for us today, to know that we will have God living with us on the new earth.

Verse 4 continuing the thought says, "and God shall wipe away all tears from their eyes, and there shall be no more death, neither sorrow, nor crying, neither shall there be any more pain, for all the former things are passed away". From this passage of scripture, we see that all these things have been present with us in heaven, but now they are no more. I need to clarify that statement, as I am sure there are some readers who will take me to task over the fact that I included death in with the sorrow, crying, and pain. True, there will be no death in heaven, but it will still be present in our minds, as death is not done away with until it is swallowed up in the lake of fire at the end of the 1,000 years.

Many of the redeemed who spent the 1,000 years in heaven with Jesus and the Father, had many questions to ask, as they looked around heaven and found that some of their friends and loved ones were not there. This made them sad and I am sure that there will be many tears shed in heaven as we go over the records of those who chose not to accept the blood of Jesus to cover their sins. A husband will be sad if his life long mate is not there enjoying heaven with him, likewise a wife will feel the same way if her husband is missing. Parents will weep because a child is not there. Children will cry if a Mommy or Daddy isn't there, or a brother or sister is missing. Grandpas and Grandmas will cry because a grandchild is not there. Many Bible scholars have portrayed heaven as a place of eternal bliss, where everyone will be happy, and sorrow does not exist. If this is how you think heaven is, I am sorry that I have to burst your bubble. In heaven all these emotions will be present with us as we go over the books and records of those, whose names were removed out of the Book of Life. It is not until the 1,000 years is over and the New Jerusalem has come down to this world, that all these mixed up emotions are wiped away. When it says, "for the former things are passed away" it means that God in his magnificent love for us will wipe out the memory of everything that makes us sad. The term "former things" means just that, everything including tears, sickness, heartache, and death. It will be as though those events in our lives had never happened. It is because of this miracle that God does, in the lives of the redeemed, that they can live in perfect joy and harmony for eternity with him. Now I know, that may make some, uncomfortable at this time, but be patient and trust in God and he will bring it to pass in his own time.

Now as God sits on his throne, he says, "behold I make all things new". Then he spoke directly to John in vision, telling him to write all this down for us to read, because he said that all these things are true and faithful. What God was saying here is, my word is reliable, you can trust in me, my child, I will not let you down. Oh what hope there is in his promises of love for each of us. Then God continued dialoguing with John, in verse 6 he said, "it is done", finished, over with. Sin is eradicated, the price is paid and the purchased ones are home where they belong. The scenario changes again, John is taken back in time to before probation closes, back to the isle of Patmos. Jesus, speaking to him said, "I am Alpha and Omega, the beginning and the end". I will give unto him and her, that is thirsty, the fountain of the water of life freely, without limit. Those who overcome will inherit all things, and I will be their God and they will be my sons and daughters. God went on to say, in verse 8, there would be a group of people who did not believe in him. Some of them were murderers, others were immoral, and some dabbled around in witchcraft, and idolatry, while others were liars. These all shall have their part in the lake of fire and brimstone, which is the second death. These people made a choice in life that led them down the path to destruction. God loved them, but in that love, he gave them the freedom to love him in return, or to refuse to, and they made their choice to turn away from him, intent on doing their own thing. Thus, he had no other alternative, than to destroy them in the fire. We will see this scene briefly in the 22nd chapter, with a few more details added to it.[3]

Now another change in scenery as one of the angels that had the seven bowls full of the wrath of God, comes and talks

---

[3] Revelation 22:14,15

to John. This angel invites him to come with him, as he wants to show John the bride, the Lamb's wife. You will recall that back in chapter 17, one of the seven angels that had a bowl, came and talked with him, showing him another woman, the false church. It will be interesting to find out if it was the same angel, who showed John the two women, when we get to heaven and talk to him.

The angel then carried John away in spirit, to a high mountain, where he showed him the great city, the holy Jerusalem coming down from God out of heaven. What a sight that must have been, for poor old John who had been sitting on the rock for so long. It had been his prison, his bottomless pit, but now he sees what his reward will be. New hope springs up in him as this view of the magnificent city passes before him. Verse 11 says that it had the glory of God, and her light was like stone most precious. This stone that is mentioned here, is not just an ordinary rock from some field, but a gemstone, one that radiates rays of light as they pass through the cut and polished sides of it. Just like the stone, those who are inside the city will have been cut and polished to perfection, by the grace of God. His goodness will radiate through them just like the light of the city.

Starting in verse 12, John was shown the city in detail. The description of it almost overwhelms our imagination, as it is so immense and beautiful. It had a great, high wall around it, with twelve gates in the wall. On each side of the city, there were three gates in the wall with the names of the twelve tribes of Israel written on them. John did not make it clear as to whether all twelve names were on each gate, or if each gate had a name of one of the tribes, written on it. It is quite likely that each gate had a single name on it, and it wouldn't surprise me if the names are arranged in the same order as they were camped around the Tabernacle in the wilderness. Beside each gate stood an angel, what he is doing there, the Bible doesn't say, but in verse 27, is says that nothing can enter through the gates except those whose names are written in the Lamb's Book of Life. So whether these angels are just greeters at the gates, or whether they are checking our citizenship cards, the Bible doesn't say.

The wall of the city has twelve foundations, and on these foundations are written the names of the twelve apostles. The fact that their names are written on the foundations, seems to imply that they have the special honor of being recognized as the foundation of the church, though the Bible does not say it in so many words. We need to be very careful when trying to understand and explain verses that are not made plain with a "thus says the Lord".

There has been much study and thought gone into the next 7 verses, namely 15 through 21. The angel did not explain to John, what it all meant, and this has led to some interesting ideas, and a bit of speculation as well. He tells us that the angel that was talking to him had a golden reed, which he measured the city with. He also measured the walls, and the gates.

In verse 16, it says that the city lies foursquare. Some take this to mean that it is cube-like, especially in light of the last part of the verse, where it says that the length and the breadth, and the height of it are equal. The term "foursquare" according to Strong's concordance, means four corners, or square, or four equal sides. So we know that the city is square, that it is 12,000 furlongs, but it is not known if this distance is on each side, or the total distance around the city. Either way, it will be a large city and there will be room for everyone. If it is 12,000 furlongs per side, it works out roughly, to about 1,500 miles per side. That is a mighty large city, in fact if you take a map of North America, and draw a line from Houston, Texas north to the Manitoba-Ontario border, on to the midway-point between the 49th parallel and the Northwest Territories, then due west to the Pacific Ocean, you will have the approximate size of the New Jerusalem. Or if you want it in simpler language, it would include all of the United States, west of a line drawn from Chicago, Illinois to Mobile, Alabama. That is a mighty large city. However John does not shed any light on how the city was measured, so we will have to wait until we get there to find out.

Next he describes the walls of the city. He saw the angel measure it, and verse 17 states that it is a 144 cubits, according to a man. In the interlinear Greek–English New Testament, it seems to indicate that the cubit measure of a man, is the same as an angel. This 144 cubits would work out to between 210–216 feet, depending on whether one uses a 17.5 inch cubit or an 18 inch one. Some translations of the Bible mention that this is the height of the wall while others do not say anything about it, leaving one to wonder if it stands for the height or width of it. It does not really matter, if it did the angel would have clarified it with John.

John gives us a rundown of the construction material used in the city, remember the angel was showing him all these things. To start with he describes the wall, saying that is was made of jasper, and the city was pure gold. This gold was not like the gold that we know today on this earth, as it was transparent like clear glass. John must have been familiar with glass, to be able to compare this gold to it. One must bear in mind that he did not say that it was glass, but only that it was transparent like glass, making it possible to look through it.

John next turns his attention to the foundations of the wall. Each of the foundations are made from a different gem stone. You can read about them, yourself in verses 19 and 20. Some Bible scholars go through all these foundations and have elaborate ideas as to what each stone stands for, but the angel was silent on that subject, and so was John. I believe we should follow their example also.

There has been some discussion on the twelve gates being made, each one from a single pearl. Now we know that by today's standards, there are no pearls large enough to make a door to a house let alone, a gate to this magnificent city, so this pearl must be either a special order, or symbolic. Let us look at verse 25 for a moment. Here it says that the gates of the city will not be shut, for there is no night there. This raises several interesting questions, for instance, if the gates are never shut, why have gates in the first place? Another question is, are these gates mentioned here, the gates that one would swing shut, or are they just the opening one would walk through? Going back to the gate being made from one pearl, is this referring to the gateposts, or archways as the case may be? Are they made from a single pearl? Heaven is referred to as the Pearl of Great Price.[4]

---

[4] Matthew 13:46

Going back to the issue of the gates never being shut, at night, John was well familiar with the practice of closing the city gate at night, so that no enemies could sneak into the city unawares. In this city, there will be no night there, neither will there be any enemies, thus there will be no need to shut the gates. The last part of verse 27 says that only those, whose names are written in the Lamb's Book of Life, will enter in through the gate.

We have skipped over a few verses, so let's go back and pick up, on them. John was very observant in his vision for he said that he did not see a temple in the city. He then went on to say that there was no need for a temple because the Lord God Almighty and the Lamb, are the temple of it. Along with this fact, he stated that the city had no need for the sun, nor the moon, as the glory of God, and the Lamb, light it up. It is hard to imagine how bright they must be. Only those who are washed in the blood and have a right to the tree of life can stand in that glorious light. Speaking of the city, John wrote that the nations of "them which are saved", are able to walk on those streets that are paved with transparent gold. The kings of the earth will bring their honor and glory, into it. What a paradise we have to look forward to. No wonder that God gave us this road map, to give us encouragement through the rough spots that were ahead of us on our journey. It will guide us from our present day, to that glorious one when we will be home with him forever.

Chapter 22

THE JOURNEY'S END

Chapter 22 is a continuation of the tour of the New Jerusalem, that the angel was showing John. In the last chapter he was shown the outside of the city, but now the angel takes him inside the city to show him around. Remember, this angel was one of the angels that had poured out the plagues of chapters 15, and 16.[1]

John now continues to describe the scenes of the vision here in the 22nd chapter. He sees a pure river of water of life, which came out of the throne of God and the Lamb. This water is not the same water that Jesus spoke of when talking to the woman by the well.[2] That water was a symbol for the gospel that Jesus wanted to share with the woman and the rest of the city, where she was from, it was a spiritual water. The water that John is shown, is a literal river of water and its origin, is the throne of God and the Lamb, showing us that they are still the sustainers of all creation. There is no reason to think that we won't need water to drink in the earth made new. We will still need to eat, to sustain our bodies there, as when he first created Adam and Eve in the beginning. Likewise we will also need water to balance our bodies chemistry. That water, will be supplied by the water from the river, of the water of life.

Not only will this water of life, fulfil our need for moisture, but it also waters the Tree of Life which grows on either side of the river, verse 2. This tree, as all trees, needs water so that it can bloom and fruit for the benefit of the redeemed. You may recall, that back in the beginning, God planted a garden in Eden. There he caused the Tree of Life to grow for Adam and Eve to eat from. As long as they ate from this tree,

---

[1] Revelation 21:9
[2] John 4:14

they would never die, as it had the power to sustain life.[3] At some point in time, God removed it from the earth so that sinful mankind could not eat from it and live forever. When he took it from the earth, he transplanted it in the heavenly Jerusalem. Now that the New Jerusalem has come down to the earth made new, John sees it there. He saw the Tree of Life bearing twelve different kinds of fruit, every month of the year. There are some who believe that each month there will be a different fruit on it, however there is no Biblical proof for or against that idea. In this, I can better understand the love of God for his people from around the world. You see, we won't be eating from the Tree of Life every day, but as we come into the city from Sabbath to Sabbath we will have access to it. Some people envision it to have apples, pears, plums, peaches, apricots, and other fruit found in North America. I am afraid these dear ones may be in for a surprise. I am sure, that God in his wisdom will have mangoes, breadfruit, durian, sour sop, and other tropical fruits, for those saints from other corners of the earth, who have different tastes than ours. As we partake of the fruit from this tree, we will be sustained.

Now I know that there may be some raised eyebrows at that last statement, but let's take a closer look at this whole picture that John has just painted for us. Notice that this water comes from the throne of God and Jesus. This water of life flows through the Tree of Life causing it to flourish and produce fruit, which in turn gives us nourishment and eternal life. You can see that through this cycle, it is Jesus and the Father who are really the sustainers of the saints.

As we study this concept, and then look at the "water of life" that Jesus offered the woman of Samaria, at the well, we see a very close resemblance of the same scenario as the tree of life. This water of life of course, was a spiritual water, which resulted in a spiritual life, this spiritual life bore spiritual fruit as she witnessed to her neighbors, resulting in eternal life for all who partook of it. What amazing lessons there are to learn from the study of God's Word.

---

[3] Genesis 2:8

In the last part of verse 2, John makes the remark that the leaves are for the healing of the nations. There have been various opinions as to what this means. This may be referring to political animosities that have prevailed among men for thousands of years, sometimes separating even loved ones.

I am sure that there are other ideas out there as well. One thing we must keep in mind is the fact that there is no sickness nor disease in heaven or on the new earth, so this healing mentioned here is not a physical healing of a disease or malady.

If you look up the word "healing" in Strong's Concordance[4], you will find some different concepts for the word. Basically it means an attendant (of sickness) or otherwise. This word is a spin-off of another word which means "adore" (God), which comes from still another word which means a "menial attendant" or a servant, as if cherishing the position. Now lets put all this together and see if we can make any sense out of it. This word "healing" actually means "a servant who wants to, or cherishes the position to adore God". But what about the leaves, are they literal leaves that want to be servants by giving shade to the saints while they lay or sit under the tree eating mangoes? Again we must turn to the concordance to see what the word "leaves" mean.[5] Here we find the word "leaves" comes from a word meaning a sprout, or an offshoot, a race or a clan, or tribe. These meanings come from another root word that means, to germinate, to grow or spring up. Could it be then, that the leaves that John saw, were symbolic of the redeemed? Were they sprouts from a vine? Jesus had told his disciples that he was the vine and they were the branches.[6] So here in Revelation, these leaves or sprouts, or offshoots, if you please, are linked up with the word "healing", and what it means. Let us see what happens when we put them together. First of all, we have the leaves or sprouts (redeemed?), then we add "healing", those who want to serve, or desires to adore God. When we put it all together, it appears that the leaves are the redeemed, who desire to

---

[4] see # 2322, 2323 and 2324
[5] see #5444, 5443, and 5453 Strong's concordance
[6] John 15:5

serve and adore God. The last part of verse 3 supports this idea, as it says that his servants shall serve him.

If the above is in fact what John saw, and the healing leaves are symbolic of the redeemed, adoring, and serving the Godhead, then the Tree of Life would have to be symbolic also as it would stand for God and Jesus. The twelve manner of fruit would have to be symbolic of the fruit of the Spirit, that Paul and Peter wrote about.[7] We will have to wait until we get to heaven to find out if this tree is literal, symbolic, or both. I hope that it is literal, as I have always been looking forward to a feast of tropical fruit.

As we continue on to verse 3, John tells us that there will be no more curse. Just what did he mean by this statement? Again there has been long and varied discussions about these words. If we turn back the pages of time, to the beginning of this worlds history, back to the book of Genesis where we have the story of the creation of this world and its inhabitants. In chapter 3 we find the story of the fall of man and woman, how they ate from the Tree of Knowledge of Good and Evil, at the suggestion of the serpent. The story goes on to describe the conversation between God, the woman and the man, and the serpent. The outcome of this conversation was that a curse, was placed on the serpent[8] because it had deceived the woman, and another curse was placed on the ground for mans part, in listening to the woman.[9] It is interesting to note that in the first book of the Bible, the curse is placed on the earth and its inhabitants, while in the last book of the Bible the curse is removed.

The removing of this curse of course comes from the fact that sin and sinners are done away with, and are no more, everything is in perfect harmony just as it was back in the Garden of Eden. God can, once again commune, face to face with his creations as he did in the beginning. The removing of the curse, of course has raised some questions in man's mind. The first curse was placed on the serpent or snake, resulting in the snake, having to crawl on it's belly for the rest

---

[7] Galatians 5:22, 23. 2 Peter 1:5-8
[8] Genesis 3:14
[9] Genesis 3:17

of it's days. The fact that the curse resulted in causing the snake to crawl on it's belly, indicates that before the curse, it had some other form of locomotion. So if snakes at creation, did not slither along on the ground as they do today, this particular snake would not have slithered up into the tree as we see snakes do now. How then did this particular snake get up in the tree, if it didn't crawl there? There are only two other ways that it could have been entwined in the branches of that tree, it either had legs and jumped into the tree, or it had wings and flew into the tree. I am not aware of any fossilized snakes, having wings or legs. In fact I do not even recall seeing or hearing of a snake fossil being found anywhere, but I am sure there must be some somewhere. One thing I do know is that the Chinese have legends and pictures of snakes that flew, away back in their history from a thousand years or more before the time of Christ. Could this be due to the fact that stories had been passed down from father to son, from the time of Adam to Noah, and then onto generations that stretched from then, to the days of the Tower of Babel, and finally into the land of China? However the idea got to China, that snakes and dragons flew through the air, is immaterial, the main thing is that they have stories passed down from generation to generation, of these creatures with wings on them. From all this, I feel safe in saying that the serpent in the book of Genesis flew into the tree, much like a bird would.

Does all this mean that there will be snakes on the earth made new? There are many people today who hate snakes, and this may all stem back to the story in Genesis, even though many of the worlds population may never have read the account. Ideas and theories have a way of growing, and being passed on, to later generations. Even among Christians, there are those who hate snakes, and who believe that there will not be snakes on the new earth. I am sorry to disappoint them, but the Bible makes it clear that there will be snakes or serpents if you please, on the earth made new. Isaiah, writing about Zion, talks about the little child playing on the hole of the asp, and the weaned child on the cockatrices' den.[10] Both

---

[10] Isaiah 11:8

these terms, asp and cockatrice, refer to snakes, so we can expect that when God makes everything new for the New Earth, he will make some new snakes as well. However, the curse will be gone and they will have the same means of locomotion as they had in the beginning, because the curse of crawling on their bellies, will be removed from them.

What about the second curse, the one placed on the ground for man's sake? What about the thorns and the thistles and the tilling of the soil? What about the sweat that the work generated, and also, the tired muscles, the aching joints? These were all part of the curse that was placed on the ground because Adam listened to Eve, but now it is removed from the earth along with the curse on the snake. No more sore backs, no more sweat burning the eyes as it runs into them from the forehead, no more torn flesh from trying to get that big luscious blackberry, out in the middle of the patch. There will be no more mosquitoes and black flies, to cause us to swell and itch. All this will be done away with, when the curse is removed from the earth made new.

The throne of God and the Lamb will be in the New Jerusalem, and all the redeemed will be his servants. We will not be treated as servants are today, but will serve him out of love for him, because of what he has done for us.

There has been some discussion on verse 5, as to what it means when it says, "there shall be no night there". Many believe that on the earth made new, that there will be no more need for the sun nor the moon, due to this statement, thus they will not be made over again, nor be in existence. We have to remember that John is being taken on a tour of the New Jerusalem, we must also keep in mind that God and the Lamb dwell there. Just the brightness of their beings gives light to the city. This does not say that outside the walls of the city, there will be no need for the sun or the moon. It only says that there will be no need for candles nor the light of the sun for us to see where we are going, for the Lord God gives us the light.

I like the next line in verse 5. It tells me that even though I am a servant of God, that he will lift me up to the position of a prince and that I will reign with him for ever and ever. Isn't that just the most exciting thought that we can have. What love the Father has for us.

The angel now tells John in verse 6, that all these sayings are faithful and true, that he can put his trust in them. John has seen a lot of the world's history pass before him, much of it was beyond his comprehension. The angel assures John, that it was God, who sent him, to reveal to his servants, the things that must shortly take place. John didn't live to see these things happen, in fact several thousand years have gone by since he wrote about the visions, and still some of these events are yet future. As we look at the events in our world today, we can know for a certainty that it is time for these events to take place.

In some Bibles, verse 7 is in red letters, indicating that these are the words of Jesus. He may have spoken direct to John in the vision, or the angel could have been relaying them to him, from Jesus. Either way, the message is the same, "behold I come quickly. Blessed is he that keeps the sayings of the prophecy of this book". Here again we find a blessing promised to those who keep the sayings of this prophecy. It is interesting that in the first chapter of Revelation verse 3, it says "blessed is he that keeps the sayings of this book", and here in the last chapter that same blessing is repeated. Again, I can not stress enough, the importance of studying and keeping, which involves memorizing, the events that have been recorded within the pages of this book. God knows that it is important for us to do, that is why he gave the message of a blessing, both, at the beginning and the end, of it.

As this vision was coming to a close, John says that when he had heard and seen the things in it, that he fell down at the feet of the angel that showed him all these things, to worship him. He was told by the angel that he was not to do it as the angel was also a fellow servant just like himself, and everyone else who keeps the sayings of this book. The angel tells him to worship God instead.

The angel then tells John that he must not seal up the prophecy or writings of this book, for the time is at hand. These events were about to begin to take place and God's children must be able to read and study them, if they are to have a safe journey through the end times.

Verses 11–13, again are spoken direct from Jesus or repeated in the first person form by the angel. He that is unjust let him be unjust still, and he that is filthy, let him be filthy still. He that is righteous, let him be righteous still, and he that is holy, let him be holy still. Behold I come quickly and my reward is with me, to give to every man according to his works. I am Alpha and Omega, the beginning and the end, the first and the last. There is no doubt as to where this message is coming from, or who it was meant for.

Jesus then continues in verse 14 by giving a blessing on all those who keep, or obey the commandments of his Father. Some translations say "blessed are those who wash their robes". Those who do, may have the right to eat from the Tree of Life, and may enter the city that John, was just shown. Jesus says in verse 16, I Jesus have sent my angel to tell to you, these things in the churches. I am the root and offspring of David, the bright and morning star.

Jesus then continues with an invitation in verse 17. The Spirit and the bride say come. And let him that hears, say come. We are to pass on the invitation to others. He continues by saying, let him who is thirsty come, and whoever will or wants to, may come and drink of the water of life freely. What an invitation that is, completely open to everyone on earth, you and me, and the drunk and the druggy, the prostitutes on the street, all are invited to come if they want to. What a magnificent God we have as our Father.

Jesus now gives a very solemn warning to everyone in verses 18 and 19. He says, "I testify, or swear, to everyone that hears or reads the prophecy of this book, if any man shall add to these sayings, God will add to him the plagues that are written in it. Furthermore, if any man shall take away from the words of this prophecy, the things written in this book, making them of no effect, God will take his name out of the book of life, and out of the holy city". This is pretty heavy stuff, and reason for us to be very careful how we preach and teach the writings of this last book that God has entrusted us with. We are to use it to guide the feet of the saints to higher ground, and in so doing have a very solemn obligation to use it carefully and wisely, for we will be held accountable for each one that may be discouraged and turns back, due to the misrepresentation of God, by you and I as we travel on this journey into time.

Verse 20, basically wraps up the content of the book. The phrase "he which testifies these things", ties the thoughts of this verse to verses 18 and 19. The words, "surely I come quickly" are spoken by the same person that says in verse 18, "for I testify unto every man". Jesus makes this last statement of his in the Bible, "surely I come quickly". Amen. It is not known for sure, if Jesus used this word "amen", as he ended his statement or if John added it in confirmation of what Jesus had just said. According to the concordance, it means or implies that a previous statement is true, certain, sure, trustworthy, so be it, or let it happen. Whoever made the statement, whether John or Jesus, we know that what Jesus said about coming quickly, is true and his word is trustworthy and it will happen.

The grace of our Lord Jesus Christ be with you all.

Chapter 23

CONCLUSION

We have covered a lot of ground, on our trip through the book of Revelation. I hope that you have enjoyed it, and that your life has been enriched by it. We have seen many things take place on our journey. We have observed the judgement, as the courtroom in heaven, was opened to our view. We saw the throne set and one sitting on it, with a two-sided book in his hand, while around the throne were twenty–four chairs, upon which sat twenty–four elders. Next, we saw the Lamb come into the throne room and take the book from him who sat on the throne. Upon taking the book, the Lamb, Jesus proceeded to open the pages one by one and go over the names of the inhabitants of this world. This is known as the Investigative Judgement, or as the Bible calls it, the cleansing of the Sanctuary. We saw Jesus open the seven seals, one by one, as different eras came under the scrutiny of those seated in the courtroom. In the closing scenes of judgement, God's children were all sealed. Then as the judgement ended we saw the seven angels given seven trumpets which they sounded one after the other, each in his assigned order. As the last or seventh trumpet sounded, we stood by and saw the wrath of God poured, out on the inhabitants of the earth, in the form of the seven last plagues. We watched as these plagues were poured out on all those who had the mark of the Beast in their forehead or in their hand. Then we beheld the glorious appearing of Jesus in the clouds of heaven as he came to claim us as his own. There was more to the story but I want to stop here and invite you to do some serious thinking.

John had done some writing earlier, as a younger man. In John 3, and reading verse 16, he wrote that God so loved the world that he gave his only Son, that whosoever believes on him, will not perish, but will have everlasting life. That, "whosoever believes", implies that everyone who has ever lived on this planet has received this invitation, but only those who believe will receive the prize. That invitation is for you and me, and we can be included in the "whosoever" group. John then continues in verse 17, by telling us that God didn't send Jesus into the world to condemn us but that through his shed blood on Calvary, he might save us.

When Jesus was talking to his disciples one time, he told them that he was going to go to his Father and prepare a place for them.[1] He then promised them, that if he went to prepare this place, he would come back and get them.[2] This same promise is extended to each, and every person on this planet who believes in him.

As the time drew near for Jesus to go back to heaven to be with his Father, he took his disciples up on the mountain one last time. He gave them some parting advice and then, he was caught up in a cloud, and ascended into heaven. As the twelve disciples stood there looking up into the sky where they had last seen their beloved Master, two angels stood beside them. These heavenly messengers, comforted them with the promise that Jesus would come back some day, in the very same way that they had seen him go into heaven.[3] This is what Jesus was talking about when he told them that he was going to his Father's house to make a place for them, that we read about earlier.

In going to be with the Father, making a place for all who believed in him, Jesus is saying, I have died for you, now I must go and be your lawyer. I must prepare my case on your behalf, so when I present it to the Father and the universe, I will win your case. When that is done then I will come back and get you. In the meantime you must wait a little while, and tell all the world what I have done on behalf of fallen man. That I not only created them, but that I love them and want them to love me in return. I want to make things like they were, in the beginning, no more dying, or crying, or aches and pains. No more sorrow or separation of loved ones. No more sin, only peace and harmony for ever. I want to walk

---

[1] John 14:2
[2] John 14:3
[3] Acts 1:9-11

with you and talk with you face to face, as I did in the Garden of Eden so long ago. This is the Gospel of Jesus Christ.

Jesus says in Revelation 3:20, Behold, I stand at the door, and knock: if any man hear my voice, and open the door, I will come in to him, and will sup with him, and he with me. Here Jesus says that he is waiting for each one of us to answer the knock at our hearts door, waiting for an invitation to come into our life. Into the life of every man, woman, and child on this earth. This is the only work that we can do to gain eternal life. This work involves the surrender of our will, to God. When we do this, then he can change our sinful nature into his sinless nature and take us to heaven, to live with him throughout eternal ages.

The Journeys End, What Will It Be?

When you've traveled this life, and come to the Journeys end,
When your freedom is gone, and you have no friend.
When in desperation, you want to know,
And you ask the question, which way do I go?
Then turn to the Bible and read it through,
For between its covers, there's a message for you.
The story is there, of a God of love,
Who watches you, from heaven above.
A story of love that no man comprehends
Of a God that is closer, than ones closest friends.
Who has promised to keep you through thick and thin,
Saying if you will love me, I'll forgive all your sin.
When the judgement is over, I'll take out my seal,
And give you a mark that you won't even feel.
When the world is in turmoil, and there's no cause to sing,
I will cover you up with the tip of my wing.
As the lightning flashes and the thunder rolls,
You'll be safely recorded on heavens scrolls.
When the wrath of God is poured out on earth,
And the boisterous crowds have ceased all their mirth.
When all we have, is the hand of God,
To guide down the road, that our Savior trod.

Will you come to the cross, at Calvary,
Accept the price it took, to set you free,
Or will you choose an easier path,
Live a life of ease and evoke Gods' wrath?
Will you, in sorrow turn away,
Because the price, is too much to pay.
At the journeys' end, where will you be,
In heaven or hell for eternity?

----- Dwight Johnson ----

How is it with you, my friend? As you have traveled on this Journey Into Time, through the Book of Revelation, will you accept Christ's invitation now? When the Savior knocks at your hearts door, will you invite him to come in so you can feast on heavenly manna? Will you say, " take my life Jesus, and make it over anew, so that I can be with you forever"? Jesus is pleading with you today. Will you give him your heart and life, will you say, "I accept your death on the cross as payment for my sins"? Or will you, in sorrow, turn away as did the rich young Ruler of Matthew 19:16–22, who wanted to be saved, but worshiped another god? Which seal, will you be sealed with, when you come to the end of the journey?

We'd love to have you download our catalog of
titles we publish at:

www.TEACHServices.com

or write or email us your thoughts,
reactions, or criticism about this
or any other book we publish at:

TEACH Services, Inc.
254 Donovan Road
Brushton, NY 12916

info@TEACHServices.com

or you may call us at:

518/358-3494